THE GIBBER EDITION

the Shabbos Shiron

Published by
Mesorah Publications, ltd.

in conjunction with

Judaica Illuminations, ltd.

The ArtScroll Mesorah Series®

First Edition, First Impression ... January 2004
First Edition, Second Impression ... July 2005

Published by Judaica Illuminations Ltd.

1664 Coney Island Ave. • Brooklyn, NY 11230 • 718-375-4600 • www.judaicailluminations.com

and Artscroll/Mesorah Ltd.
and Distributed by Mesorah Publications, Ltd.

4401 Second Avenue • Brooklyn, NY 11232 • 718-921-9000 • www.artscroll.com

Distributed in Israel by
SIFRIATI / A. GITLER
6 Hayarkon Street
Bnei Brak 51127, Israel

Distributed in Europe by
LEHMANNS
Unit E, Viking Industrial Park, Rolling Mill Rd.
Jarrow, Tyne and Wear, NE32 3DP, England

Distributed in Australia and New Zealand by
GOLDS WORLD OF JUDAICA
3-13 William Street
Balaclava, Melbourne 3183, Victoria, Australia

Distributed in South Africa by
KOLLEL BOOKSHOP
Shop 8A Norwood Hypermarket
Norwood 2196, Johannesburg, South Africa

Table Edition: ISBN: 1-57819-994-8

Slipcase Edition: ISBN: 1-57819-995-8

Printed in Canada

Table of Contents

Guide to Reading the Transliteration

In our transliteration, we follow the NCSY precedent, using Ashkenazic pronunciation. Consonants are read as they sound in English, except for "ch" (ח,כ,ך) which is pronounced as in challah. The "silent" Hebrew letters — א and ע, whenever they appear, and ה, when it appears at the end of a word — are not represented. Although the letter ה is not usually pronounced when it appears at the end of a word, there are exceptions to the rule. These exceptions are indicated in Hebrew by a dot inside the letter — הּ. In transliteration the ה appears as a final h and is preceded by a vowel.

A consonant is usually pronounced together with the vowel following it. Thus, הַמֶּלֶךְ, "hamelech," is pronounced "ha-me-lech," and not "ham-el-ech." Hyphens are used to indicate exceptions to this rule.

When two consonants appear in tandem (except for those that are pronounced as a single sound, such as, ch, sh, tz), the first ends a syllable and the second begins a new syllable. Thus, וּבְנֵה, "uvnay," is pronounced "uv-nay"; אֶקְרָא, "ekro," is pronounced "ek-ro" not "e-kro."

Vowels are pronounced as follows:

a	אַ	as in hurr**a**h	i	אִ	or אִי	as in mach**i**ne
o	אָ	as in **o**ften	u	אֻ	or אוּ	as in l**u**nar
ō	אֹ	or אוֹ as in p**o**st	oy	אֹי	as in b**oy**	
ay	אֵ	or אֵי as in p**ay**	ai	אַי	as in **ai**sle	
e	אֶ	as in l**e**g				

The sounded sh'va (בְּ) is represented by an apostrophe (b') and is pronounced similarly to the indistinct a in ago.

Hyphens are used to separate syllables that might otherwise be slurred into each other (e.g., מֵעַתָּה is transliterated "may-ato" not "ma-yato").

Capital letters are not used in Hebrew. However, for the convenience of the reader, the transliteration uses a capital letter to indicate the beginning of a verse or a sentence and proper nouns. Additionally, capitals are used to indicate Divine Names which may not be pronounced except as part of a Scriptural verse or within a prayer.

THE SHABBOS SHIRON
is *lovingly dedicated*
to the memories of

Charles Goldner
אלימלך חיים בן ירמיהו ע"ה
and
Kate Ettlinger Goldner
מינדל בת משולם ע"ה

יבלח"ט *and*
in honor of

Isadore and Ruth Gibber שיחיו
יצחק בן אריה ליב
רחל בת דוד בנימין

Our dear parents have taught and continue to
teach by their example. We are the
beneficiaries of their dedication to
Shabbos and the precious tenets of Judaism.

May this Shiron enhance the Shabbos tables of
others as they have enhanced ours.

**Debbie and Elliot Gibber
and family**

Acknowledgments

ith the completion of The Shabbos Shiron, the Manuscript Shiron series has, with the help of God, come full circle. Early editions of the Hebrew and Hebrew/English Shiron, as well as special editions for Bar/Bat Mitzvah and the Jewish wedding, have enhanced hundreds of celebrations from Albany to Australia. Beauty without meaning, however, is like a body without a soul; the external trappings may be attractive, but it is devoid of purposeful content. By commissioning the series, Debbie and Elliot Gibber have enriched the Shabbos experience and added immeasurably to the beautiful world of Judaica.

The original Manuscript Shiron was commissioned by the Gibbers to mark their eldest son's Bar Mitzvah. With each subsequent publication, another dimension has been incorporated into the aesthetic appreciations of Judaism. The Shabbos Shiron has been, in essence, a work in progress, adding layer upon layer of illumination, meaning and commentary to the original calligraphy and design.

The more we learn, the more we need to know. The Jewish community is not satisfied with a cursory treatment of material. A deeper understanding of the contents will hopefully translate into a more profound appreciation of Judaism itself.

As an artist and a student of Torah, I hope to visually express the deep-felt passion for the messages of our Sages, which transmit and translate the Word of God. If I am fortunate on some level to faithfully share those messages through my images, then the palette which is my pulpit will hopefully do justice to both. Artistry, like life itself, is a never-ending, ever-emerging process. The colors vary, the styles can take on different hues, as long as the final product is an expression of the soul. Talent and creativity are gifts – and responsibilities – to craft the work of the hand, the feeling of the heart and the understanding of the mind into a product which glorifies the One Who has graciously endowed us.

I have been particularly fortunate to have been associated with the ArtScroll family for many years. From Elliot and Dave Schwartz of ArtScroll Printing, I have learned about many aspects of technical production and the printing industry. From Rabbi Meir Zlotowitz and Rabbi Nosson Scherman, two of the most prolific disseminators of Torah today, I have learned so much about the meaningful interplay of literary artistry and visual aesthetics. ArtScroll has set the standard in Jewish publishing, and each of their works is another gem in the crown of Torah. Additionally, they have graciously enhanced this volume by allowing me to make use of their transliteration, and have shared their expertise in editing. I echo the sentiments of thousands worldwide in offering my blessings that they continue their magnificent contributions to add treasures of Jewish learning.

The Illuminated Pirkei Avos was my most recent publication distributed by ArtScroll. Gedalia Zlotowitz, Avraham Biderman and Eli Kroen have been most helpful then, and continue to be of great assistance in marketing. David Schulman of Kromar Printing had shared his technical expertise and creativity to enhance the finished product.

Artistry, like life itself, is a never-ending, ever-emerging process.

The typesetting of Shloimie Nussbaum has helped take my (often inscrutable) longhand into its preliminary typeset form, accurately and patiently. Yaakov Gerber and Yitzchok Saftlas of Bottom Line Design have once again shared their creative computer graphics and professional expertise to enhance my artistic images. I appreciate the transliteration of Chaya Chava Shulman, who helped make the original Hebrew text accessible to the Hebraically challenged. Mrs. Tova Finkelman assisted Rabbi Nosson Scherman שליט"א, in editing the manuscript, and offered many constructive suggestions to allow for greater facility in reading.

A major addition to this edition was the laws section. In a clear, concise style, the information captures the important elements of the Shabbos table, and adds to a greater appreciation of the Shabbos experience. Working on the laws together with my dear son, Rabbi Avi Weinrib, a young *talmid chochom* learning and teaching in the Chicago Community Kollel, was the ultimate *nachas*. May we merit to collaborate on many more Torah projects together. A special thank you to Rabbis Ephraim Friedman, Ari Friedman, Moshe Rosenstein, Sachi Allswang and Horav Dovid Zucker שליט"א, who reviewed the *halachah* section.

Friends, colleagues and study partners have had a profound impact on my works, consciously and subtly. My dear friend, Rabbi Yaakov Solomon, has excelled in his literary artistry and creative outreach efforts. I was privileged to work with him on earlier art/research volumes on Bar Mitzvah and Bat Mitzvah. Study partners R' Yisroel Hisiger, R' Shmuel Danziger, R' Noson Tzvi Cohen and Dr. Chaim Weiss have often been sounding boards for Torah insights, and I value their friendship in learning.

Mention must be made of some of the incredible individuals and organizations, though there are certainly many, many more, that have shared their infectious enthusiasm for Judaism with thousands of Jews who yearn to learn. Dear friend, Rabbi Avrohom Jacobovitz, director of Machon L'Torah in Detroit, first inspired some of his friends and colleagues to share the gift of Shabbos with others. I was privileged to be among them. Rabbi Itchie Lowenbraun and AJOP, Rabbi Ephraim Buchwald and NJOP, Partners in Torah, Aish HaTorah, JEP, Gateways and the hundreds of community *kiruv* groups around the world, have touched the lives of thousands, and inspired a generation to discover Judaism. The NCSY Bencher and the movement it represents, has done so much to make Judaism's spirit and song accessible to thousands. Hopefully, we can build upon the foundation that it has established.

I am fortunate to be able to learn from some masters of inspiration and learning. My esteemed Rav, Horav Eliezer Ginsburg שליט"א, and the encyclopedic knowledge of my Rebbe, Horav Shmuel Yosef Lercher שליט"א, have taught volumes, in text and in character, at our *Bais Hamedrash,* Agudath Israel Snif Zichron Shmuel. I am privileged to learn lessons of Torah and lessons for living from two Torah luminaries, Horav Avrohom Schorr שליט"א, and Horav Elya Brudny שליט"א. My foundations in learning and love for Torah are a credit to the Yeshiva of Hartford, Talmudical Yeshiva of Philadelphia, Mirrer Yeshiva of Brooklyn and Jerusalem. May I be a worthy disciple to share the lessons of Torah that their selfless Rebbeim have taught.

Though *any* talent is a God-given gift, it has to be nurtured and developed. I owe a tremendous debt of gratitude to the heavenly emissaries who help me share my vision of beautiful and meaningful Judaica. I am grateful for the confidence they have in me to faithfully translate subtle messages into visual images on profound Torah texts.

Helene שתחי' and Zyg ע"ה Wolloch commissioned the calligraphy and commentary of the Haggadah in memory of the Holocaust.

I owe a debt of gratitude to Ira and Ingeborg Rennert and Diana and Morad Roshanzamir. They commissioned the books *Bar Mitzvah: Its Observance and Significance,* and *Transitions: The Bat Mitzvah Treasury*, respectively. These have enhanced the understanding of these celebrations, giving them additional meaning.

Rachel and Jack Gindi are patrons of the original scrolls of the *Megillot of Redemption* series on the Five Megillot. Lenore and Stanley Weinstein have helped share the beauty of King David's *tefillos* with the commissioning and publication of *Hallel.* Mr. and Mrs. Rudolph Tessler have embarked with me on a work-in-progress, *Letters of Eternity: The Aleph-Bais Treasury.* Hopefully, we will share their messages together over the coming years. Fred and Cheryl Halpern join me in illuminating the *berachos* in their family heirloom edition, *Shaarei Berachah.*

A special note of appreciation to dear friends Harvey and Naomi Wolinetz, who commissioned my largest work to date, Pirkei Avos/Ethics of the Fathers. In the three and one half years it took to complete the original manuscript, and with the publication of the Collector's Edition and popular editions, we have been humbled by the response. May we continue to see Torah *nachas* and may Hashem answer all our prayers.

My beloved parents, Mr. and Mrs. Chaim Weinrib שיחיו, my dear father-in-law, Rav Leib Isbee זצ"ל, and יבל"ח, my mother-in-law, Mrs. Rose Isbee תחי', deserve my eternal gratitude. They have been inspirational role models and teachers to our family, transmitting the beauty of our heritage to their children.

My wife, Miriam, partner in my every endeavor, role model and inspiration for our family, has helped make our Shabbos experience truly a touch of the World to Come. May we continue to enjoy nachas from our wonderful children and grandchildren.

And to the Master Artist who has given me a gift. I thank You for the heart to be sensitive to the beauty of Your creations; I thank You for the eyes that at times see that which may be hidden from others; I thank You for the mind to comprehend in some measure the depth of Your Torah; and I thank You for the hand to faithfully transcribe that which You have shown me. May I be worthy of being a brush in the Hand of God.

Yonah Weinrib
Shevat 5764

I owe a tremendous debt of gratitude to the heavenly emissaries who help me share my vision of beautiful and meaningful Judaica.

The Shabbos Table:
THE ALTAR BEFORE GOD

The Shabbos Table:
The Altar Before God

 young lady spent a Shabbos at the home of a traditionally observant family. Not coming from such a background herself, this highly intelligent, quite sophisticated professional wanted to experience the Shabbos that friends had told her about. She came away from her taste of Shabbos overwhelmed. "Was it the food? The singing? The words of Torah? The kids?" her friends asked. "It may have been all of them," she answered. "All I know is that when I will have a family, I want my Shabbos to look like *that!*"

What is it about the Shabbos table that makes it so special? One can go to different countries, varied types of communities, homes whose ancestry is traced to Ashkenazic, Sephardic or *chassidic* roots, and each has its own special quality that makes its Shabbos table unique. Judaism is an experiential way of life; theoretical or philosophical lectures about the nature and quality of the Shabbos table cannot measure up to one Shabbos experience.

In essence, the Shabbos table is a microcosm of all that is precious in Judaism. God said to Moses, "I have a wonderful present in My inner treasure house, and its name is Shabbos. Go tell the Jewish People that I wish to give it to them" (Talmud, *Shabbos* 10b). God's statement to the Jewish People about the gift of Shabbos is a message about how to best appreciate it. Come into God's domain if you wish to fully savor His Shabbos. This holy day has to be felt, seen, tasted and embraced by all of one's senses to be enriched by all that it has to offer *(Sfas Emes)*.

Let us examine the elements of Shabbos and try to glean a deeper appreciation of God's present to the Jewish People.

טעמו וראו כי טוב ה' – "Taste and see that God is good" (Psalms 34:9). Perhaps King David is sharing some of the components that help one perceive the goodness of God. Though each ethnic group lays claim to food that has its own unique character, traditional Jewish food simply tastes good. From tried and true recipes that have been handed down through the generations, to haute cuisine cookbooks that present Shabbos and festival food with panache, Jewish food is unique because it is garnished with a healthy dose of spirituality. Standard Jewish Shabbos fare, the challah, the fish, the soup, the cholent and kugel, and all of the טעמו / taste-sensitive elements, are rightfully in the domain of the woman of the home.

Judaism, however, cannot just be tasted; it has to be visible as well. The master of the household will often orchestrate the proceedings at the Shabbos table. From the ritual order of the actual elements of the meal, to sharing and eliciting words of Torah, to presenting thoughts and ideas in the spirit of the day, he is charged with visibly demonstrating Shabbos. Just as any Jewish *balebuste,* or homemaker, couldn't possibly invite guests without adequately preparing for them, a guest as exalted as the Shabbos Queen

Come into God's domain if you wish to fully savor His Shabbos. This holy day has to be felt, seen, tasted and embraced by all of one's senses to be enriched by all that it has to offer

needs forethought and preparation by the wife *and* the husband. The table is bedecked in Shabbos finery, an aura of tranquility fills the home, husband and wife have worked arduously to ensure that each detail is in order as Shabbos arrives.

What are the elements that make a beautifully prepared meal on a Friday night or Saturday into an uplifting Shabbos meal worthy of its name? What does an observer see about Shabbos that gives him or her a glimpse into the beauty of Judaism? The Caesar asked Rabbi Yehoshua ben Chananya about the wonderful aroma of his Shabbos food. "What spice do you put into your food?" he asked the Rabbi. "We have a spice called Shabbos", he told the Caesar. "Please give some to us!" he requested. Rabbi Yehoshua replied, "For those who safeguard the Shabbos, it will be beneficial; for those who do not, it will be of no help." (Talmud, *Shabbos* 119a).

Culinary expertise can add taste to a dish, but the true enhancement of flavor comes from the Shabbos experience. As any great cook can tell you, you can follow a recipe and measure each ingredient exactly, but the taste may vary slightly from week to week. It is no different with the Shabbos meal. The wonderful food, the camaraderie of friends, the warmth of the family, words of Torah, soulful or lively songs and angelic children can all add up to a successful recipe for Shabbos. If we see beyond the luscious challah, hear *zemiros* with a sensitive ear, watch the harmony of a husband and wife sharing together, surrounded by family and friends, the playful children (even if they sometimes quarrel), we see the radiance of Shabbos, truly a touch of the World to Come.

Time — In a technologically sophisticated society like ours, brilliant minds come up with innovative devices to save time – and today's man and woman are always running. If we prayed for a 36-hour day, we could fill it up with things to do, and then some, and we'd ask for more time. The fast food, instant access, DSL, express lanes for *everything* are supposedly there to help us achieve a quality of life that we often find elusive. There's often little opportunity to savor the moment, because we are already on to the next item on our agenda.

Shabbos is general, and the Shabbos table in particular, give today's man, woman and family a treasured opportunity to actually spend time, *meaningful* time, with each other. "Food on the fly" just isn't the taste of Shabbos that our Sages envisioned. Shabbos is a weekly chance to reconnect with each other, even if the rest of the week has offered less and less time in which to do so. There are longer Shabbos meals and shorter ones, and each family can gauge how to best appreciate the additional benefit of Shabbos – the precious gift of time.

Family — We all enjoy the beauty of the Passover Seder, perhaps the most widely celebrated ritual in Judaism. With the festive background of matzos and wine (and, of course, a most delicious repast prepared by the woman of the home, the culinary commander-in-chief), generations sit together and relate the story of our Exodus from Egypt. Often it is a multi-generational experience; grandparents sharing our national and often personal history with children and grandchildren, faithfully transmitting the tenets of our faith. Through story and song, food and family, the links to our beautiful heritage are forged, and children relive our slavery and ultimate redemption.

If crafted correctly, the Shabbos table can become a weekly *seder*. Extended family and friends join with the nuclear family to create a bond that transcends age differences and personal levels of observance. The unity and joint sense of purpose that bring children, their parents and grand-parents together at the Shabbos table, make it a meaningful vehicle to transmit the beauty of our heritage.

Food — גדול לגימה שמקרבת רחוקים – Great is the provision of food, because it brings together individuals who were distant (Talmud, *Sanhedrin* 103b). Food creates a bond. The invitation to someone to join a family at their Shabbos table is not merely a way to satisfy his hunger; it is an invitation to become part of the extended family. Shabbos foods are deeply rooted in custom and tradition (see section on Shabbos Foods), and beckon the invitee to enjoy the warmth of the family as much as the warmth of the food. The *mitzvah* of *hachnosos orchim* means more than greeting guests. הכנסה means to allow one to enter, and that assumes that for the duration of his stay, the guest will not merely partake of the food, but become part of the family.

Words of Torah — A Shabbos table becomes enhanced when Torah thoughts on the portion of the week, upcoming festivals, philosophy and other areas of Jewish interest are discussed. The table becomes an informal classroom where concepts are learned, knowledge is dissemi-nated, and the concept of the primacy of Torah as a force in our lives becomes reinforced. Just as at the Passover Seder the commandment of "and you shall tell your son" (*Shemos* 13:8) comes alive as a father shares lessons about faith in God with his children, so it is with Shabbos. The father demonstrates to his children that the Torah which I study is important, and the lessons which you are taught lay the foundation for your future. The depth of Torah can be underscored when one question or thought is examined by different commentators.

Zemiros and Song — Singing at the Shabbos table is not only limited to those with beautiful voices. The messages of our songs are found in themes expressed in the *zemiros* which date back hundreds of years, or the contemporary tunes with lyrics from our prayers or Psalms. The *zemiros* are the songs of our soul, the haunting melodies that reflect the pain of our exile and our longing to return to our homeland. Upbeat refrains express the exultation of Shabbos, and our pride as Jews. These are the domain of everyone, the musically-gifted and those whose expansive heart on Shabbos exceeds their ability to stay on key.

Our Sages describe Shabbos as an inheritance. Shabbos, with its accompanying rituals, songs and experiences, is often handed down from generation to generation.

"Bequeath to us, Hashem, our God, with love and with desire, Your holy Shabbos" *(Shabbos liturgy)*. Our Sages describe Shabbos as an inheritance. Shabbos, with its accompanying rituals, songs and experiences, is often handed down from generation to generation. We build upon the traditions that we have seen, adding touches of our own to enhance the Shabbos experience for ourselves and our children. The *zemiros* and songs that we sing at the table are the melodic background that Shabbos provides for the harmony of Creation.

Parents, Children and Relationships — In addition to transmitting Jewish teachings to our children, the Shabbos table affords us the opportunity to impact positively on our children's development. The pedagogic skill and Solomonic wisdom that parents must possess to be successful with their children are often called into play at the Shabbos table. Let's face it; kids are kids. The attention span they can be expected to have at an adult-oriented Shabbos meal is limited, and *our* patience as parents has to make allowances for theirs as children.

A refrain sometimes heard is, "I could *never* invite guests to my home for Shabbos, the way my kids act!" The discomfort and misbehavior of young children at mealtime is axiomatic; the way we react to them is our statement about Jewish principles in child rearing. Children offer a meaningful dimension to the Shabbos table, for it offers them a chance to share their learning and experiences during the week, and an opportunity for parents to interact meaningfully with them.

Friendships and Bonding — "Either friendship or death!" The statement uttered by *Choni HaMa'agol,* sage of the *Mishnah* (Talmud, *Ta'anis* 23a), points to the importance of human companionship. People need friends, and meaning is added to life when social interaction is positively directed, with the Shabbos table as a most agreeable host. A network and sense of community develops where friends meet like-minded individuals. Married couples extend their families in friendship to the unattached and share camaraderie, warmth and lessons for life.

Most importantly, an individual at a Shabbos table is perforce an ambassador of God. He or she conveys, subtly or otherwise, the teachings of Torah they have learned and the Torah lifestyle that they live. We are all teachers, sharing the messages about what it means to be Jewish to all those who are willing to learn from us.

Spirituality — By its very nature, the spiritual dimension of Shabbos cannot be tasted or seen, but must be experienced. It touches all of the elements outlined above, and it transforms the secular into the holy, the simple into the special. Filtered through the prism of Torah, day to day experiences are elevated to a higher plane, and infused with a touch of the Divine.

The Ultimate Shabbos Experience — The many dimensions discussed above are some of the ingredients that help create a successful Shabbos recipe. The varied expressions that make each family's table unique are the beautiful tapestry that represents our nation. Some have more food than *zemiros,* others will be heavy on words of Torah while lighter on the camaraderie, still others will have a rich assortment of all of these. The best combination is one which enables each of the participants to come away from the Shabbos table inspired, until they can't wait to experience another beautiful Shabbos.

The *Midrash* (*Shemos* 5:18) relates the interchange between Moses and Pharaoh, when the former was growing up in the palace of the king. The Jews were enslaved and Moses felt their pain. "Pharaoh," said Moses, "if the Jews work incessantly, they will not be productive workers in the service of the king." "What is your recommendation?" Pharaoh asked Moses. "Give them one day to rest and recharge their energies, and in that way you will maximize the benefits you derive from them." Moses selected the day of Shabbos, and even before the Jews received the Torah, Shabbos was designated as the day in which they not only physically rested, but were spiritually uplifted.

What did the Jews in Egypt do on Shabbos? One would imagine that after a week filled with back-breaking work, they would merely collapse from exhaustion. The *midrash* tells us otherwise. Families would sit together and review scrolls called the *megillos,* or scrolls of redemption. Rav Yaakov Kamenetsky z"l posits that they contained the psalm מזמור שיר ליום השבת, a song for the Shabbos day. In this chapter there is in fact, no discussion of Shabbos at all. A focal concept is the suffering of the righteous and the prospering of the wicked. The psalm concludes that ultimately evildoers will be destroyed and the righteous will live on. Passed on from their ancestors, the Patriarchs, they were told of the salvation that was promised to the Jewish nation, and how they would reach the Promised Land as God's Chosen People.

The Jews in Egypt spent their Shabbos as a time of hope and inspiration. They would divest themselves of the pain and worry of their grueling week, and the stories and messages that were passed down from their fathers enabled them to push through till the following week. They lived with the faith that God would correct the injustices they suffered, and punish the Egyptians.

Perhaps this was the forerunner of our present-day Shabbos experience. We struggle to get through the week, overcoming the work, the obstacles and the difficulties that each of us face. We seek the refuge of our day of rest and contentment. We elevate the physical and enable our spirits to spend the Shabbos as a day of inspiration. We share words and songs that give us hope and a sense of anxious anticipation. The messages of Sages of old carry us beyond the exile, and we live awaiting a better tomorrow. The days of work and creative activity will end, and surrounded by family and friends, we will bask in the radiance of the World to Come.

We seek the refuge of our day of rest and contentment. We elevate the physical and enable our spirits to spend the Shabbos as a day of inspiration.

Erev Shabbos:
PREPARING FOR SHABBOS

Shabbos is compared to a queen, and a guest of such lofty stature deserves to be accorded her proper honor. From the clothes we wear to the foods we serve, to the physical activities in which we are engaged in anticipation of our special guest, we demonstrate our excitement at the arrival of Shabbos.

In the Wilderness, the Jews were commanded to construct a *mishkan*, or Tabernacle, a physical structure that would be a repository for the Divine Presence. Gold, silver, wood, textiles and hides were the physical trappings that would be infused with sanctity, enabling the sublime presence of God to be accorded a resting place on earth. Just as Jews were ennobled to have a spatial way-station for holiness, so, too, Shabbos affords us the opportunity to create a Divine resting place in the dimension of time. The greater the preparations in anticipation of the Shabbos, the greater its impact upon ourselves and our family.

Preparing for Shabbos was not viewed by our Sages as menial work, but as an exalted and spiritual activity. Even work which easily could have been delegated to servants was undertaken by the Rabbis themselves. Preparations to greet the Shabbos Queen were likened to greeting the *Shechinah,* the Divine Presence itself. (Talmud, *Shabbos 119a*)

- Rav Papa would prepare the wicks to be used in the oil lamps for Shabbos.
- Rav Zeira would kindle the fire for Shabbos.
- Rav Nachman the son of Yitzchok would busy himself incessantly with buying the necessary items for Shabbos. "If Rav Avina and Rav Ashi, the great Torah scholars, would pay me a visit, wouldn't I busy myself acquiring the finest foods in *their* honor? Surely, I must do the same for Shabbos."
- Rav Chisda sliced beets for the Shabbos meal.
- Rav Abahu would sit and fan the fire in the oven to help in the preparation of Shabbos meals.
- Rava would salt the Shabbos fish.

There are times in life when one's preparations can be almost as important as his accomplishments. The feeling of *nachas* at a Bar Mitzvah and the joy of a wedding day become enhanced by the months of preparations which preceded it. Indeed, the preparation becomes an end in itself. We extend a vacation by constantly thinking about it, we elevate a simcha by planning for it, we enhance the Shabbos experience by adequately preparing for it. We work and we work, and sheer exhaustion is the only result. But when we invest our time to prepare for Shabbos, God gives us *His* Shabbos, a gift from the innermost chambers of the Almighty.

We extend a vacation by constantly thinking about it, we elevate a simcha by planning for it, we enhance the Shabbos experience by adequately preparing for it.

Preparing for Shabbos
This World and the World to Come

ur Sages viewed life and living with a clarity that far surpasses our myopic vision. The parables drawn from everyday life share a glimpse of the world as it is meant to be seen. "One who toils on *erev* Shabbos will eat on Shabbos; if he doesn't toil then, from what will he eat on Shabbos" (Talmud, *Avodah Zarah 3a*).

The six days of the week, when one is engaged in physical activities, are the *erev* Shabbos, the eve of Shabbos of life. When Shabbos finally arrives, a feeling of tranquility descends, and all work comes to a halt. We are at ease, knowing that we are preparing to partake of the actual day of rest for which we have prepared. If we prepare, we eat; if we do not, we go hungry.

On a cosmic level, the Sages viewed the six days of physical activity as a parallel to our earthly existence. We toil, we plan, we build and we create, yet the fruits of our labors are not necessarily meant to be enjoyed in this world. Judaism does not eschew the pleasures of life. Rather, it allows us to partake of them in a more profound sense, for a greater purpose. We are preparing for *The* Shabbos, the day of eternal Shabbos – the World to Come. Every action, each good deed performed during our lifetime is an investment for eternity.

> An intern working long and hard hours in the hospital realizes that his efforts in pursuing a livelihood far exceed those of his non-professional counterparts. "Why put in such long hours? Look at your friend, he's getting by with fewer hours and half the effort?" his friends would chide him. Upon entering the medical field and earning far more than his non-professional colleague, the efforts he expended are now justified as a meaningful investment toward a greater reward.

To derive a lesson about the temporal and eternal life from the six days of creation and Shabbos, we must have a better understanding of these days and their relationship to Shabbos. According to some *halachic,* Jewish legal authorities, Shabbos is unique in that there is a Torah commandment to prepare for it. We build a *succah* on *Succos*, eat *matzah* on Passover, put on *tefillin* each day, yet these are the actual fulfillments of those *mitzvos*; there is no explicit commandment to prepare for their performance. Although any performance is enhanced by forethought and adequate preparation, the Torah wants us to take time and effort to ensure the proper observance of Shabbos. To the extent that we prepare ourselves to appropriately greet the Shabbos, to that extent we will fully appreciate its holiness.

Shabbos: Day of Contentment
In the Talmud and Midrash

◈ Rav Zeira said, "Initially, when I saw the Rabbis running to a lecture on Shabbos, I felt they were desecrating the sanctity of the day. When I heard the teaching that one should always run to hear Jewish legal discussions, I, too, would run." (Talmud, *Berachos* 6a).

◈ R' Shimon bar Yochai and his son R' Elazar left the cave in Peki'in where they hid from the Romans for thirteen years. When they ultimately left the cave, they saw an old man running just before sundown on *erev* Shabbos, holding two myrtle branches. "Why do you carry these? We asked him. "I am bringing them to honor the Shabbos. One is for זכור, to remember the Shabbos, and one is for שמור, to safeguard the Shabbos" (Talmud, *Shabbos* 33b).

◈ These two aspects of Shabbos represent the Jews' obligation to remember the Shabbos by observing its positive commandments, and safeguarding it by refraining from transgressing its prohibitions. Two candles (at least) are lit on erev Shabbos, one for זכור and one for שמור. One who is exacting in the *mitzvah* of lighting the Shabbos candles will merit children who are Torah scholars. Similarly, one who maintains the custom of having fragrant myrtle in honor of the Shabbos, merits the same reward, as the righteous are likened to myrtles (*Maharsha* ibid.).

◈ "If you proclaim the Shabbos day 'honored,' and you honor it by not being involved in your personal affairs, pursuing your own needs or discussing forbidden matters — then you will delight in Hashem" (Isaiah 58:13). The Talmud looks at Shabbos as a day in which we involve ourselves in spiritual matters and divest ourselves of the mundane. One's clothing on Shabbos should not be like the clothing he wears all week; the way we walk and talk on Shabbos is different from that of the weekday. We are dressed in special clothes designated for Shabbos, and our conversation should not involve any business matters (Talmud, *Shabbos* 113a).

◈ If the Jewish people would safeguard two consecutive Shabbosos, being conscientious to uphold all of its *halachic* aspects, we would be immediately redeemed (Talmud, *Shabbos* 118b).

◈ The *Mishnah* (*Pirkei Avos* 5:19) lists ten things that were created on the eve of the first Shabbos, just before sundown. There was a tremendous amount of creative activity by God as the weekdays were about to come to a close. Perhaps this explains why preparations are so hectic on every Friday just before Shabbos arrives. Just as the first days of creation ended with a tremendous flurry of activity before the advent of Shabbos, so too, it is with our lives. Hopefully, our day of rest will also in some way mirror that of the Creator.

Laws of Erev Shabbos
Preparing for Shabbos

🍥 To properly honor Shabbos, one should be personally involved in Shabbos preparations, even if one has household help.

🍥 Although, ordinarily, one should avoid household activity before morning davening, necessary Shabbos preparations are permissible.

🍥 It is considered a special honor to the Shabbos to make one's own *challah,* rather than using store-bought *challah.*

🍥 One should avoid doing laundry on Friday in order to devote one's full attention to Shabbos preparations.

🍥 One should shower or bathe on Friday in hot water in honor of Shabbos.

🍥 It is proper to groom one's hair and fingernails on Friday in honor of the Shabbos.

🍥 One should avoid sitting down to a meal from three hours before Shabbos in order to begin the Friday night meal with a hearty appetite. "Hours" are calculated by dividing the number of hours from sunrise to sunset by twelve. These are known as *"sha'os zmaniyos",* seasonal hours. However, one should avoid entering Shabbos overly hungry.

🍥 It is proper to cover all tables in the home in honor of Shabbos.

🍥 It is a *mitzvah* to taste the Shabbos foods on Friday to ensure that the seasoning and spices are as desired.

🍥 One honors Shabbos by setting aside special clothing to wear on this holy day. One should not differentiate his mode of dress, whether in Shul, at home, or even spending the entire Shabbos by himself. Special clothing is in honor of the day regardless of the company.

🍥 It is proper for women to be dressed for Shabbos before lighting candles.

🍥 It is an honor to Shabbos that the table be fully set before the man of the home arrives from shul.

One must remove challah *from dough, which has a thick consistency and is made from wheat, barley, spelt, oats or rye. If it has 43*$^{1}/_{5}$ *egg measures, one must make a blessing. Once an olive-sized measure is removed, it should be thoroughly burned.*

הַפְרָשַׁת חַלָּה

בָּרוּךְ אַתָּה יְיָ אֱלֹהֵינוּ מֶלֶךְ הָעוֹלָם אֲשֶׁר קִדְּשָׁנוּ בְּמִצְוֹתָיו וְצִוָּנוּ לְהַפְרִישׁ חַלָּה מִן הָעִסָּה:

יְהִי רָצוֹן מִלְּפָנֶיךָ יְיָ אֱלֹהֵינוּ וֵאלֹהֵי אֲבוֹתֵינוּ שֶׁהַמִּצְוָה שֶׁל הַפְרָשַׁת חַלָּה תִּתְחַשֵׁב כְּאִלּוּ קִיַּמְתִּיהָ בְּכָל פְּרָטֶיהָ וְדִקְדּוּקֶיהָ. וְתֵחָשֵׁב הֲרָמַת הַחַלָּה שֶׁאֲנִי מְרִימָה כְּמוֹ הַקָּרְבָּן שֶׁהֻקְרַב עַל הַמִּזְבֵּחַ שֶׁנִּתְקַבֵּל בְּרָצוֹן. וּכְמוֹ שֶׁלְּפָנִים הָיְתָה הַחַלָּה נְתוּנָה לַכֹּהֵן וְהָיְתָה זוֹ לְכַפָּרַת עֲוֹנוֹת כָּךְ תִּהְיֶה לְכַפָּרָה לַעֲוֹנוֹתַי. וְאָז אֶהְיֶה כְּאִלּוּ נוֹלַדְתִּי מֵחָדָשׁ נְקִיָּה מֵחֵטְא וְעָוֹן. וְאוּכַל לְקַיֵּם מִצְוַת שַׁבָּת קֹדֶשׁ וְהַיָּמִים הַטּוֹבִים עִם בַּעֲלִי (וִילָדֵינוּ) לִהְיוֹת נִזּוֹנִים מִקְּדוּשַׁת הַיָּמִים הָאֵלּוּ וּמֵהַשְׁפָּעָתָהּ שֶׁל מִצְוַת חַלָּה יִהְיוּ יְלָדֵינוּ נִזּוֹנִים תָּמִיד מִיָּדָיו שֶׁל הַקָּבָּ"ה בְּרוֹב רַחֲמָיו וַחֲסָדָיו, וּבְרֹב אַהֲבָה. וְשֶׁתִּתְקַבֵּל מִצְוַת חַלָּה כְּאִלּוּ נָתַתִּי מַעֲשֵׂר וּכְשֵׁם שֶׁהֲרֵינִי מְקַיֶּמֶת מִצְוַת חַלָּה בְּכָל לֵב, כָּךְ יִתְעוֹרְרוּ רַחֲמָיו שֶׁל הַקָּבָּ"ה לְשָׁמְרֵנִי מִצַּעַר וּמִמַּכְאוֹבִים כָּל הַיָּמִים אָמֵן:

22

In the Holy Temple, a part of our produce was removed and given to the priestly family, the kohanim. (Numbers 15:18) A portion of the challah was given to the kohein. He was dependent on the largesse of the Israelites, and they in turn, needed his offerings as an atonement for the sins of the Jewish nation.

The blessing is only recited if the requisite amount of flour is used, approximately five pounds. One is required to separate challah even if less flour is used, but without a blessing.

Separating Challah

Blessed are You, Hashem our God, King of the Universe, who has sanctified us by His commandments and commanded us to separate the challah from the dough.

Boruch atoh Adōnoy, Elōhaynu melech ho-ōlom, asher kidshonu b'mitzvōsov, v'tzivonu l'hafrish challoh min ho'isoh.

Since Judaism advocates experiencing Shabbos, the best way to appreciate the mitzvah of challah is by making (and eating) it.

Ingredients

5 pounds flour, 1 cup oil, 3 tbsp. salt, 4 eggs
4 ounces fresh yeast, 4 cups warm water, 1½ cups sugar

Directions

Put flour, salt and sugar in a bowl, form a well in the flour.

Dissolve yeast into 2 cups of the warm water with 1 tbsp. sugar.

Pour into the well — let sit for five minutes until yeast bubbles.

Add oil, eggs and the rest of the water.

Knead well until the dough becomes smooth and elastic.

It should spring back when pressed with the fingertips.

When dough rises, separate a piece the size of an olive, and thoroughly burn it.

When more than 5 lbs. of flour are used, recite the blessing above.

Form loaves. Brush lightly with egg beaten with 1 tsp. of sugar.

Bake at 350° for 45-50 minutes until golden brown.

The Sign of Shabbos

habbos is called a sign, אות, between the Jews and their Creator. This sign attests to God's role in creating the world in six days and resting on the seventh, Shabbos. The Talmud says that one who willfully desecrates the Shabbos is reckoned as if he transgressed the entire Torah. So fundamental is Shabbos to the Jewish people that one who undermines its sanctity has demonstrated his disregard for the Torah and all its precepts.

The *Chofetz Chaim* (1839-1933) explains the exalted status of Shabbos with the following parable. A shopkeeper displayed a shingle over his store announcing to his townsfolk that he was preparing to embark on a career as a craftsman. Weeks were spent readying the shop for customers. With his new tools on hand, it appeared that he was now ready to accept commissions for work. To their surprise, the townspeople arrived at the store one day to find the doors locked and the shutters down. "Obviously, the shopkeeper must be involved in a personal matter, which precluded him from opening today," they thought. The scene repeated itself on the following day. "Maybe the shopkeeper had a family *simcha* which took him out of town," they surmised. A third day passed, as did a fourth, and again, the shutters were down and the doors locked. The townspeople continued to speculate about the shopkeeper's absence.

At the end of the week, the townspeople came to the store, but this time the scene was different. Not only were the doors locked, but the shingle had been removed. As long as the sign was displayed over the store, the people knew that the owner was still operating. Once the sign was down, they knew sadly that the shopkeeper was, unfortunately, no longer in business.

Shabbos is the sign that we proudly display, proclaiming our unique relationship with the Creator. We may stumble in our personal and collective observance, but our fealty to God and His traditions is underscored as long as we maintain Shabbos observance. Once the sign between us has, heaven forbid, been removed, on some level, the business is closed. The pre-eminent position that Shabbos plays is an eternal testimony to the relationship between God and the Jews.

Candle Lighting:
ILLUMINATING THE SHABBOS

Prayers through the Generations

he young man studying in the great Ponovez Yeshiva in Bnei Brak was stopped by one of his teachers. Familiar with the secular nature of his student's family, the Rebbe wondered how it came to be that he should pursue a life of Torah study in Ponovez. "Actually," said the student, "my family left the path of Torah long ago. Both my grandfather and grandmother grew up on an irreligious *kibbutz* and, upon marriage, they agreed to continue their secular lifestyle – with one exception. My grandmother lit candles every Friday night, a tradition she inherited from her mother. There was really no other semblance of tradition, but this was the one practice that she kept each week.

Her candle-lighting was accompanied by a fervent prayer for her children. As the State of Israel had been recently established, she prayed that her children grow to be as great as David Ben-Gurion, Prime Minister of Israel. Her choice of role model reflected her limited understanding of the definition of greatness. At the time, he was the symbol of leadership in our country, and she hoped that her children and descendants would follow in his footsteps."

The student continued the saga. "My grandfather, Zalman Oran, was a close friend of the Prime Minister, and served in his cabinet. At an important meeting regarding the nature of the State, my grandfather was asked to accompany Ben-Gurion to meet Rav Avrohom Yeshayah Karelitz, the great Chazon Ish. After the meeting, the two Israeli dignitaries commented about the aura cast by this great Torah Sage, his wisdom and noble bearing. My grandfather came home and reverently told my grandmother about their inspiring encounter with greatness. 'I have met an angel!' my grandfather exclaimed. That Friday night, my grand-mothers prayer had a different message: 'May my children merit to be great ... like the Chazon Ish.' Heartfelt prayers, sincerely uttered by a Jewish mother at the time of candle-lighting, helped her descendant develop into a student worthy of studying in the great Ponovez Yeshiva.

As Shabbos begins, the prayers, the tears and heartfelt requests of each Jewish mother ascend heavenward with the light of the Shabbos candles.

Laws of Candle Lighting
Illuminating the Shabbos

☙ The candles should be lit 18-20 minutes before sundown. In Jerusalem, the custom is to light 40 minutes before sundown. If one is running late, the candles can be lit until sundown. If one is unsure if sundown has arrived, one should not light candles.

☙ The earliest time one can light candles is 1 ¼ hours before sundown (seasonal hours). If one lights before this time, he/she has not fulfilled the obligation and should light again with a new blessing. One should be especially aware during the summer months when accepting "early Shabbos" that they are lighting at the proper time.

☙ When lighting candles, one should hold the match or candle to the wick until the candle is fully lit.

☙ There is a basic difference between men and woman regarding the blessing recitation at candle lighting. Blessings over *mitzvos* are generally recited immediately preceding the performance of the *mitzvah*. However, once a woman recites the blessing over the candles, she automatically accepts Shabbos. It would therefore be forbidden for women to light the candles after recitation of the blessing. The accepted custom is to first light the candles, cover one's eyes (as not to benefit from the light until after recitation of the blessing), recite the blessing, and then uncover one's eyes and enjoy the light of the candles. Men, however, do not accept Shabbos until sundown or upon reciting the Shabbos prayers, and should first recite the blessing and then light the candles.

In situations of need one may make a conditional acceptance of Shabbos enabling them to light candles without fully accepting Shabbos. A competant halachic authority should be consulted.

☙ The custom is to wave one's hands over the candles (towards one-self) before reciting the blessing after lighting, to usher in the Shabbbos.

☙ The prevalent custom is to light two candles. Many add an additional candle for each child. However, if one is away from home, only two candles are lit.

☙ There is a time-honored custom that charity is given before candle lighting.

☙ Following candle lighting, it is an opportune moment to pray for the health and success of one's family. (See page 30)

Laws of Candle Lighting
Illuminating the Shabbos

- There are three reasons we light candles before Shabbos: 1) To honor the day, as candles are often lit during festive occasions. 2) Eating by candlelight enhances the Shabbos meal. 3) To avoid stumbling and disturbing the peace of Shabbos.

- Based on the second reason it is most appropriate that the candles are lit on or near the table where the Shabbos meal is being eaten. Based on the third reason one should have some form of light in all rooms that will be occupied throughout Shabbos.

- The candles should be lit specifically for Shabbos. If they were lit for any other purpose they should be extinguished and lit again solely in honor of Shabbos.

- Candle lighting for the entire household is generally incumbent on the woman of the home, since she is usually the one most involved in running it. The husband should be involved by setting up and preparing the candles to be lit.

- If the woman of the home will be away on Shabbos, her husband should light. If he is also away, a daughter above the age of twelve should light. If not, a boy over thirteen should light.

- In a situation where the husband is traveling, there is no need for him to light where he is. If his wife is traveling, the custom is for her to light where she is. If both husband and wife are traveling together, they should light where they are. If they are in separate places, each has their own obligation to light where they are.

- If one plans to sleep at home but eat outside the home, two options apply. Preferably, the candles should be lit at home before Shabbos begins. However, this is only an option if some benefit is derived from the candles after nightfall. This would mean either before leaving or upon returning home one should derive benefit from the light of the candles. If this is not an option, one should arrive at his hosts' home before Shabbos, and light there.

- When at a hotel for Shabbos, one should light either in the hotel room or on his private table. At the very least the candlelight should be in a place that will benefit those sitting there. If this is not an option, one should additionally turn on an electric light in the room with the intent to fulfill their obligation of lighting candles. Regarding the blessing a competant *halachic* authority should be consulted.

בָּרוּךְ

אַתָּה יְיָ אֱלֹהֵינוּ מֶלֶךְ
הָעוֹלָם אֲשֶׁר קִדְּשָׁנוּ בְּמִצְוֹתָיו
וְצִוָּנוּ לְהַדְלִיק נֵר שֶׁל שַׁבָּת:

יְהִי רָצוֹן

לְפָנֶיךָ יְיָ אֱלֹהַי וֵאלֹהֵי אֲבוֹתַי, שֶׁתְּחוֹנֵן
אוֹתִי (וְאֶת אִישִׁי, וְאֶת בָּנַי, וְאֶת בְּנוֹתַי,
וְאֶת אָבִי, וְאֶת אִמִּי) וְאֶת כָּל קְרוֹבַי;
וְתִתֶּן לָנוּ וּלְכָל יִשְׂרָאֵל חַיִּים טוֹבִים
וַאֲרוּכִים, וְתִזְכְּרֵנוּ בְּזִכְרוֹן טוֹבָה וּבְרָכָה;
וְתִפְקְדֵנוּ בִּפְקֻדַּת יְשׁוּעָה וְרַחֲמִים;
וּתְבָרְכֵנוּ בְּרָכוֹת גְּדוֹלוֹת; וְתַשְׁלִים בָּתֵּינוּ;
וְתַשְׁכֵּן שְׁכִינָתְךָ בֵּינֵינוּ, וְזַכֵּנִי לְגַדֵּל בָּנִים
וּבְנֵי בָנִים חֲכָמִים וּנְבוֹנִים, אוֹהֲבֵי יְיָ, יִרְאֵי
אֱלֹהִים, אַנְשֵׁי אֱמֶת, זֶרַע קֹדֶשׁ, בַּיְיָ דְּבֵקִים,
וּמְאִירִים אֶת הָעוֹלָם בַּתּוֹרָה וּבְמַעֲשִׂים טוֹבִים,
וּבְכָל מְלֶאכֶת עֲבוֹדַת הַבּוֹרֵא. אָנָּא שְׁמַע אֶת
תְּחִנָּתִי בָּעֵת הַזֹּאת, בִּזְכוּת שָׂרָה וְרִבְקָה
וְרָחֵל וְלֵאָה אִמּוֹתֵינוּ, וְהָאֵר נֵרֵנוּ שֶׁלֹּא
יִכְבֶּה לְעוֹלָם וָעֶד, וְהָאֵר פָּנֶיךָ וְנִוָּשֵׁעָה, אָמֵן:

FRIDAY NIGHT

BLESSED are You, Hashem, our God, King of the universe, who has sanctified us with His commandments and commanded us to kindle the light of Shabbos

Boruch atoh Adōnoy Elōhaynu melech ho-ōlom, asher kidshonu b'mitzvōsov v'tzivonu l'hadlik nayr shel Shabbos.

MAY IT BE Your will, Hashem our God, and the God of our forefathers, that You grace me (and my husband, and sons and daughters, and my father and my mother) and all my relatives, and give to us and to all of Israel a good and long life; that You remember us favorably and with a blessing; that You recall us with salvation and mercy; and that You bless us with plentiful blessings, that You make our homes complete, and that You should make Your Divine Presence dwell among us. Grant us the merit to raise children and grandchildren who are wise and understanding, who love Hashem and fear Him. Men of truth, holy offspring, who cleave to Hashem and who enlighten the world with Torah and good deeds, and with all work in the service of the Creator. I plead with You, Hashem, hear my prayer at this time in the merit of Sarah, Rebecca, Rachel and Leah, our matriarchs. And illuminate our candles that they may never be extinguished for ever and ever. And let Your Countenance shine upon us that we may be saved. Amen.

Y'HI ROTZŌN l'fonecho, Adōnoy Elōhai v'Elōhay avōsai, she-t'chōnayn ōsi (v'es ishi, v'es bonai, v'es bnōsai, v'es ovi, v'es imi) v'es kol k'rōvai; v'sitayn lonu u'lchol Yisroayl chayim tōvim va'aruchim, v'sizk'raynu b'zichrōn tōvoh u'vrochoh, v'sifk'daynu bifkudas y'shu'oh v'rachamim, u'svor-chaynu b'rochos g'dōlōs, v'sashlim botaynu, v'sashkayn Sh'chinoscho baynaynu. V'zakayni l'gadayl bonim uvnay vonim chachomim u'nevōnim, ōhavay Adonoy, yiray Elōhim, anshay emes, zera kōdesh ba'Adōnoy d'vaykim um'irim es ho-ōlom baTōrah uvma-asim tōvim u'vchol m'leches avōdas habōray. Ono shma es t'chinosi ho'ays hazōs bizchus Soroh, v'Rivkoh v'Rochel v'Layoh imōsaynu, v'ho'ayr nayraynu shelō yichbeh l'ōlom vo-ed. V'ho-ayr ponecho v'nivoshay-oh. Omayn.

Candle-Lighting
In the Talmud and Midrash

One who is regularly accustomed to light candles (a reference to Shabbos and Chanukah candles), will merit to havs sons that are Torah scholars (Talmud, *Shabbos* 23b). *Maharsha* comments that the masculine verb רגיל, rather than the feminine, רגילה, is used. This is to underscore the husband's role in the *mitzvah* of candle lighting. He may prepare the candles, singe the wicks, or pour the oil in the candelabra. It is his responsibility to ensure that his wife lights candles at the proper time.

One of the miracles that occurred during Sarah's lifetime was that the candles she lit on Friday night would burn until the following week. (Additionally, there was a blessing found in the challah she baked and there was a cloud, representing God-liness, hovering above her tent *(Midrash Rabbah)* When Isaac took Rivka as a wife, the Torah relates: "And Isaac brought her [Rivka] into the tent of his mother, Sarah." Rashi quotes the *Midrash* that these supernatural occurrences had stopped with Sarah's death. When Isaac married Rivka and these three occurrences returned, it was as if Sarah's tent had become revived through Rivka, a heavenly corroboration of Isaac's choice of a wife.

The *mitzvah* of candle-lighting is primarily incumbent on the woman of the home. When Eve ate of the fruit from the Tree of Knowledge in Gan Eden, she brought death to the world. If man would have lived in a state of perfection, there would be no need for the atonement of death. Since the first woman was responsible for the "extinguishing the light of the world" by bringing death to mankind, she is forever charged with restoring that illumination by kindling the Shabbos lights (*Orach Chaim* 263:3).

If you (the children of Israel) safeguard the candles of Shabbos, I (Hashem) will safeguard the candles of Zion (*Yalkut Shimoni, Beha'aloscha*). God's protection of the Land of Israel and the bringing of the ultimate redemption will reflect the care and concern we display for candle-lighting and the Shabbos itself.

Candle-Lighting
In the Talmud and Midrash

◦ Two objects are likened to the lamp and the illumination of the flame; the soul of man and the mitzvos of Hashem כי נר מצוה ותורה אור (משליו:כג). "Because the mitzvah is like the lamp and the torah is light" (Proverbs 6:23). Man's soul is compared to a candle, as the verse states "נר ה' נשמת אדם", the soul of man is like the lamp of Hashem. God challenges man to be exacting in the performance of *mitzvos*. If you are careful to safeguard Hashem's lamp, His *mitzvos*, then He will safeguard your lamp, your soul" (*Devarim Rabbah* 2).

◦ If one has only enough money to buy wine for Kiddush or oil for Chanukah candle-lighting, he should buy oil to kindle the Chanukah lights, because that *mitzvah* is extremely beloved. If one has only enough money to buy oil for Shabbos, or oil for Chanukah lights, Shabbos takes precedence over Chanukah. Lighting candles in the home on Shabbos brings peace and tranquility, and the Torah stresses the importance of harmony in the Jewish home (*Rambam,* Laws of Chanukah 4:13, based on Talmud, *Shabbos* 23b).

◦ The man of the home must say to his family members on *erev* Shabbos, before dark, "Did you tithe (as one may not tithe on Shabbos)? Did you construct an eruv (a partition enabling carrying from one domain to the next, עירובי חצירות and עירובי תחומין)? Kindle the Shabbos lights! (Talmud, *Shabbos* 34a). The first two subjects are asked as questions, while the request to light the Shabbos candles is a directive from the husband to his wife, as it is obvious whether his wife has lit the Shabbos candles. The woman of the home acts as her husband's emissary in this *mitzvah*, enabling him to have a share in the *mitzvah* (*Aishel Avrohom*).

◦ "And God blessed the seventh day" (*Bereishis* 2:3). With what did He bless it? With light! (*Midrash Rabbah*)

of Shabbos descends upon the Jewish home, we bless our daughters that they live a life of holiness.

Interestingly, the paragons of greatness after which young men are directed to pattern their lives are Ephraim and Menashe, rather than the Patriarchs, Abraham, Isaac and Jacob. After Joseph was reunited with his father Jacob, he told him: "In you will Israel be blessed; may God make you like Ephraim and Menashe," and he placed Ephraim before Menashe (*Bereishis* 35:14) although Menashe was the elder brother. Throughout the generations, fathers have blessed their sons to be like the grandchildren of Jacob, the two sons of Joseph.

What made these two young men worthy of being the focus of parental blessings for generations to come?

The messages of Torah are timeless. The blessing that was applicable in Egypt three thousand years ago to Ephraim and Menashe speaks to the young man of today's day and age as well. Joseph, a viceroy of Egypt, was responsible for governing the country. When his father Jacob came down to Egypt at the end of his life, to some extent he found the tranquility that had evaded him until then. He was able to spend his remaining years in Torah study, with Ephraim as his partner. Menashe was his father's assistant in running the affairs of state.

As the children of Joseph and the grandchildren of Jacob, their upbringing would certainly be fitting for the family of our forefathers. Yet they were the first children raised totally in a foreign country whose mores and customs were antithetical to the values they were taught at home. The pervasive danger of a morally bankrupt society was of great concern to Jacob, and their ability to grow as scions of the house of Jacob made them the source for blessing for all time. A father in today's society passes on the blessing which echoes from generations past. "May you be like Ephraim and Menashe, who grew up in an environment where Torah values did not reign supreme, yet remained faithful to its precepts."

In Jacob's blessing there is another word of caution. "And he placed Ephraim *before* Menashe." Ephraim, who personified an unswerving loyalty to Torah and its study, took priority over Menashe. It was important for Menashe to be active in affairs of state and matters of the material world, but that would always be secondary to the pursuit of Torah and its ideals. The blessing for all generations carries with it the import of Jacob's words. For all time, may your priorities be correctly ordered, and may matters of the spirit take precedence over material affairs.

Blessing of the Children

A story is told of the *chassid* who came to beseech his Rebbe for a blessing that his son grow to be a Torah scholar. "A blessing? You are asking for a blessing from *me*? Hashem is the source of all blessings, and I am not empowered to bestow blessings upon individuals. But you! You can pray, and *no one* can pray better than you!"

On Friday night as they light the Shabbos candles, Jewish mothers are given the keys to unlock storehouses of goodness for their children. Upon their return from synagogue, Jewish parents bless their children, beseeching God to make them God-fearing and righteous. We pray to God that our daughters emulate the character traits of the Matriarchs, Sarah, Rebecca, Rachel and Leah. Their kindness, their modesty, their compassion and their selflessness made them the role models for future generations of young women.

We bless our daughters that they follow the example of the Matriarchs. As the foundational pillars of our nation, they create the spiritual base for all future generations. Our commentators question the grammatical structure of the verse חכמת נשים בנתה ביתה, "The wisdom of women built her home" (Proverbs 14:1). Why does the verse begin using the plural form, *women*, and then use the singular form, *her* home?

To successfully create the spiritual and emotional environment necessary to sustain a Jewish home, a woman requires more than her merit alone. She brings with her the character traits, the wisdom and the faith that are the legacy of her mother, grandmother and all the generations since the Matriarchs. It is these *women* who help build *her* home and provide her with the necessary tools to pass on these characteristics to her descendants.

Sarah, who helped Abraham promote the concept of one God to the world, was a role model for teaching the value of personal modesty to future generations. Rebecca, young as she was, rushed to do *chesed*, acts of lovingkindness, and taught this virtue to young women by example. Self-sacrifice became ingrained in our spiritual fiber when Rachel selflessly allowed Leah to marry Jacob, giving her secret signals to save her sister from humiliation. "There was no person who praised God until Leah" (*Midrash*). She recognized that one must be thankful to Hashem for the seemingly commonplace as well as for the miraculous. As the holiness

Friday Night

It is customary for parents to bless their sons on Friday night
after returning from synagogue

בִּרְכַּת לַבָּנִים

יְשִׂימְךָ אֱלֹהִים
כְּאֶפְרַיִם וְכִמְנַשֶּׁה

יְבָרֶכְךָ יְיָ וְיִשְׁמְרֶךָ
יָאֵר יְיָ פָּנָיו אֵלֶיךָ וִיחֻנֶּךָּ
יִשָּׂא יְיָ פָּנָיו אֵלֶיךָ וְיָשֵׂם לְךָ שָׁלוֹם

וַיְבָרְכֵם
בַּיּוֹם הַהוּא

וַיִּגְדַּל
הַנַּעַר

Y'SIMCHO
*Elōhim
k'Efray-im
v'chiMnashe.*

May Hashem
make you like
Ephraim and Menashe.

Y'VORECH'CHO
*Adōnoy v'yishm'recho.
Yo-ayr Adōnoy panov
aylecho vichuneko.
Yiso Adōnoy
panov aylecho
v'yosaym l'cho
sholōm.*

May Hashem bless you
and safeguard you.

May Hashem illuminate
His countenance to you,
and be gracious to you.

May Hashem lift His
countenance to you and
grant you peace

Friday Night

It is customary for parents to bless their daughters on Friday night after returning from synagogue

מִצַת לְבָנוֹת

יְשִׁימֵךְ אֱלֹהִים
כְּשָׁרָה רִבְקָה רָחֵל וְלֵאָה

יְבָרֶכְךָ יְיָ וְיִשְׁמְרֶךָ
יָאֵר יְיָ פָּנָיו אֵלֶיךָ וִיחֻנֶּךָּ
יִשָּׂא יְיָ פָּנָיו אֵלֶיךָ וְיָשֵׂם לְךָ שָׁלוֹם

Y'SIMAYCH
Elōhim
k'Soro Rivko
Rochayl v'Layo.

Y'VORECH'CHO
Adōnoy v'yishm'recho.
Yo-ayr Adōnoy panov
aylecho vichuneko.
Yiso Adōnoy
panov aylecho
v'yosaym l'cho
sholōm.

May Hashem
make you like Sarah,
Rebecca, Rachel and Leah.

May Hashem bless you
and safeguard you.

May Hashem illuminate
His countenance to you,
and be gracious to you.

May Hashem lift His
countenance to you and
grant you peace

SHOLOM ALEICHEM — *Sholom Aleichem is a relatively recent addition to the Friday night sequence of prayers and rituals, apparently authored by the 17th century Kabbalists. Initially, there was some question as to whether or not it should be included in our texts.*

When a person leaves the synagogue on Friday night, he is escorted home by two ministering angels; one good and one evil. If upon arrival home, the candles are lit, the table is set and the beds are made, the good angel declares, "So may it be next Shabbos!" Begrudgingly, the evil angel must answer, "Amen!" If, however, the candles are not lit, the table is not set and the beds are unmade, the evil angel proclaims, "So may it be next Shabbos!" The good angel must reluctantly answer. "Amen!" (Talmud, Shabbos 119a).

EACH OF THE FOLLOWING PHRASES IS
REPEATED THREE TIMES

שָׁלוֹם עֲלֵיכֶם מַלְאֲכֵי הַשָּׁרֵת מַלְאֲכֵי עֶלְיוֹן מִמֶּלֶךְ מַלְכֵי הַמְּלָכִים הַקָּדוֹשׁ בָּרוּךְ הוּא:

בּוֹאֲכֶם לְשָׁלוֹם מַלְאֲכֵי הַשָּׁלוֹם מַלְאֲכֵי עֶלְיוֹן מִמֶּלֶךְ מַלְכֵי הַמְּלָכִים הַקָּדוֹשׁ בָּרוּךְ הוּא:

בָּרְכוּנִי לְשָׁלוֹם מַלְאֲכֵי הַשָּׁלוֹם מַלְאֲכֵי עֶלְיוֹן מִמֶּלֶךְ מַלְכֵי הַמְּלָכִים הַקָּדוֹשׁ בָּרוּךְ הוּא:

צֵאתְכֶם לְשָׁלוֹם מַלְאֲכֵי הַשָּׁלוֹם מַלְאֲכֵי עֶלְיוֹן מִמֶּלֶךְ מַלְכֵי הַמְּלָכִים הַקָּדוֹשׁ בָּרוּךְ הוּא:

Apparently, the manner in which one appreciates each Shabbos is critical. If the Shabbos experience this week is positive, if our preparations to welcome the Shabbos Queen are adequate, then we receive a celestial approbation of our actions. "So may it be next Shabbos!" "One mitzvah will lead to another" (Pirkei Avos 4:2). The cumulative effect of our Shabbos observance will impact the lives of our family members, and we will be able to greet God's heavenly emissaries each week.

Some commentators question the inclusion of the last verse of Sholom Aleichem, צאתכם לשלום, as part of the text. In essence, we are asking our heavenly escorts to leave, bidding them a peaceful journey! One would hope that the angels would derive great satisfaction from remaining during the meal and seeing its proper observance. During the week we need the assistance of the ministering angels to help bring our prayers before the Heavenly Throne. We lack the merit to propel our heartfelt pleas heavenward and need emissaries to assist us. On Shabbos, with the table set and the appropriate preparations for this holy day accomplished, we become ennobled to plead our own cause. We bid our heavenly escorts farewell, and imbued with the sanctity of the day, we begin our Shabbos in the embrace of the Creator.

Each phrase is recited three times

PEACE upon you

O ministering angels, angels of the Exalted One — from the King Who reigns over kings, the Holy One, Blessed is He.

MAY YOUR COMING be for peace, O angels of peace, angels of the Exalted One — from the King who reigns over kings, the Holy One, Blessed is He.

BLESS ME for peace, O angels of peace, angels of the Exalted One from the King Who reigns over kings, the Holy One, Blessed is He.

MAY YOUR DEPARTURE be to peace, O angels of peace, angels of the Exalted One — from the King who reigns over kings, the Holy One, Blessed is He.

SHOLŌM ALAYCHEM
mal-achay ha-shorays, mal-achay elyōn,
Mimelech malchay ham'lochim,
Hakodōsh boruch hu.

BOR'CHUNI L'SHOLŌM
mal-achay ha-sholōm, mal-achay elyōn,
Mimelech malchay ham'lochim,
Hakodōsh boruch hu.

BŌ-ACHEM L'SHOLŌM
mal-achay ha-sholōm, mal-achay elyōn,
Mimelech malchay ham'lochim,
Hakodōsh boruch hu.

TZAYS'CHEM L'SHOLŌM
mal-achay ha-sholōm, mal-achay elyōn,
Mimelech malchay ham'lochim,
Hakodōsh boruch hu.

כִּי מַלְאָכָיו יְצַוֶּה לָּךְ לִשְׁמָרְךָ בְּכָל דְּרָכֶיךָ.
יְיָ יִשְׁמָר צֵאתְךָ וּבוֹאֶךָ, מֵעַתָּה וְעַד עוֹלָם.

רִבּוֹן כָּל הָעוֹלָמִים אֲדוֹן כָּל הַנְּשָׁמוֹת, אֲדוֹן הַשָּׁלוֹם.
מֶלֶךְ **אַבִּיר**, מֶלֶךְ **בָּרוּךְ**, מֶלֶךְ **גָּדוֹל**,
מֶלֶךְ **דּוֹבֵר** שָׁלוֹם, מֶלֶךְ **הָדוּר**, מֶלֶךְ **וָתִיק**, מֶלֶךְ **זָךְ**, מֶלֶךְ **חַי** הָעוֹלָמִים,
מֶלֶךְ **טוֹב** וּמֵטִיב, מֶלֶךְ **יָחִיד** וּמְיֻחָד, מֶלֶךְ **כַּבִּיר**, מֶלֶךְ **לוֹבֵשׁ** רַחֲמִים,
מֶלֶךְ **מַלְכֵי** הַמְּלָכִים, מֶלֶךְ **נִשְׂגָּב**, מֶלֶךְ **סוֹמֵךְ** נוֹפְלִים, מֶלֶךְ **עוֹשֶׂה**
מַעֲשֵׂה בְרֵאשִׁית, מֶלֶךְ **פּוֹדֶה** וּמַצִּיל, מֶלֶךְ **צַח** וְאָדוֹם, מֶלֶךְ **קָדוֹשׁ**,
מֶלֶךְ **רָם** וְנִשָּׂא, מֶלֶךְ **שׁוֹמֵעַ** תְּפִלָּה, מֶלֶךְ **תָּמִים** דַּרְכּוֹ.

מוֹדָה אֲנִי לְפָנֶיךָ, יְיָ אֱלֹהַי וֵאלֹהֵי אֲבוֹתַי, עַל כָּל הַחֶסֶד אֲשֶׁר עָשִׂיתָ
עִמָּדִי וַאֲשֶׁר אַתָּה עָתִיד לַעֲשׂוֹת עִמִּי וְעִם כָּל בְּנֵי בֵיתִי
וְעִם כָּל בְּרִיּוֹתֶיךָ בְּנֵי בְרִיתִי, וּבְרוּכִים הֵם מַלְאָכֶיךָ הַקְּדוֹשִׁים
וְהַטְּהוֹרִים שֶׁעוֹשִׂים רְצוֹנֶךָ. אֲדוֹן הַשָּׁלוֹם, מֶלֶךְ שֶׁהַשָּׁלוֹם שֶׁלּוֹ, בָּרְכֵנִי
בַּשָּׁלוֹם, וְתִפְקֹד אוֹתִי וְאֶת כָּל בְּנֵי בֵיתִי, וְכָל עַמְּךָ בֵּית יִשְׂרָאֵל, לְחַיִּים
טוֹבִים וּלְשָׁלוֹם.

מֶלֶךְ עֶלְיוֹן עַל כָּל צְבָא מָרוֹם, יוֹצְרֵנוּ יוֹצֵר בְּרֵאשִׁית, אֲחַלֶּה
פָנֶיךָ הַמְּאִירִים שֶׁתְּזַכֶּה אוֹתִי וְאֶת כָּל בְּנֵי בֵיתִי
לִמְצוֹא חֵן וְשֵׂכֶל טוֹב בְּעֵינֶיךָ וּבְעֵינֵי כָל בְּנֵי אָדָם וְחַוָּה, וּבְעֵינֵי
כָל רוֹאֵינוּ, לַעֲבוֹדָתֶךָ. וְזַכֵּנוּ לְקַבֵּל שַׁבָּתוֹת מִתּוֹךְ רוֹב שִׂמְחָה, וּמִתּוֹךְ
עֹשֶׁר וְכָבוֹד, וּמִתּוֹךְ מְעוּט עֲוֹנוֹת. וְהָסֵר מִמֶּנִּי וּמִכָּל בְּנֵי בֵיתִי וּמִכָּל
עַמְּךָ בֵּית יִשְׂרָאֵל כָּל מִינֵי חֹלִי, וְכָל מִינֵי מַדְוֶה, וְכָל מִינֵי דַלּוּת
וַעֲנִיּוּת וְאֶבְיוֹנוּת. וְתֶן בָּנוּ יֵצֶר טוֹב לְעָבְדְּךָ בֶּאֱמֶת וּבְיִרְאָה וּבְאַהֲבָה.
וְנִהְיֶה מְכֻבָּדִים בְּעֵינֶיךָ וּבְעֵינֵי כָל רוֹאֵינוּ, כִּי אַתָּה הוּא מֶלֶךְ הַכָּבוֹד,
כִּי לְךָ נָאֶה, כִּי לְךָ יָאֶה.

אָנָּא מֶלֶךְ מַלְכֵי הַמְּלָכִים, צַוֵּה לְמַלְאָכֶיךָ מַלְאֲכֵי הַשָּׁרֵת, מְשָׁרְתֵי
עֶלְיוֹן, שֶׁיִּפְקְדוּנִי בְּרַחֲמִים, וִיבָרְכוּנִי בְּבוֹאָם לְבֵיתִי בְּיוֹם קָדְשֵׁנוּ.
כִּי הִדְלַקְתִּי נֵרוֹתַי, וְהִצַּעְתִּי מִטָּתִי, וְהֶחֱלַפְתִּי שִׂמְלוֹתַי לִכְבוֹד יוֹם הַשַּׁבָּת,
וּבָאתִי לְבֵיתְךָ לְהַפִּיל תְּחִנָּתִי לְפָנֶיךָ, שֶׁתַּעֲבִיר אַנְחָתִי, וָאָעִיד אֲשֶׁר
בָּרָאתָ בְּשִׁשָּׁה יָמִים כָּל הַיְצִיר, וָאֶשְׁנֶה וָאֲשַׁלֵּשׁ עוֹד לְהָעִיד עַל כּוֹסִי
בְּתוֹךְ שִׂמְחָתִי, כַּאֲשֶׁר צִוִּיתַנִי לְזָכְרוֹ, וּלְהִתְעַנֵּג בְּיֶתֶר נִשְׁמָתִי אֲשֶׁר נָתַתָּ
בִּי. בּוֹ אֶשְׁבּוֹת כַּאֲשֶׁר צִוִּיתַנִי לְשָׁרְתֶךָ, וְכֵן אַגִּיד גְּדֻלָּתְךָ בְּרִנָּה. וְשִׁוִּיתִי
יְיָ לְקִרְאָתִי, שֶׁתְּרַחֲמֵנִי עוֹד בְּגָלוּתִי, לְגָאֳלֵנִי וּלְעוֹרֵר לִבִּי לְאַהֲבָתֶךָ,
וְאָז אֶשְׁמוֹר פִּקּוּדֶיךָ וְחֻקֶּיךָ בְּלִי עֶצֶב, וְאֶתְפַּלֵּל כַּדָּת כָּרָאוּי וְכַנָּכוֹן.
מַלְאֲכֵי הַשָּׁלוֹם, בּוֹאֲכֶם לְשָׁלוֹם, בָּרְכוּנִי לְשָׁלוֹם, וְאִמְרוּ בָּרוּךְ לְשָׁלְחֵנִי
הֶעָרוּךְ, וְצֵאתְכֶם לְשָׁלוֹם, מֵעַתָּה וְעַד עוֹלָם, אָמֵן סֶלָה.

For His Angels, He will charge for you, to protect you in all your ways. May Hashem protect your going and returning, from this time and forever.

Master of All Worlds, Lord of all souls, Lord of peace, mighty King, blessed King, great King, King who bespeaks peace, glorious King, ancient King, pure King, King Who gives life to the universe, good and beneficent King, unique and singular King, powerful King, King robed in mercy, King Who reigns over kings, exalted King, King Who raises the fallen, King who sustains the works of creation, King Who redeems and rescues, King Who is pure and ruddy, holy King, exalted and lofty King, King Who hears prayers, King whose way is flawless.

I Thank You Hashem, my God and the God of my fathers for all the kindness You have done with me and which You shall do for me, for all the members of my household, and for all Your creatures who are my fellows. And blessed are Your holy and pure angels who do Your will. Lord of peace, King to whom peace belongs, bless me with peace, and consider me, and my entire household and Your entire people, the house of Israel, for a good life and for peace.

O King, Who is Exalted and above all the heavenly host, our Creator, Molder of creation, I beseech Your resplendent countenance that You privilege me and the members of my household to find favor and good understanding in Your eyes, and in the eyes of all men, and the eyes of all who see us, so that we may serve you. Make us worthy to welcome Sabbaths with great joy, wealth and honor, and amid fewness of sins. Remove from me and from all the members of my household and from all Your people Israel, all kinds of sickness, all kinds of pain, and all kinds of need, poverty and destitution. And give us a positive desire to serve You with honesty, with awe and with love. May we command respect in Your eyes and in the eyes of all who see us, for You are the King of Glory, for whom respect is seemly and fitting.

Please, King Who reigns over kings, command Your angels, the ministering angels, servants of the Exalted One, to consider me with mercy, and bless me when they enter my home on our holy day. For I have kindled my lights, prepared my bed, and changed my clothes to honor the Sabbath, and I have come to Your house me to entreat You to banish my sighs, and I will testify that You created all creation in six days, and I shall repeat and will again testify a third time over my cup, joyfully, as You commanded me, to be mindful of observing the Sabbath, and to take pleasure in the additional soul which You have placed within me. I shall rest on it, as You have commanded me, to serve You, and I will tell of Your greatness with joyous song. I have set Hashem before me that You may have mercy on me in my exile, to redeem me and to arouse my heart's love for You. Then I shall observe Your laws and Your decrees without suffering, and I will pray correctly, appropriately and fittingly.

O angels of peace, come in peace, bless me for peace, pronounce a blessing over my prepared table, and depart in peace, from this time and forever. Amen. Selah.

אֵשֶׁת חַיִל

אֵשֶׁת חַיִל מִי יִמְצָא וְרָחֹק מִפְּנִינִים מִכְרָהּ:
בָּטַח בָּהּ לֵב בַּעְלָהּ וְשָׁלָל לֹא יֶחְסָר: גְּמָלַתְהוּ טוֹב
וְלֹא רָע כֹּל יְמֵי חַיֶּיהָ: דָּרְשָׁה צֶמֶר וּפִשְׁתִּים
וַתַּעַשׂ בְּחֵפֶץ כַּפֶּיהָ: הָיְתָה כָּאֳנִיּוֹת סוֹחֵר מִמֶּרְחָק
תָּבִיא לַחְמָהּ: וַתָּקָם בְּעוֹד לַיְלָה וַתִּתֵּן טֶרֶף לְבֵיתָהּ
וְחֹק לְנַעֲרֹתֶיהָ: זָמְמָה שָׂדֶה וַתִּקָּחֵהוּ מִפְּרִי כַפֶּיהָ
נָטְעָה כָּרֶם: חָגְרָה בְעוֹז מָתְנֶיהָ וַתְּאַמֵּץ זְרוֹעֹתֶיהָ:
טָעֲמָה כִּי טוֹב סַחְרָהּ לֹא יִכְבֶּה בַלַּיְלָה נֵרָהּ:
יָדֶיהָ שִׁלְּחָה בַכִּישׁוֹר וְכַפֶּיהָ תָּמְכוּ פָלֶךְ: כַּפָּהּ פָּרְשָׂה
לֶעָנִי וְיָדֶיהָ שִׁלְּחָה לָאֶבְיוֹן: לֹא תִירָא לְבֵיתָהּ
מִשָּׁלֶג כִּי כָל בֵּיתָהּ לָבֻשׁ שָׁנִים: מַרְבַדִּים
עָשְׂתָה לָּהּ שֵׁשׁ וְאַרְגָּמָן לְבוּשָׁהּ: נוֹדָע בַּשְּׁעָרִים בַּעְלָהּ
בְּשִׁבְתּוֹ עִם זִקְנֵי אָרֶץ: סָדִין עָשְׂתָה
וַתִּמְכֹּר וַחֲגוֹר נָתְנָה לַכְּנַעֲנִי: עֹז
וְהָדָר לְבוּשָׁהּ וַתִּשְׂחַק לְיוֹם אַחֲרוֹן: פִּיהָ
פָּתְחָה בְחָכְמָה וְתוֹרַת חֶסֶד עַל לְשׁוֹנָהּ: צוֹפִיָּה הֲלִיכוֹת בֵּיתָהּ
וְלֶחֶם עַצְלוּת לֹא תֹאכֵל: קָמוּ בָנֶיהָ
וַיְאַשְּׁרוּהָ בַּעְלָהּ וַיְהַלְלָהּ: רַבּוֹת בָּנוֹת
עָשׂוּ חָיִל וְאַתְּ עָלִית עַל כֻּלָּנָה: שֶׁקֶר הַחֵן
וְהֶבֶל הַיֹּפִי אִשָּׁה יִרְאַת יְיָ הִיא תִתְהַלָּל: תְּנוּ
לָהּ מִפְּרִי יָדֶיהָ וִיהַלְלוּהָ בַשְּׁעָרִים מַעֲשֶׂיהָ:

FRIDAY NIGHT

A Woman of Valor

who can find? Far beyond pearls is her worth. Her husband's heart trusts in her and he shall lack no fortune. She repays his good but never his harm. All the days of her life she seeks out wool and flax and her hands work willingly. She was like the merchant's ships. From afar she brings her bread. From sleep she arises while it is still night, to give food to her household and what is due to her maidens. She thinks of a field and buys it. From the fruits of her labor she planted a vineyard. With might she girded her loins and strengthened her arms. She feels that her venture is good, her lamp is not snuffed out at night, her hand reaches out for the distaff, and her palms support the spindle. She extends her palm to the poor and sends her hand out to the destitute. She fears not snow for her household, for her household is attired in scarlet wool. Fine carpets she made for herself, of linen and purple wool is her clothing. Well known in the councils is her husband, when he sits among the elders. Strength and splendor are her clothing, and she awaits with joy the very last day. Her mouth she opens with wisdom and the lesson of lovingkindness is on her tongue. She keeps watch over the ways her household and eats not of the bread of laziness. Her children arise and praise her, her husband, and he lauds her. Many are the daughters who have achieved valor, but you surpassed them all. Charm is false and beauty is futile. A woman who fears Hashem, she should be praised. Give to her from the fruits of her labor and let her be praised in the gates by her very own deeds.

AYSHES CHA-YIL mi yimtzo, v'rochōk mip'ninim michroh.   Botach boh layv baloh, v'sholol lō yechsor.   G'molas-hu tōv v'lō ro, kōl y'may cha-yeho.   Dor'sho tzemer ufishtim, vata-as b'chayfetz kapeho.   Hoy'so ko-oniyōs sōchayr, mimerchok tovi lachmoh.   Vatokom b'ōd lailoh, vatitayn teref l'vaysoh, v'chōk l'na-arōseho.   Zom'mo sode vatikochayhu, mip'ri chapeho not'o korem.   Chog'roh b'ōz mosneho, vat'amaytz z'rō-ōseho.   To-amo ki tōv sachroh, lō yichbe balailo nayroh.   Yodeho shil'cho vakishōr, v'chapeho tom'chu folech.   Kapoh por'so le-oni, v'yodeho shil'cho lo-evyōn.   Lō siro l'vaysoh misholeg, ki chol baysoh lovush shonim.   Marvadim os'so loh, shaysh v'argomon l'vushoh.   Nōdo bash'orim baloh, b'shivtō im ziknay oretz.   Sodin os'so vatimkōr, vachagōr nos'no lak'na-ani.   Ōz v'hodor l'vushoh, vatis-chak l'yōm acharōn.   Piho pos'cho v'chochmo, v'sōras chesed al l'shōnoh.   Tzōfiyoh halichōs baysoh, v'lechem atzlus lō sōchayl.   Komu voneho vai-ash'ruho, baloh vai-hal'loh.   Rabōs bonōs osu cho-yil, v'at olis al kulono.   Sheker hachayn v'hevel hayōfi, isho yir-as Adōnoy hi sis-halol.   T'nu loh mip'ri yodeho, vihal'luho vash'orim ma-aseho.

his lyrical praise to the "woman of valor" is taken in its entirety from chapter 31 of the Book of Proverbs by King Solomon. Though some *midrashic* sources describe this allegorically, referring variously to the Shabbos Queen, Torah or the Divine Presence, these do not discount the simple literal interpretation, extolling the woman of the home as its mainstay. The fact that the woman of the home is used as an allegory for such lofty concepts points to her exalted status in the eyes of our Sages. The א-ב acrostic is used in certain significant chapters of Psalms – אשרי, Chapter 119, and others, to signify the all-encompassing nature of the subject. Each of the 22 letters of the Hebrew alphabet is used to extol the subject of Aishes Chayil, from א to ת, spanning the gamut of experience.

The *Midrash* (*Bereishis* 11:8) says that each day of the week found a partner in the days of creation; Sunday had Monday, Tuesday had Wednesday, Thursday had Friday. The day of Shabbos petitioned before its Creator, "Who will my partner be?" "The Children of Israel," replied God. "They will be your partner." Shabbos has so much to offer, but who in creation will be worthy of internalizing its lessons? The Children of Israel can fully appreciate this heavenly gift, and will become recipients of God's lovingkindness (*Sfas Emes*). Based on this *midrash*, the *aishes chayil* referred to is the Shabbos Queen.

Other commentaries (*Eitz Yosef*, in the name of the *Gaon* of Vilna) see *Aishes Chayil* as an allusion to the Torah itself. The word חיל has the numerical equivalent of 48, a reference to the 48 traits through which Torah is acquired (*Pirkei Avos* 6:6). The Torah is so exalted that it is difficult to find anything that can equal it.

Judaism recognizes and lauds the role of the *aishes chayil*. Her multifaceted roles make her the mainstay of the home. Mother, wife, caregiver, organizer, educator, culinary coordinator, and often a provider for many of the material aspects of the home. The aura that the Jewish home exhudes generally reflects the character that she helps create, and the physical components that grace the Shabbos table are a result of her efforts during the week. "One who toils on *erev* Shabbos will eat on Shabbos" (Talmud, *Avodah Zara* 3a).

The beauty of the Shabbos table, the aura of tranquility, an immaculate home worthy of greeting the Shabbos Queen, are a credit to the efforts of each Jewish *aishes chayil*. The man of the home is often the breadwinner, providing for the material needs of the household. It is each woman of valor who artfully crafts them into the fabric of the Jewish home, nurtured with love, caring, warmth and compassion.

At the end of this masterful song of praise extolling the role of the Jewish woman, King Solomon adds a sentence which requires interpretation. "Charm is false and beauty is futile. A woman who fears Hashem, she should be praised." Are charm and beauty indeed so meaningless? While excessive attention to these traits would border on vanity, is there no place in Judaism for characteristics that can ennoble the Jewish woman?

In truth, charm and beauty can be likened to the integer zero. Standing alone, they have no inherent value. They often reflect an elusive pursuit of beauty that the secular world has glorified, though it may be a superficial veneer beclouding true inner charm. Ten zeros grouped together add up to nothing; once the number one is placed in front of them, however, it gives them all value. The fear of Hashem, establishing a wholesome set of priorities for the important aspects of life, exalts beauty and charm and enables them to truly enhance the *aishes chayil*.

Aishes Chayil
A Woman of Valor

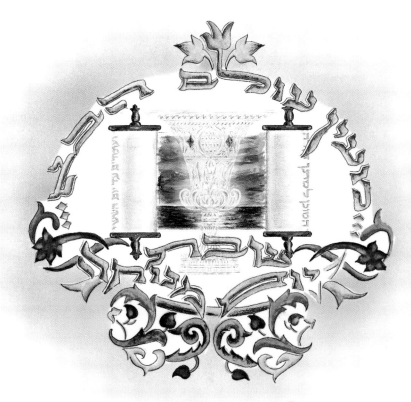

Friday Night:
THE GATEWAY TO SHABBOS

Laws of Friday Night Kiddush
Sanctifying the Shabbos

- After reciting Kiddush at least 2.22 oz should be drunk, preferably in one swallow. If this proves to be difficult, one should at least attempt to finish the required amount within two minutes' time. The maximum allotted time is nine minutes.

- When reciting Kiddush for others, the leader should have specific intent to fulfill the obligation of those listening and those listening should have specific intent to fulfill their obligation by hearing the Kiddush recited.

- Ideally, all participants listening to Kiddush, should taste of the wine. The best way to distribute the wine is to first pour off wine for the others into a separate glass before drinking from the Kiddush cup.

- The wine should be drunk while seated. Participants should remain silent until one has drunk and the leader has finished drinking the required amount.

- Kiddush must be recited at the place where one intends to eat. After Kiddush recitation, one should begin eating as soon as possible.

- One must consume a proper meal after Kiddush. This is defined as either an entire Shabbos meal (which is preceded by the washing ritual. see below), or at least a minimum of an olive-size amount of cake, cookies or foods from the five species of grain: wheat, oats, spelt, barley and rye. This is the volume measurement which equals the amount of food that would displace slightly less than one fluid oz. of liquid. Another option, though less preferred, would be to drink at least 3.3 oz. of wine or grape juice. This should be in addition to the wine or grape juice one drinks for Kiddush.

- If one plans to eat the required amount at a different table from where Kiddush was recited, he should have this in mind while reciting Kiddush.

- One can only eat the required amount in a separate room from where he recited Kiddush if he had this in mind while reciting Kiddush, and the second room is visible from where he recited Kiddush.

- One cannot recite Kiddush in one building and then eat the required amount in a separate building.

- Even if one has fulfilled his own obligation for Kiddush, he may exempt someone else who has not. This is based on the principle of *arvus*, that each Jewish person is responsible for his fellow man.

Laws of Friday Night Kiddush
Sanctifying the Shabbos

- It is a Biblical obligation to hear or recite Friday night Kiddush.

- Both men and woman are equally obligated in the *mitzvah* of Kiddush.

- One should begin training his children to listen to Kiddush starting from 5-6 years of age.

- Upon returning from shul, one should recite Kiddush as soon as possible.

- Once Shabbos begins, one may not eat or drink before reciting or hearing Kiddush.

- The Kiddush cup should be held in the palm of the right hand with one's fingers wrapped around it. One who is left handed should hold the cup in his left hand.

- The cup should be held at least four inches above the table.

- There are various customs regarding whether to stand or sit while reciting Kiddush. Some stand during the entire Kiddush. Others sit during the entire Kiddush. A third custom is to stand while reciting the first paragraph of "*Yom Hashishi*" and to sit for the remainder of Kiddush.

- The Kiddush begins with the words "*Vai-hi erev,*" which are recited in an undertone.

- When beginning the words "*Yom Hashishi*" one should gaze at the candles.

- The cup used for Kiddush should be whole, without cracks or holes, and able to rest steadily on its base.

- One may use a disposable cup if no metal or glass cup is available.

- The cup should hold a minimum of 4.42 oz. and be filled to the rim.

- Kiddush can be made on either wine or grape juice.

- Kiddush should not be made from the remnants of wine which has been drunk. If one wishes to reuse wine for Kiddush, he should follow this procedure: First, *additional* wine should be poured from the wine bottle into the cup. One should then pour the entire contents of the cup back into the bottle. This wine can then be reused for Kiddush.

- The cup being used for Kiddush should first be washed out.

- The challah should be covered while reciting Kiddush.

סֵדֶר לֵיל שַׁבָּת

(בלחש) וַיְהִי עֶרֶב וַיְהִי בֹקֶר:

יוֹם הַשִּׁשִּׁי

וַיְכֻלּוּ הַשָּׁמַיִם וְהָאָרֶץ
וְכָל צְבָאָם: וַיְכַל אֱלֹהִים
בַּיּוֹם הַשְּׁבִיעִי מְלַאכְתּוֹ
אֲשֶׁר עָשָׂה. וַיִּשְׁבֹּת
בַּיּוֹם הַשְּׁבִיעִי מִכָּל
מְלַאכְתּוֹ אֲשֶׁר עָשָׂה:
וַיְבָרֶךְ אֱלֹהִים אֶת יוֹם הַשְּׁבִיעִי וַיְקַדֵּשׁ
אֹתוֹ כִּי בוֹ שָׁבַת מִכָּל מְלַאכְתּוֹ אֲשֶׁר
בָּרָא אֱלֹהִים לַעֲשׂוֹת:

סַבְרִי מָרָנָן וְרַבָּנָן וְרַבּוֹתַי:

בָּרוּךְ אַתָּה יְיָ אֱלֹהֵינוּ מֶלֶךְ הָעוֹלָם
בּוֹרֵא פְּרִי הַגָּפֶן:

בָּרוּךְ אַתָּה יְיָ אֱלֹהֵינוּ מֶלֶךְ הָעוֹלָם
אֲשֶׁר קִדְּשָׁנוּ בְּמִצְוֹתָיו וְרָצָה בָנוּ
וְשַׁבַּת קָדְשׁוֹ בְּאַהֲבָה וּבְרָצוֹן הִנְחִילָנוּ
זִכָּרוֹן לְמַעֲשֵׂה בְרֵאשִׁית. (כִּי הוּא יוֹם)
תְּחִלָּה לְמִקְרָאֵי קֹדֶשׁ זֵכֶר לִיצִיאַת
מִצְרָיִם. (כִּי בָנוּ בָחַרְתָּ וְאוֹתָנוּ קִדַּשְׁתָּ
מִכָּל הָעַמִּים) וְשַׁבַּת קָדְשְׁךָ בְּאַהֲבָה
וּבְרָצוֹן הִנְחַלְתָּנוּ: בָּרוּךְ אַתָּה יְיָ
מְקַדֵּשׁ הַשַּׁבָּת:

Friday Night Kiddush

The first line is said in an undertone

And it was the evening and it was the morning

THE SIXTH DAY.

And the heavens and the earth were completed and all of their hosts. And God completed on the seventh day His work which He had done. And he rested on the seventh day from all His work which He had done, and God blessed the seventh day and sanctified it, for He rested from all His work which He had created to do.

Attention our masters and our teachers:

BLESSED are You, Hashem, our God, King of the Universe, who creates the fruit of the vine.

BLESSED are You, Hashem, our God, King of the Universe, who has sanctified us with His commandments and was pleased with us and His holy Shabbos, with love and with pleasure He bequeathed to us a remembrance of creations. For this day is the first of the holy convocations, a memorial to our exodus from Egypt. For You chose us and sanctified us from all nations, and Your holy Shabbos with love and pleasure You bequeathed to us.

BLESSED are You, Hashem, who sanctifies the Shabbos.

(vai-hi erev vai-hi vo-ker)

YŌM HASHISHI.

Vai-chulu hashoma-yim v'ho-oretz v'chol tz'vo-om. Vai-chal Elōhim ba-yōm hash'vi-i m'lachtō asher osoh, va-yishbōs ba-yōm hash'vi-i mikol m'lachtō asher osoh. Vai-vorech Elōhim es yōm hash'vi-i vai-kadaysh ōsō, ki vō shovas miko'l m'lachtō asher boro Elōhim la-asōs.

WHOEVER MAKES KIDDUSH ON WINE
ON FRIDAY NIGHT, HIS DAYS ARE LENGTHENED IN THIS WORLD, AND YEARS OF LIFE ARE ADDED TO HIM IN THE WORLD TO COME.

Savri moronon v'rabonon v'rabōsai:

BORUCH *ato Adōnoy Elōhaynu melech ho-ōlom, bō ray p'ri hagofen.*

All present respond: *Omayn*

BORUCH *ato Adōnoy Elōhaynu melech ho-ōlom, asher kid'shonu b'mitzvōsov v'rotzo vonu, v'Shabbos kodshō b'ahavo uvrotzōn hinchilonu zikorōn l'ma-asay v'rayshis. Ki hu yōm t'chilo l'mikro-ay kōdesh, zaycher litzi-as Mitzro-yim. Ki vonu vocharto, v'ōsonu kidashto mikol ho-amim v'Shabbos kodsh'cho b'ahavo uvrotzōn hinchaltonu. Boruch ato Adōnoy, m'kadaysh ha-Shabbos.*

All present respond: *Omayn*

Netilas Yodayim
Ritual Washing Before Bread

אֱלֹהֵינוּ מֶלֶךְ הָעוֹלָם אֲשֶׁר קִדְּשָׁנוּ בְּמִצְוֹתָיו וְצִוָּנוּ עַל נְטִילַת יָדָיִם:

BLESSED are You, Hashem, our God, King of the Universe, Who has sanctified us with His commandments, and commanded us to wash the hands.

BORUCH atoh Adōnoy, Elōhaynu Melech ho'ōlom, asher kid'shonu b'mitzvōsov, v'tzivonu al netilas yodayim.

 hough this blessing is recited when one washes his hands before eating bread, the literal meaning of *netilas yodayim* is "to raise the hands." Some have the custom of reciting the phrase, שְׂאוּ יְדֵיכֶם קֹדֶשׁ וּבָרְכוּ אֶת ה', "Raise your hands in holiness, and bless Hashem." Once the hands have been washed and are in a state of cleanliness, one should avoid having water that washed the area above the wrist fall fall back down onto his fingers. This can be practically accomplished by raising the hands upward after washing.

An additional requirement for washing is that a cup be used, rather than washing directly under a faucet. In Aramaic, a cup is called a *natal*, hence the blessing *al netilas yodayim*.

The exalted status of the table upon which one eats, and certainly the Shabbos table, invests it with a measure of sanctity that transcends the mundane and touches the Divine. The *kohen*, or priest, would have to wash his hands and feet in the *kiyor*, the washbasin, before doing the service in the Temple. Ritual purity laws were applicable when the Temple was extant, and the *kohanim*, priests, had to wash their hands lest they defile *terumah* by merely touching it. *Terumah* was a

portion of the produce given by the Jews to the *kohanim*, and had to be eaten by them in a state of ritual purity. To ensure that these laws were upheld by the *kohanim*, who might have unwittingly come into contact with a spiritually unfit object during the day, the Rabbis instituted that washing should be done by all Jews before eating bread. Additionally, the Rabbis instituted washing as an added measure of cleanliness and sanctity (Talmud, *Chulin* 106a, and *Tosfos* ibid.). Even though the Temple does not exist today, the Rabbis maintained the practice nonetheless. We are hopeful that the Temple will be rebuilt and the laws of purity will once again apply.

In *Vayikra* 11:44 it states וְהִתְקַדִּשְׁתֶּם וִהְיִיתֶם קְדֹשִׁים, "and you shall sanctify yourselves and you shall be holy." The *Midrash* derives the following laws from that verse: "And you shall sanctify yourselves"– this refers to the washing with water at the beginning (of the meal), for *netilas yodayim*, "and you shall be holy," – this refers to washing at the end of the meal before Grace after Meals is recited. The law is Rabbinically ordained, with an allusion from the verse in *Vayikra*. The Talmud (ibid.) says that one fulfills a *mitzvah* by washing his hands, that of adhering to the dictates of the Sages.

Laws of Netilas Yodayim
Washing Before Bread

- One performs a ritual washing before eating bread by first pouring one cup of water twice on his right hand followed by twice on his left. The same would be true for one who is left handed.

- The cup used for washing should be whole, without holes or cracks.

- Each cup's pouring should contain a minimum of 3.3 oz of water.

- After washing one should first rub his wet hands together and then recite the following blessing: *Baruch ata...al netilas yodayim.* The blessing should be recited before one dries his hands.

- One should refrain from speaking once he has begun washing.

- One should not dry his hands on his clothing.

- Preferably, the washing should not take place in the washroom. If there is no other place available, one should not dry his hands until after exiting the washroom.

- The water should come in direct contact with one's hands, therefore obstructions, i.e. rings, should be removed before washing.

- The water should be poured up until the wrist.

- Care should be taken to dry the hands well after washing. One should not begin eating until after his hands are totally dry.

- If one's wet hands are touched by someone who has not yet washed, he is required to rewash his hands. A second blessing is not made.

- Talking should be avoided until after swallowing a piece of bread. If necessary, one is permitted to talk about anything pertaining to the cutting of the bread, i.e. "Please bring the knife." etc.

- One should avoid needless delaying between washing and the cutting of the bread.

Netilas Yodoyim
In the Talmud and Midrash

The Talmud (*Bava Metzia* 24a) relates an incident in which a silver goblet was stolen from the home of the host by one of his guests. Mar Zutra Chasida noticed one young scholar wash his hands, and wipe them on his friend's garment. "He is the thief!" Mar Zutra Chasida proclaimed. Upon questioning, the guest admitted that indeed he had stolen the goblet. Mar Zutra Chasida reasoned: One who shows callous disregard of someone else's property and can use his friend's garment as a wash-towel, is suspect of a much more severe crime in interpersonal monetary dealings.

Although the Rabbis indicate that the minimum requirement of water for ritual washing of the hands before bread is a *revi'is* (approximately 3.3 ounces), one should pour water on his hands in abundance. Rav Chisda said, "I washed with full handfuls of water and received full handfuls of heavenly goodness (Talmud, *Shabbos* 62b).

One who has callous disregard for *netilas yodayim* will become impoverished (ibid.). An allusion to this fact is that the acronym for ידים נטילת על is עני, a poor person. If one holds this important *mitzvah* in disdain, he will receive the punishment of poverty (*Levush*).

Rava defined callous disregard of the *mitzvah* of *netilas yodayim* as one who does not wash at all. One who washes, but only uses the minimum requirement of water and does not rub his hands together is exempt from this severe punishment (ibid.).

Foods which are traditionally dipped into liquids require one to wash his hands, however, no blessing is recited (Talmud, *Pesachim* 115a). The Torah allusion of קדושים והייתם והתקדשתם "and you shall make yourselves holy," which requires washing before a meal, refers to staple foods only, such as bread. A common examole is dipping the *karpas*, or greens, into salt water at the Passover Seder.

One who eats bread without drying one's hands is considered as if he ate ritually impure bread (Talmud, *Sotah* 4b). The purpose of washing is to imbue a sense of sanctity into man, and if he doesn't wash or dry his hands appropriately, he is causing defilement rather than sanctity.

The students of R' Yisroel of Salant once noticed their Rebbe washing his hands with water in a very sparing manner. The puzzled students knew that in Jewish law one is commended for using a great deal of water for *netilas yodayim*. "Why was our teacher being so frugal?" they respectfully asked him. "Do you know where we get the water with which we wash our hands?" asked R' Yisroel. "The maid-servant has to go outside to the well, lower her pitcher, and go back many times until there is enough water for all of us to wash. How can I be exacting in the fulfillment of a *mitzvah* at someone else's expense?"

Blessing for Bread
Sustenance from the Earth

BLESSED are You, Hashem, our God, King of the Universe, Who brings forth bread from the ground.

BORUCH atoh Adōnoy, Elōhaynu Melech ho'ōlom, hamōtzi lechem min ho'oretz.

f one would think about the process of how seeds are planted, nourished, grown, cut and processed into the foods we eat, he would realize that the entire order is nothing short of miraculous. Why should stalks of wheat grow from a single seed? Why doesn't a barley stalk grow if we plant a wheat seed? Why does the plant begin to take root only *after* it decomposes and becomes seemingly useless?

We take these events for granted only because they seem to be a natural part of the world order. There is nothing "natural" about these occurences or how we sustain ourselves with staples of life from a simple seed. When Adam sinned in the Garden of Eden, the process of procuring the basics of life changed forever. Whereas before the sin trees bore fruits of all kinds, henceforth thorns and thistles would grow. Initially, all types of produce were available for Adam with no effort; after he sinned, earning a livelihood became a struggle for survival.

בזעת אפיך תאכל לחם, "With the sweat of your countenance you will eat bread" (*Bereishis* 3:19). The lesson for Adam and all of mankind was that man would have to work extremely hard to wrest his livelihood from an unyielding earth. R' Samson Raphael Hirsch notes that לחם, bread, is found in the root of מלחמה, war, as a daily battle is waged to put "bread on one's table." The effort exerted, says R' Hirsch, is not limited to the

face, the פנים, but rather involves his אפים, his entire countenance. The majestic seat of his insight and being which should be reserved for helping man master his world, has been denigrated by being pressed into assisting him in the mundane tasks of survival.

The battle, the מלחמה, unfortunately, is not limited to man's attempted conquest of his environment. In the area of eking out his subsistence, man must often pit himself against his fellow man. The energy expended to earn his daily keep becomes further diluted when he must struggle with his fellow man. Man hopes to carve out his territory, to achieve his modest successes, to fight for his very existence.

The blessing we make on bread differs from those made on fruits and vegetables, and bespeaks the tremendous effort needed to eat his daily bread. With fruits and vegetables, we acknowledge God in His role as a Creator, "Who creates the fruit of the tree", בורא פרי העץ, or the "fruit of the ground", בורא פרי האדמה. Many fruits and vegetables are ready to eat, with minimal effort expended to enhance the produce. The luscious array of foods grown from the earth are available for consumption, and we readily acknowledge God as the Creator of those foods. The miracle of these fruits, enabling a seed to develop into a life-giving tree, allows us to offer our humble thanks to the Creator who shared these gifts with us.

The blessing our Rabbis designated for bread is המוציא לחם מן הארץ, "Who brings forth bread from the land." The sweat involved in planting a seed and ultimately baking bread is tremendous, the efforts are extensive, the personal involvement often arduous — and our thanks to God for being part of the process must be overwhelming and everlasting. Indeed, many of the Torah prohibitions on Shabbos relate to forbidden activities in working the earth. The eleven prohibitions, called סידורא דפת, the order of the bread, relate to those steps necessary to make a seed into a piece of bread.

The Talmud (*Shabbos* 73a) lists the necessary steps that were employed in the Tabernacle which are the prototypes of forbidden creative activity on Shabbos. Those of סידורא דפת – sowings, plowing, reaping, gathering together, threshing, winnowing, selecting, grinding, sifting, kneading and baking, finally result in the piece of bread to eat. The fragrant aroma that wafts through a bakery in action belies the arduous efforts it took to reach that point.

In every struggle, one must look to see the positive. After generations of back-breaking toil to bring food from the earth, the descendants of Adam were despondent. The curse to Adam and his descendants had indeed been fulfilled, and with their primitive resources their plight seemed helpless — until Noah was born. "And he called him Noah, saying, 'This one will bring us ease from our work and from the toil of our hands, from the earth which God has cursed'" (*Bereishis* 5:29). Until Noah was born, there were no tools available to plow the land, and though man would sow wheat, thorns would grow. The birth of Noah heralded a new era for mankind. The struggle was still there, but God equipped man with the tools to wage battle.

We live in the most technologically sophisticated period since man was created. What was once science fiction has become a reality. We do things today better, faster and cheaper than did our ancestors, and we pride ourselves on the gadgetry and conveniences which have enhanced the quality of our lives. Yet ... the struggle continues, as it did in the time of Adam. With the sweat of our countenance we persist, and indeed, God has greatly eased the process. As we sit down with two challos on our beautifully bedecked Shabbos table, by saying the *hamotzi* blessing, we pause briefly with our humble statement to our Creator. At times it comes with great difficulty, but today, more than ever, I thank You. I thank You for being able to partake of Your beneficence, I thank You for enabling me to overcome the obstacles set out as I earn my provisions, and I thank You for allowing me to be a partner in the process of bringing forth bread from the earth.

As we sit down with two challos on our beautifully bedecked Shabbos table, by saying the hamotzi blessing, we pause briefly with our humble statement to our Creator.

Laws of Hamotzi
Staple of Life

- The blessing of *hamotzi* should be recited over two whole loaves of bread or matzo. These breads are referred to as *lechem mishnah,* the double portion of bread. This commemorates the extra measure of *manna* that fell for the Jews in the Wilderness on Friday.

- Both men and women who are reciting *hamotzi* are obligated in *lechem mishnah*. Children reciting *hamotzi* should also be taught to do so.

- A crack in the challah would not render it broken, unless, upon lifting the smaller half, the larger part would break off.

- If two loaves attach during baking, one may separate them and they can be considered two whole loaves. If only one whole loaf is available it should be used with a second piece of challah. If no whole loaves are available, one should recite *hamotzi* on two pieces of challah.

- One should remove both breads from any bags or wrappings.

- Frozen bread may be used if no other bread is available.

- The challos should be placed one on top of the other. On Friday night the bottom challah should be cut first; on *Shabbos* day the top challah is cut first. On Festivals, the top challah is cut first even at night.

- On Friday night to avoid "passing over the mitzvah" one should place the lower bread closer to oneself while reciting the blessing.

- Before reciting the blessing, one makes an indentation in the bread where one intends to cut.

- One begins by announcing, *"birshus"* – With your permission… as a sign of respect, as well as alerting all who are present to pay attention to the blessing.

- One should place all ten fingers on the challah. He should raise both loaves when reciting the name of God in the blessing of *hamotzi*.

- After reciting the blessing, one slices a piece of challah, eats it, then slices and passes the remaining challah to the others present. Kabbalistically, the challah should be dipped into salt three times before eating.

- One should place the challah in front of those present rather than directly into their hands or throwing it.

- One should not walk or talk until after swallowing a piece of bread.

Hamotzi – Staple of Life
In the Talmud and Midrash

One is obligated to make the blessing over two whole challahs on Shabbos, based on the verse, (*Shemos* 16:22) "And it was on the sixth day (Friday), that they gathered a double portion of food." This is called לחם משנה (Talmud, *Shabbos* 117b).

The two loaves of challah, לחם משנה, that are eaten on Shabbos correspond to the extra portion of manna that fell on Friday when the Jews were in the Wilderness. The manna fell on the earth and was covered by a white, frost-like dew. To commemorate this event, the Shabbos table is covered with a white tablecloth, and the challahs are covered with a challah cover (*Elyah Rabbah* 271:16).

The blessing recited over bread takes priority over the blessing on wine, if one has both foods before him. Therefore, in terms of *halachic* priority one should really say the blessing of *hamotzi* on the challah before *borei pri hagefen* on the wine. This creates a difficulty, since one may not eat before making Kiddush, which is said over the wine. To avoid "passing over the *mitzvah*" of challah, we make sure the challah is covered during Kiddush, so it is not "embarrassed" by being deemed *halachically* inferior (*Tur, Orach Chaim* 271).

If one eats bread without drying his hands, it is considered as if he ate ritually impure bread (Talmud, *Sotah* 4b).

At the time when Hashem told Adam "Thorns and thistles will grow for you," he began crying. When He said, "With the sweat of your countenance you will eat bread," he was appeased (Talmud, *Shabbos* 118a).

The manna which fell for the Jews in the Wilderness was a barometer which measured their righteousness. The Torah calls manna various terms in different verses. It is called לחם, bread, signifying that it was baked; עגות, cakes, a pre-baking process, and טחון, it must be ground up to be eaten. How are the various terms reconciled? For the righteous, the manna fell baked, as ready-to-eat bread. For those who were less righteous, the food had to be baked, but was somewhat ready; for the evildoers, it was totally unprocessed. They had to convert the manna into flour, bake it and only then could they partake of it (Talmud, *Yoma* 75a).

When the angels came to visit Abraham in the guise of wayfarers, (*Bereishis* 18:5) he said to them, "And I will take a piece of bread (for you)". God said to Abraham, "You said 'I will give you a piece of bread,' by your life (a promise), I will shower down upon your descendants bread from the heavens" (*Bereishis Rabbah* 48). The acts of kindness performed by our forefathers were not singular actions, but impacted on their descendants generations later to make them recipients of Hashem's goodness.

Shabbos Foods:
TASTES OF TRADITION

Shabbos Foods

The customs and traditions that have been handed down from generation to generation and from various communities have withstood the test of time. Customs are not innovations of particularly creative individuals, but are firmly rooted precepts that have helped maintain Judaism throughout the long exile. "The custom of our forefathers is in our hands" (Talmud, *Beitzah* 5b), is the badge of honor worn proudly by those who cling to the traditions of their ancestors.

Food is part of life. No celebration in any culture is complete without it. Food can serve as the backdrop of an affair, the focus of attention or merely complement a program or set of activities. In Judaism, food in general, and Shabbos food in particular, has a spiritual dimension that makes certain foods staples in their communities.

The menu chosen for the Shabbos meal is a unique combination of foods which reflect the nature of the day, מעין עולם הבא, a touch of the World to Come. The "otherworldly" quality of food served at the Shabbos meal parallels the food that will in fact be served to the righteous at the end of time. The Talmud (*Bava Basra* 75a) enumerates three foods which will be part of that exalted banquet. These are the feast of the leviathan fish, the meat of the *shor habor*, the wild ox, and the wine which was stored away since the time of Creation. We partake of foods which are truly a semblance of the World to Come. *(Mateh Moshe)*

CHALLAH -

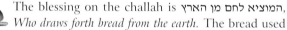

The blessing on the challah is המוציא לחם מן הארץ, *Who draws forth bread from the earth.* The bread used on Shabbos has the distinction of being called by its own name, challah, to remind the woman of the home to separate challah, a portion of the dough, before baking it. If the appropriate amount of flour is used (see Laws of Hamotzi), a special blessing and prayer are recited. *(Taamei Minhagim)*

The custom is to make *hamotzi* on *lechem mishneh,* to commemorate the double portion of manna that fell for the Jews in the Wilderness. *Arizal* notes that it is customary to have twelve loaves at the Shabbos meal to commemorate the *lechem hapanim,* the "show bread", which was brought in the Tabernacle. The bread stayed warm miraculously from the eve of Shabbos when it was baked, until the following Shabbos. They were taken off on Shabbos and eaten by the *kohanim,* the priests. We recall this blessing as we use the twelve *challos,* also alluded to in some of the *zemiros.*

Some women have the custom of braiding six strips of dough to form each challah. Since one uses *lechem mishneh,* the *challos* allude to the twelve "show breads" that were brought in the Tabernacle *(Iyun Tefillah).*

Elyah Rabbah discourages the practice of having twelve challos, as we are unfamiliar with their Kabbalistic symbolism. The Shinover Rav justifies

Customs are not innovations of particularly creative individuals, but are firmly rooted precepts that have helped maintain Judaism throughout the long exile.

the custom of using two challos, as well as the allusion to the twelve *challos*. Each elongated challah, held vertically, resembles the letter "ו", which has the numerical value of six; with two *challos,* the allusion to the twelve *challos* is correct.

It is customary to place the *challos* over each other. The bottom challah should be cut first on Friday night, the top challah on Shabbos day. To avoid the problem of "passing over the *mitzvah*," the lower challah should be moved closer on Friday night so that it is the first challah that we encounter when we are ready to say *hamotzi*.

Hamotzi Customs -

One places all the fingers on the challos when reciting the *hamotzi* blessing. In the blessing of *hamotzi*, there are ten words. Additionally, there are ten *mitzvos* which relate to the planting and harvesting of the grain in preparation for making bread.

1. It is forbidden to plow with a donkey and an ox together.
2. It is forbidden to plant two species together.
3. One must leave the forgotten sheaf of wheat for the poor.
4. One must leave a corner, *peah*, of the field uncut.
5. When one harvests the field, *leket,* the gleanings of the field should be left for the poor.
6. The first fruit, *bikkurim* must be given from the seven species with which the Land of Israel is praised.
7. *Terumah*, a portion offered to the *kohein*, the priest.
8. *Maaser rishon*, a first tithe.
9. *Maaser sheni*, a second tithe.
10. Separating challah from the dough.

To allude to these prohibitions and positive commandments, we hold the challah with ten fingers during the recitation of *hamotzi* (*Tur* 167:7).

Maharal (*Nesivos Olam*, chapter 18) notes that there are ten blessings which Yitzchok bestowed upon Yaakov when he bestowed upon him the blessing of ויתן לך (*Bereishis* 27:28-29). The benefits of heaven and earth in regard to produce and bounty are mentioned, and perhaps the ten blessings also apply to *hamotzi*. Ten laws which apply to the cup of wine used in *bircas hamazon*, are also mentioned in Jewish law.

Challah Impressions -

It is customary to make a slight impression or mark with the knife before the challah is fully cut and *hamotzi* is recited (*Magen Avraham* 274:1). It is preferable not to delay eating the challah after making the blessing of *hamotzi*. One cannot cut through the challos because on Shabbos they must be whole. An impression is made so that the master of the home will know where he should cut the challah and still minimize the pause between the blessing and eating (*Machtzis Hashekel*).

When the challah is sliced on Shabbos, it is placed on a plate or tray and the assembled take their own piece. Handing a piece of challah to someone resmbles the custom of mourning, wherein the bereaved takes food from others. Alternatively, we ask God in *bircas hamazon* that we not be dependent on the gifts of flesh and blood. It is improper to throw the challah, since it is disrespectful to the subject of the blessing (*Mishnah Berurah* 267:18). There are some who have the custom to gently toss the challah. Since the table of man is compared to the altar, we replicate some of the actions which took place there. The *aimurim*, animal innards which fall off the altar, were tossed back on the altar into the fire. Therefore, the custom in some *chassidic* and other communities is to follow that practice (*Chasam Sofer*).

FISH –
It is customary to eat fish at the Shabbos meal. (*Magen Avrohom*, chapter 242 suggests this for all three Shabbos meals.) During the Great Deluge, all mankind and animals were destroyed except Noah and his family. Animals were killed because they had corrupted their mating practices, and were destroyed together with the human race, which was totally immoral. The only animal life that did not succumb was the fish, because it did not follow the practice of the animals. On Shabbos, the most elevated of days, we eat fish, the most elevated of living species (*Minhag Yisroel Torah*).

B'nei Yissaschar offers an alternate reason for eating fish on Shabbos. Fish were formed on the fifth day of creation, man was created on the sixth day, and Shabbos was the seventh. There is a three-fold blessing that is present when we join these three elements, and "the three-fold strand will not easily be severed" (Ecclesiastes 4:12). When man eats fish on Shabbos, he will reap the benefits of these three blessings.

Eating gefilte fish has some practical *halachic* advantages over eating whole fish with bones. On Shabbos, one must be careful not to be *borer*, selecting and removing inedible items from edible matter. The laws of Shabbos are quite complex, and though there are ways to eat fish with bones, gefilte fish circumvents the problem (*Minchas Shabbos*).

LUKSHEN SOUP –
Some attribute eating soup on Shabbos to the phrase כי מלאכיו יצוה לך. *For His angels, He will command for you* is said on Friday night before Kiddush. The final letters of the phrase spell the word זויהך, the Yiddish word for soup. Lukshen are eaten to symbolize unity. Just as the lukshen get intertwined with one another, Shabbos is seen as a day of togetherness and peace (R' Pinchos of Koritz). Others see in it a contraction of the word לא קשין, it is not difficult. Our Rabbis tell us that earning a livelihood is קשין, difficult, as the splitting of the Red Sea. On Shabbos, the day of blessing, we plead to God that earning our livelihood should not be difficult (*Minhag Yisroel Torah*).

Fish were formed on the fifth day of creation, man was created on the sixth day, and Shabbos was the seventh.

When man eats fish on Shabbos, he will reap the benefits of these three blessings.

KUGEL -

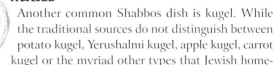

Another common Shabbos dish is kugel. While the traditional sources do not distinguish between potato kugel, Yerushalmi kugel, apple kugel, carrot kugel or the myriad other types that Jewish home-makers have created, there is a reason why kugel has become standard Shabbos fare. *Rema* (*Orach Chaim* 242) writes that in some places there was a custom to eat *mulysa* or *pashtida* on Friday night to commemorate the manna the Jews ate in the Wilderness. *Pashtida* is commonly referred to as our kugel, or a knish-like food. Just as the manna was covered with a layer of dew above and below it, the kugel is made with a covering above and beneath a type of filling, often meat. Since on Shabbos the manna did not fall, as there was a double portion on Friday, we have a remembrance of it by eating the manna-like kugel.

Another explanation for the custom of eating kugel is based on an additional allusion to the manna. The shape of the manna was round, expressed in Hebrew as כעיגול, like a circle (Talmud, *Yoma* 75a), a word which sounds like our kugel (or *kigel*, according to *chassidic* pronunciations).

CHOLENT -

The tasty, stew-like dish which is served on Shabbos day originated hundreds of years ago. The reason for it dates back to the time of the Saducees, *Tzedukim*, a heretical sect of Jews that denied the teachings of the Oral Torah. The Torah states (*Shemos* 35:3) "You shall not kindle fire in any of your dwellings on the Sabbath day." While the Rabbis understood the verse as a prohibition against kindling any new flame on Shabbos, the Saducees took it literally (*Rema, Orach Chaim* 257). They sat in the dark all Shabbos, not having any flame in their homes at all. In contradistinction to their teachings, we specifically keep our food warm overnight, cooked on the fire that was lit before Shabbos. The word "cholent" is derived from the word שלן, *it stayed overnight*, a reference to the way the food was cooked.

Eating cholent on Shabbos was not only enacted to enable us to enjoy Shabbos delicacies. It is a reaffirmation of the teachings of our Sages that has helped maintain our nation. Our fealty to the traditions of our ancestors has linked us to earlier generations, and has kept the Written and Oral Torah alive. The symbolism is profound, and the teachings are eternal. With the proper intent, we eat foods on Shabbos that are rooted in tradition, physically satisfying and spiritually uplifting.

Others see the eating of hot foods on Shabbos as a litmus test of one's dedication to the Rabbinic teachings. If one does not eat them because he says there is a prohibition to do so, one must investigate to see if he is in fact a heretic (*Mateh Moshe* 470, in the name of *Abudraham*). Delighting in Shabbos, *oneg* Shabbos, however, is relative to each individual. If eating hot foods on Shabbos is distasteful to him, he should certainly refrain from doing so.

SALT -

When making hamotzi, the challah is dipped into salt three times. Salt was used in the Temple for the sacrifices, "on all your sacrifices you should offer salt". (*Vayikra* 2:13) In the beginning of Creation, the waters were split, some remaining below and some remaining in the heavens.

The lower waters complained to the Almighty, "It is our desire to be close to our King!" They wished to be placed in the heavens as were the upper waters. The "covenant of salt" (ibid) is the promise made to appease them. Whenever a sacrifice was offered, salt, a by-product of water, was also offered. Since our table is compared to the altar before God, we have salt on the table at all times.

SHABBOS TREATS -

"And you shall call Shabbos a delight" (Isaiah 58:13). Delighting in the Shabbos means allowing ourselves to partake of physical delicacies to create a positive atmosphere for spiritual growth. Just as the manna had whatever taste its owner desired (Talmud *Yoma* 75a), we partake of a full range of special treats especially in honor of the Shabbos. Additionally, one should recite one hundred blessings every day. In the *amidah* prayer, *shemoneh esrei* said during the week, there are nineteen blessings. Including the blessings said three times daily and those recited in the morning prayers, saying this many blessings is not particularly difficult. On Shabbos, when the *shemoneh esrei* has only seven blessings, our Rabbis gave us the opportunity to reach our one hundred-blessing goal by encouraging us to say additional blessings on food. Since there are many complicated laws regarding foods, their blessings and requirements, it is helpful to be well-versed in these laws, or to speak to a *halachic* authority.

"Borrow on My account and I will repay you" (*Talmud,* Beitzah 15b). This directive from God is to enjoy all of the delicacies which life has to offer, even when we have to borrow to pay for it. It is God's testimony to the Jewish people that He will enable us to provide for beautifully prepared Shabbos meals. We delight on a day when He delights, and we find peace and contentment in all that He has given us.

Delighting in the Shabbos means allowing ourselves to partake of physical delicacies to create a positive atmosphere for spiritual growth

Allusions for Shabbos Foods

he many foods we eat on Shabbos, the delight in the physical aspects of the day, are all methods of enhancing our Shabbos. The specific dishes we eat have particular significance, as mentioned, each with a given reason why it became customary to consume it on Shabbos.

In Judaism, *gematria*, or numeric equivalent, has particular significance. Each Hebrew character has a numeric value, i.e., א = 1, ב = 2, י = 10, כ = 20, etc. An extension of the *gematria* principle is the מספר קטן, or lower number value, looking at the unit numbers rather than at the tens and hundreds equivalent. Hence, י = 10 in the regular counting system, and in the *mispar katan* formula it is equal to 1. For example, אמת = א = 1, מ = 40, ת = 400. The zeros are dropped and the מספר קטן is 9.

Since Shabbos is the seventh day of the week, it would be logical to have the number 7 prominently featured in areas relating to Shabbos. This is particularly true regarding the foods we eat.

challah / חלה = 5 + 30 + 8 = 43 (4 + 3 = 7)

fish / דג = 4 + 3 = 7

wine / יין = 70 = 7

soup / מרק = 100 + 200 + 40 = 340 (3 + 4 = 7)

candle / נר = 250 (2 + 5 = 7)

meat / בשר = 502 (5 + 2 = 7)

This allusion, attributed to the *Gaon* of Vilna and other commentators, points to the Divine element found in even the most mundane actions. The spirit of Shabbos is found in all that we do, and the foods that enable us to enjoy the Shabbos are part of God's Divine commandments.

Zemiros Shabbos:

SONGS OF THE SOUL

סדר ליל שבת

this song was composed by moshe ben kalonymus, who lived at the end of the 10th century. it praises those who observe shabbos properly.

כל מקדש שְׁבִיעִי כָּרָאוּי לוֹ. כָּל שׁוֹמֵר שַׁבָּת כַּדָּת מֵחַלְּלוֹ.
שְׂכָרוֹ הַרְבֵּה מְאֹד עַל פִּי פָעֳלוֹ. אִישׁ עַל
מַחֲנֵהוּ וְאִישׁ עַל דִּגְלוֹ: א. וְהֹבֵי יְיָ הַמְחַכִּים בְּבִנְיַן אֲרִיאֵל. בְּיוֹם הַשַּׁבָּת שִׂישׂוּ וְשִׂמְחוּ
כִּמְקַבְּלֵי מַתַּן נַחֲלִיאֵל. גַּם שְׂאוּ יְדֵיכֶם קֹדֶשׁ וְאִמְרוּ לָאֵל. בָּרוּךְ יְיָ אֲשֶׁר
נָתַן מְנוּחָה לְעַמּוֹ יִשְׂרָאֵל: ד. דּוֹרְשֵׁי יְיָ זֶרַע אַבְרָהָם אוֹהֲבוֹ. ה. מְאַחֲרִים
לָצֵאת מִן הַשַּׁבָּת וּמְמַהֲרִים לָבוֹא. ו. שְׂמֵחִים לְשָׁמְרוֹ וּלְעָרֵב עֵרוּבוֹ.
זֶה הַיּוֹם עָשָׂה יְיָ נָגִילָה וְנִשְׂמְחָה בוֹ: ז. זִכְרוּ תּוֹרַת מֹשֶׁה בְּמִצְוַת שַׁבָּת
גְּרוּסָה. ח. חֲרוּתָה לַיּוֹם הַשְּׁבִיעִי כְּכַלָּה בֵּין רֵעוֹתֶיהָ מְשֻׁבָּצָה. ט. הוֹרִים
יְרֵשׁוּהָ וִיקַדְּשׁוּהָ בְּמַאֲמַר כָּל אֲשֶׁר עָשָׂה. וַיְכַל אֱלֹהִים בַּיּוֹם הַשְּׁבִיעִי
מְלַאכְתּוֹ אֲשֶׁר עָשָׂה: י. יוֹם קָדוֹשׁ הוּא מִבּוֹאוֹ וְעַד צֵאתוֹ. כָּל זֶרַע יַעֲקֹב
יְכַבְּדוּהוּ כִּדְבַר הַמֶּלֶךְ וְדָתוֹ. ל. לָנוּחַ בּוֹ וְלִשְׂמוֹחַ בְּתַעֲנוּג אָכוֹל וְשָׁתוֹ.
כָּל עֲדַת יִשְׂרָאֵל יַעֲשׂוּ אוֹתוֹ: מ. מָשׁוֹךְ חַסְדְּךָ לְיוֹדְעֶיךָ אֵל קַנָּא וְנוֹקֵם. נ. נוֹטְרֵי
לַיּוֹם הַשְּׁבִיעִי זָכוֹר וְשָׁמוֹר לְהָקֵם. ש. שַׂמְּחֵם בְּבִנְיַן שָׁלֵם בְּאוֹר פָּנֶיךָ תַּבְהִיקֵם.
יִרְוְיֻן מִדֶּשֶׁן בֵּיתֶךָ וְנַחַל עֲדָנֶיךָ תַשְׁקֵם: ע. עֲזוֹר לַשּׁוֹבְתִים בַּשְּׁבִיעִי
בֶּחָרִישׁ וּבַקָּצִיר עוֹלָמִים. פ. פּוֹסְעִים בּוֹ פְּסִיעָה קְטַנָּה סוֹעֲדִים בּוֹ לְבָרֵךְ
שָׁלֹשׁ פְּעָמִים. צ. צִדְקָתָם תַּצְהִיר כְּאוֹר שִׁבְעַת הַיָּמִים. יְיָ אֱלֹהֵי יִשְׂרָאֵל
הָבָה תָמִים:(יְיָ אֱלֹהֵי יִשְׂרָאֵל אַהֲבַת תָּמִים: יְיָ אֱלֹהֵי יִשְׂרָאֵל תְּשׁוּעַת עוֹלָמִים:)

this song of joy was composed by a medieval poet named moshe.

מְנוּחָה וְשִׂמְחָה אוֹר לַיְּהוּדִים. יוֹם
שַׁבָּתוֹן יוֹם מַחֲמַדִּים.
שׁוֹמְרָיו וְזוֹכְרָיו הֵמָּה מְעִידִים. כִּי לְשִׁשָּׁה כָּל בְּרוּאִים וְעוֹמְדִים:
שׁ. שְׁמֵי שָׁמַיִם אֶרֶץ וְיַמִּים. כָּל צְבָא מָרוֹם גְּבוֹהִים וְרָמִים.
תַּנִּין וְאָדָם וְחַיַּת רְאֵמִים. כִּי בְּיָהּ יְיָ צוּר עוֹלָמִים:
ה. הוּא אֲשֶׁר דִּבֶּר לְעַם סְגֻלָּתוֹ. שָׁמוֹר לְקַדְּשׁוֹ מִבּוֹאוֹ וְעַד
צֵאתוֹ שַׁבַּת קֹדֶשׁ יוֹם חֶמְדָּתוֹ. כִּי בוֹ שָׁבַת אֵל מִכָּל מְלַאכְתּוֹ:
ב. בְּמִצְוַת שַׁבָּת אֵל יַחֲלִיצָךְ. קוּם קְרָא אֵלָיו יָחִישׁ לְאַמְּצָךְ.
נִשְׁמַת כָּל חַי וְגַם נַעֲרִיצָךְ. אֱכוֹל בְּשִׂמְחָה כִּי כְבָר רָצָךְ:
ב. בְּמִשְׁנֶה לֶחֶם וְקִדּוּשׁ רַבָּה. בְּרוֹב מַטְעַמִּים וְרוּחַ נְדִיבָה.
יִזְכּוּ לְרַב טוּב הַמִּתְעַנְּגִים בָּהּ. בְּבִיאַת גּוֹאֵל לְחַיֵּי הָעוֹלָם הַבָּא:

FRIDAY NIGHT

This zemer was composed by Moshe ben Klonymus of the 10th century, a variation of which is found in Machzor Vitry. Its primary theme, noted in the א-ב acrostic, praises those who are exacting in their Shabbos observance, and the reward awaiting them. The zemer underscores the joy experienced by those who faithfully adhere to the laws of Shabbos, and the gladness awaiting them when the Holy Temple in Jerusalem will be rebuilt.

KŌL M'KADAYSH sh'vi-i koro-uy lō,
Kol shomer Shabbos kados maychal'lō,
S'choro harbay m'od al pi fo'olō,
Ish al machanayhu, v'ish al diglō.

Ōhavei Adōnoy hamchakim l'vinyan ari-ayl,
B'yōm haShabbos sisu v'simchu
kimkablay matan nachali-ayl,
Gam s'eu y'daychem kōdesh v'imru lo-Ayl,
Boruch Adōnoy asher nosan m'nuchoh
l'amo Yisrō-ayl.

Dorshay Adōnoy, zera Avrohom ōhavō,
Ham-acharim lotzays min haShabbos,
um'maharim lovō,
U'smaychim l'shomrō ul-orayv ayruvō,
Zeh ha-yōm osoh Adōnoy, nogiloh v'nism'cho vō.

Zichru Tōras Mōshe, b'mitzvas Shabbos g'ruso,
Charusoh layōm hashvi-i, k'chaloh
bayn ray-ōseho meshubotzo,
Tehōrim yiroshuho, vikadshuho
b'ma-amar kol asher oso,

Vay'chal Elōhim ba-yōm hashvi'i
m'lachto asher osō.

Yōm kodosh hu, mibō-ō v'ad tzaysō,
Kōl zera Ya'akōv y'chabduhu
kidvar hamelech v'dosō,
Lonuach bo v'lismoach b'sa-anug ochol v'shosō,
Kol adas Yisroel, ya-asu osō.

M'shōch chasd'cho l'yōd-echo, Ayl kanō v'nokem,
Nōtray layōm hashvi'i zochor v'shomor l'hokaym,
Samchaym b'vinyan sholaym, b'or ponecho tavhikaym,
Yirv'yun mideshen baysecho,
vnachal adonecho sashkaym.

Azōr lashovsim bashvi-i,
bechorish uvakotzir ōlomim,
Pōs-im bo p'si-oh k'tanoh,
sō-adim bo l'voraych sholōsh p'omim,
Tzidkosom tatzhir k'or shivas hayomim,
Adōnoy Elōhay Yisro-ayl hovoh somim,
(Adōnoy Elōhay Yisro-ayl, ahavas tomim,
Adōnoy Elōhay Yisroel, t'shu'as ōlomim.)

The author משה, a Medieval composer, affixed his name to the opening sentences of this zemer. Resting on Shabbos and enjoying its delicacies can become spiritually imbued activities. Observing Shabbos's positive precepts and safeguarding it by not transgressing any prohibitions, bring an exalted sense of contentment to the individual. The gift of Shabbos is given to God's treasured nation, the Jewish People.

MENUCHOH V'SIMCHOH,
ōr lay-hudim
Yōm Shabbosōn, yōm machamadim,
Shōmrov v'zōchrov haymoh m'idim,
Ki l'shishoh, kōl bru-im v'ōmdim.

Sh'may shoma-yim, eretz v'yamim,
Kol tz'vo morōm, g'vōhim v'romim
Tanin v'odom, v'chayas r'aymim,
Ki b'Yoh Adōnoy tzur ōlomim.

Hu asher diber l'am segulosō,
Shomōr l'kadshō mibō-ō v'ad tzaysō,

Shabbos kōdesh yōm chemdosō,
Ki vō shovas Ayl mikol m'lachtō.

B'mitzvas Shabbos Ayl yachalitzoch,
Kum k'ro aylov yochish l'amtzoch,
Nishmas kol chai, vgam na-aritzoch,
Echōl b'simchoh ki k'vor rotzoch.

B'mishneh lechem v'kiddush rabboh,
B'rōv mat-amim v'ruach n'divoh,
Yizku l'rav tuv hamis-angim boh,
B'vi-as gō-ayl, l'cha-yay ho'ōlom habo

סֵדֶר לֵיל שַׁבָּת

THIS SONG PRAISES THE SABBATH, WHILE ENUMERATING SOME OF ITS LAWS. IT WAS COMPOSED BY MENACHEM BEN MAKHIR OF RATISBON IN THE 11th CENTURY.

מַה יְּדִידוּת מְנוּחָתֵךְ, אַתְּ שַׁבָּת הַמַּלְכָּה.
בְּכֵן נָרוּץ לִקְרָאתֵךְ בּוֹאִי כַלָּה נְסוּכָה.
לְבֻשׁ בִּגְדֵי חֲמוּדוֹת, לְהַדְלִיק נֵר בִּבְרָכָה. וַתֵּכֶל כָּל הָעֲבוֹדוֹת.
לֹא תַעֲשׂוּ מְלָאכָה: לְהִתְעַנֵּג בְּתַעֲנוּגִים בַּרְבּוּרִים וּשְׂלָיו וְדָגִים:

מֵעֶרֶב מַזְמִינִים, כָּל מִינֵי מַטְעַמִּים, מִבְּעוֹד יוֹם מוּכָנִים, תַּרְנְגוֹלִים
מְפֻטָּמִים, וְלַעֲרוֹךְ כַּמָּה מִינִים, שְׁתוֹת יֵינוֹת מְבֻשָּׂמִים, וְתַפְנוּקֵי
מַעֲדַנִּים, בְּכָל שָׁלֹשׁ פְּעָמִים: לְהִתְעַנֵּג בְּתַעֲנוּגִים בַּרְבּוּרִים וּשְׂלָיו וְדָגִים:

נַחֲלַת יַעֲקֹב יִירָשׁ, בְּלִי מְצָרִים נַחֲלָה. וִיכַבְּדוּהוּ עָשִׁיר וָרָשׁ, וְתִזְכּוּ
לִגְאֻלָּה. יוֹם שַׁבָּת אִם תִּשְׁמֹרוּ, וִהְיִיתֶם לִי סְגֻלָּה. שֵׁשֶׁת יָמִים
תַּעֲבֹדוּ, וּבַשְּׁבִיעִי נָגִילָה: לְהִתְעַנֵּג בְּתַעֲנוּגִים בַּרְבּוּרִים וּשְׂלָיו וְדָגִים:

חֲפָצֶיךָ בּוֹ אֲסוּרִים, וְגַם לַחֲשׁוֹב חֶשְׁבּוֹנוֹת. הִרְהוּרִים מֻתָּרִים, וּלְשַׁדֵּךְ
הַבָּנוֹת, וְתִינוֹק לְלַמְּדוֹ סֵפֶר, לַמְנַצֵּחַ בִּנְגִינוֹת, וְלַהֲגוֹת בְּאִמְרֵי שֶׁפֶר,
בְּכָל פִּנּוֹת וּמַחֲנוֹת: לְהִתְעַנֵּג בְּתַעֲנוּגִים בַּרְבּוּרִים וּשְׂלָיו וְדָגִים:

הִלּוּכָךְ תְּהֵא בְנַחַת, עֹנֶג קְרָא לַשַּׁבָּת. וְהַשֵּׁנָה מְשֻׁבַּחַת, כְּדָת נֶפֶשׁ
מְשִׁיבַת. בְּכֵן נַפְשִׁי לְךָ עָרְגָה. וְלָנוּחַ בְּחִבַּת, בַּשּׁוֹשַׁנִּים סוּגָה, בּוֹ
יָנוּחוּ בֵּן וּבַת.   לְהִתְעַנֵּג בְּתַעֲנוּגִים בַּרְבּוּרִים וּשְׂלָיו וְדָגִים:

מֵעֵין עוֹלָם הַבָּא, יוֹם שַׁבָּת מְנוּחָה. כָּל הַמִּתְעַנְּגִים בָּהּ, יִזְכּוּ
לְרוֹב שִׂמְחָה. מֵחֶבְלֵי מָשִׁיחַ, יֻצָּלוּ לִרְוָחָה. פְּדוּתֵנוּ תַצְמִיחַ. וְנָס
יָגוֹן וַאֲנָחָה: לְהִתְעַנֵּג בְּתַעֲנוּגִים בַּרְבּוּרִים וּשְׂלָיו וְדָגִים:

THIS SONG WAS COMPOSED BY ARI Z'L, THE FAMOUS 16th CENTURY KABBALIST OF SAFED.

יוֹם זֶה לְיִשְׂרָאֵל

אוֹרָה וְשִׂמְחָה שַׁבַּת מְנוּחָה:

צִוִּיתָ פִּקּוּדִים בְּמַעֲמַד הַר סִינַי, שַׁבָּת וּמוֹעֲדִים לִשְׁמוֹר בְּכָל שָׁנַי.
לַעֲרוֹךְ לְפָנַי מַשְׂאֵת וַאֲרוּחָה, שַׁבַּת מְנוּחָה: יוֹם זֶה לְיִשְׂרָאֵל

חֶמְדַּת הַלְּבָבוֹת לְאֻמָּה שְׁבוּרָה, לִנְפָשׁוֹת נִכְאָבוֹת נְשָׁמָה יְתֵרָה.
לְנֶפֶשׁ מְצֵרָה יָסִיר אֲנָחָה, שַׁבַּת מְנוּחָה: יוֹם זֶה לְיִשְׂרָאֵל

קִדַּשְׁתָּ בֵּרַכְתָּ אוֹתוֹ מִכָּל יָמִים, בְּשֵׁשֶׁת כִּלִּיתָ מְלֶאכֶת עוֹלָמִים.
בּוֹ מָצְאוּ עֲגוּמִים הַשְׁקֵט וּבִטְחָה שַׁבַּת מְנוּחָה: יוֹם זֶה לְיִשְׂרָאֵל

לְאִסּוּר מְלָאכָה צִוִּיתָנוּ נוֹרָא, אֶזְכֶּה הוֹד מְלוּכָה אִם שַׁבָּת אֶשְׁמוֹרָה.
אַקְרִיב שַׁי לַמּוֹרָא מִנְחָה מֶרְקָחָה שַׁבַּת מְנוּחָה: יוֹם זֶה לְיִשְׂרָאֵל

חַדֵּשׁ מִקְדָּשֵׁנוּ זָכְרָה נֶחֱרֶבֶת, טוּבְךָ מוֹשִׁיעֵנוּ תְּנָה לַנֶּעֱצֶבֶת. בְּשַׁבָּת
יוֹשֶׁבֶת בְּזֶמֶר וּשְׁבָחָה שַׁבַּת מְנוּחָה: יוֹם זֶה לְיִשְׂרָאֵל

FRIDAY NIGHT

The middle section of this zemer contains the acrostic for the author, Menachem ben Makhli of Rassbon in the 11th century. The Shabbos Queen is exalted through the physical enjoyment of fish and fowl, complementing the spiritual dimension of the day. The laws of Shabbos are outlines, and the actions, speech and thought of the Jews make it a semblance of the World to Come.

MAH Y'DIDUS *m'nuchosaych,*
at Shabbos hamalkoh,
B'chayn norutz kikrosaych, bō-i chaloh n'suchoh,
L'vush bigday chamudōs, l'hadlik nayr bivrochoh,
Vataychel kol ho-avōdōs, lō sa-asu m'lochoh.
  L'his-anayg b'sa-anugim
  Barburim uslov v'dogim.

May'erev mazminin, kol minay mat-amim,
Mib-ōd yōm muchanim, tarn'gōlim m'futomim,
V'la'arōch kamoh minim, sh'sōs yaynōs m'rusomim,
V'safnukay ma-adamin, b'chol sholosh p'omim.
  L'his-anayg b'sa-anugim
  Barburim uslov v'dogim.

Nachalas Ya-akōv yirosh, b'li m'tzorim nachaloh,
Vichabduhu oshir vorosh, v'sizku lig-uloh,
Yōm Shabbos im tishmōru, vih'yisem li s'guloh,
Shaysheshes yomim ta-avōdu, uvashvi-i nogiloh.
  L'his-anayg b'sa-anugim
  Barburim uslov v'dogim.

Chafotzecho boh asurim,
v'gam lachashōv cheshbōnōs,
Hirhurim mutorim, ulshadaych habanōs,
V'sinōk l'lamdō sayfer,
lamnatzayach binginōs,
V'hahagōs b'imray shefer, b'chol pinōs umachanōs.
  L'his-anayg b'sa-anugim
  Barburim uslov v'dogim.

Hiluchoch t'hay v'nachas, ōneg k'ro LaShabbos,
V'hashaynoh m'shubachas, kados nefesh m'shivas,
B'chayn nafshi l'cho orgoh, v'lonuach b'chibas,
Kashōshanim, sugoh, bō yonuchu bayn uvas.
  L'his-anayg b'sa-anugim
  Barburim uslov v'dogim.

May-ayn ōlom habo, yōm Shabbos m'nuchoh,
Kol hamis-angim boh, yizku l'rōv simchoh,
Maychevlay moshiyach yutzolu lirvochoh,
P'dusaynu satmiyach, v'nos yogōn va'anochoh.
  L'his-anayg b'sa-anugim
  Barburim uslov v'dogim

This zemer as it appears is an abridged form of the extended version found in Otsar HaTefillos and other siddurim. The full version contains an acrostic with the name Yitzchak Luria chazak, and is attributed to Arizal, the great Kabbalist Rav Yitzchak Luria. The day of Shabbos brings spiritual contentment and the Neshama yesairah, additional soul, that enters the Jew on Shabbos, enhances his tranquil spirit.

Yōm zeh l'Yisro-ayl, *ōroh v'simchoh,*
Shabbas m'nuchoh.
Tziviso pikudim b'ma-amad har Sinai,
Shabbos umō-adim lishmōr b'chol shonay,
La-arōch l'fonay mas'ays va'aruchoh,
Shabbos m'nuchoh.
  Yōm zeh l'Yisro-ayl...

Chemdas halvovōs l'umoh sh'vuroh,
Linfoshōs nich-ovos n'shomoh y'sayroh,
L'nefesh m'tzayrosh yosir anochoh,
Shabbos m'nuchoh.
  Yōm zeh l'Yisro-ayl...

Kidashto, bayrachto ōsō mikol yomim,
B'shayshes kiliso m'leches ōlomim,

Bō motzu agumim hashkayt uvit-choh,
Shabbos m'nuchoh.
  Yōm zeh l'Yisro-ayl...

L'isur m'lochoh tzivisonu nōro,
Ezkeh hōd m'luchoh im Shabbos eshmōroh,
Akriv shai lamōro minchoh merkochoh,
Shabbos m'nuchoh.
  Yōm zeh l'Yisro-ayl...

Chadaysh mikdoshaynu zochroh nechereves,
Tuvcho mōshi-aynu t'noh lane-etzeves,
B'Shabbos yōsheves b'zemer ushvochoh,
Shabbos m'nuchoh.
  Yōm zeh l'Yisro-ayl...

סֵדֶר לֵיל שַׁבָּת

THIS SONG OF PRAISE TO GOD WAS COMPOSED BY YISRAEL BEN MOSHE OF NAJARA, A FAMOUS
16ᵗʰ CENTURY LINGUIST AND KABBALIST, AND A STUDENT OF ARI Z'L.

יָהּ רִבּוֹן עָלַם וְעָלְמַיָּא. אַנְתְּ הוּא מַלְכָּא מֶלֶךְ
מַלְכַיָּא. עוֹבַד גְּבוּרְתֵּךְ וְתִמְהַיָּא. שְׁפַר
קֳדָמָךְ לְהַחֲוָיָא: יָהּ רִבּוֹן עָלַם וְעָלְמַיָּא. אַנְתְּ הוּא מַלְכָּא מֶלֶךְ מַלְכַיָּא:

שְׁבָחִין אֲסַדֵּר צַפְרָא וְרַמְשָׁא. לָךְ אֱלָהָא קַדִּישָׁא דִּי בְרָא כָל נַפְשָׁא.
עִירִין קַדִּישִׁין וּבְנֵי אֱנָשָׁא. חֵיוַת בָּרָא וְעוֹפֵי שְׁמַיָּא.
יָהּ רִבּוֹן עָלַם וְעָלְמַיָּא. אַנְתְּ הוּא מַלְכָּא מֶלֶךְ מַלְכַיָּא:

רַבְרְבִין עוֹבְדָיךְ וְתַקִּיפִין. מָכִיךְ רְמַיָּא וְזַקִּיף כְּפִיפִין.
לוּ יְחֵיה גְבַר שְׁנִין אַלְפִין. לָא יֵעוֹל גְּבוּרְתֵּךְ בְּחֻשְׁבְּנַיָּא.
יָהּ רִבּוֹן עָלַם וְעָלְמַיָּא. אַנְתְּ הוּא מַלְכָּא מֶלֶךְ מַלְכַיָּא:

אֱלָהָא דִּי לֵה יְקַר וּרְבוּתָא. פְּרוֹק יַת עָנָךְ מִפֻּם אַרְיָוָתָא.
וְאַפֵּיק יַת עַמָּךְ מִגּוֹ גָלוּתָא. עַמָּךְ דִּי בְחַרְתְּ מִכָּל אֻמַּיָּא.
יָהּ רִבּוֹן עָלַם וְעָלְמַיָּא. אַנְתְּ הוּא מַלְכָּא מֶלֶךְ מַלְכַיָּא:

לְמִקְדָּשָׁךְ תּוּב וּלְקֹדֶשׁ קֻדְשִׁין. אֲתַר דִּי בֵה יֶחֱדוּן רוּחִין וְנַפְשִׁין.
וִיזַמְּרוּן לָךְ שִׁירִין וְרַחֲשִׁין. בִּירוּשְׁלֵם קַרְתָּא דְשֻׁפְרַיָּא.
יָהּ רִבּוֹן עָלַם וְעָלְמַיָּא. אַנְתְּ הוּא מַלְכָּא מֶלֶךְ מַלְכַיָּא:

THIS SONG OF THANKSGIVING IS ATTRIBUTED BY SOME TO THE TANNA RABBI SHIMON BAR YOCHAI.

צוּר מִשֶּׁלּוֹ אָכַלְנוּ בָּרְכוּ אֱמוּנַי. שָׂבַעְנוּ
וְהוֹתַרְנוּ כִּדְבַר יְיָ:

הַזָּן אֶת עוֹלָמוֹ רוֹעֵנוּ אָבִינוּ. אָכַלְנוּ אֶת לַחְמוֹ וְיֵינוֹ שָׁתִינוּ.
עַל כֵּן נוֹדֶה לִשְׁמוֹ וּנְהַלְלוֹ בְּפִינוּ. אָמַרְנוּ וְעָנִינוּ אֵין קָדוֹשׁ כַּיְיָ:
צוּר מִשֶּׁלּוֹ אָכַלְנוּ בָּרְכוּ אֱמוּנַי. שָׂבַעְנוּ וְהוֹתַרְנוּ כִּדְבַר יְיָ:

בְּשִׁיר וְקוֹל תּוֹדָה נְבָרֵךְ לֵאלֹהֵינוּ. עַל אֶרֶץ חֶמְדָּה טוֹבָה שֶׁהִנְחִיל
לַאֲבוֹתֵינוּ. מָזוֹן וְצֵדָה הִשְׂבִּיעַ לְנַפְשֵׁנוּ. חַסְדּוֹ גָּבַר עָלֵינוּ וֶאֱמֶת יְיָ:
צוּר מִשֶּׁלּוֹ אָכַלְנוּ בָּרְכוּ אֱמוּנַי. שָׂבַעְנוּ וְהוֹתַרְנוּ כִּדְבַר יְיָ:

רַחֵם בְּחַסְדֶּךָ עַל עַמְּךָ צוּרֵנוּ. עַל צִיּוֹן מִשְׁכַּן כְּבוֹדֶךָ זְבוּל בֵּית
תִּפְאַרְתֵּנוּ. בֶּן דָּוִד עַבְדֶּךָ יָבוֹא וְיִגְאָלֵנוּ. רוּחַ אַפֵּינוּ מְשִׁיחַ יְיָ:
צוּר מִשֶּׁלּוֹ אָכַלְנוּ בָּרְכוּ אֱמוּנַי. שָׂבַעְנוּ וְהוֹתַרְנוּ כִּדְבַר יְיָ:

יִבָּנֶה הַמִּקְדָּשׁ עִיר צִיּוֹן תְּמַלֵּא. וְשָׁם נָשִׁיר שִׁיר חָדָשׁ וּבִרְנָנָה נַעֲלֶה.
הָרַחֲמָן הַנִּקְדָּשׁ יִתְבָּרַךְ וְיִתְעַלֶּה. עַל כּוֹס יַיִן מָלֵא כְּבִרְכַּת יְיָ:
צוּר מִשֶּׁלּוֹ אָכַלְנוּ בָּרְכוּ אֱמוּנַי. שָׂבַעְנוּ וְהוֹתַרְנוּ כִּדְבַר יְיָ:

FRIDAY NIGHT

The author, Rabbi Yisrael ben Moshe Najara, was one of the disciples of the Arizal in the 16th century. It is somewhat unique among the zemiros, since it was written in Aramaic and not in Hebrew. It extols the greatness and omnipotence of God. The zemer ends with a heartfelt plea to God to end our exile and return to Jerusalem and the Holy Temple.

YOH RIBŌN olam v'olma-yo,
Ant'hu malko melech malcha-yo.
Ōvad g'vurtaych v'simha-yo,
Sh'far kodomoch l'hachavayoh.
    Yoh ribon olam v'olma-yo,
    Ant Hu malko melech malcha-yo.

Sh'vochim asadayr tzafro v'ramsho,
Loch Eloho kadisho di v'ro kol nafsho,
Irin kadishin u'vnay enosho,
Chayvas b'ro, v'ōfay sh'ma-yo.
    Yoh ribōn olam v'olma-yo,
    Ant Hu malko melech malcha-yo.

Rav'rvin ōvdaych v'sakifin,
Mochich r'ma-yo v'zakif k'fifin,

Lu yichyeh g'var, sh'nin alfin,
Lo yay'ōl g'vurtaych b'chushb'nayo.
    Yoh ribōn olam v'olma-yo,
    Ant Hu malko melech malcha-yo.

Eloho di layh y'kar ur'vuso,
P'rōk yas onoch mipum ary'voso.
V'apayk yas amaych, migōy goluso,
Amaych di v'chart mikol umayo.
    Yoh ribōn olam v'olma-yo,
    Ant Hu malko melech malcha-yo.

L'mikdoshoch tuv, ul'kōdesh kudshin,
Asar di vay yechedun ruchin v'nafshin,
Vizamrun loch shirin v'rachashin,
Birushlaym karto d'shufrayo.
    Yoh ribōn olam v'olma-yo,
    Ant Hu malko melech malcha-yo.

This zemer, attributed by some to Rabbi Shimon bar Yochai, parallels the zemer, or invitation to participants to join the leader in Grace After Meals. It includes a reference to God sustaining mankind (הזן), the Land of Israel (הארץ) and the rebuilding of Jerusalem (בונה ירושלים). Dover Shalom describes the zemer's theme based on the Midrash Bereishis. When passersby would visit Abraham, they would extol his kindness after they ate and drank their fill. "Don't thank me," Abraham would say, "extol the virtues of the One Who really sustained you."

TZUR MISHELŌ ochalnu,
borchu emunai,
Sovanu v'hōsarnu, k'dvar Adonoy.

Hazon es ōlomō, rō'aynu ovinu,
Ochalnu es lachmō, v'yaynō shosinu.
Al kayn nōdeh lishmō, unhal'lō b'finu,
Omarnu v'oninu, ayn kodōsh ka'Adōnoy.
    Tzur mishelō ochalnu, borchu emunay,
    Sovanu v'hōsarnu, k'dvar Adōnoy.

B'shir v'kol tōdoh, n'voraych l'Elōhaynu,
Al eretz chemdoh tovoh, shehinchil la'avōsaynu,
Mōzōn v'tzaydoh, hisbi-a l'nafshaynu,
Chasdō govar olaynu, v-emes Adōnoy.
    Tzur mishelō ochalnu, borchu emunay,
    Sovanu v'hōsarnu, k'dvar Adōnoy.

Rachaym b'chasdecho, al amcho tzuraynu,
Al Tziyōn mishkan kevōdecho,
z'vul bays tif-artaynu,
Ben Dovid avdecho, yovō v'yig-olaynu,
Ruach apaynu, m'shiyach Adōnoy.
    Tzur mishelō ochalnu, borchu emunay,
    Sovanu v'hōsarnu, k'dvar Adōnoy.

Yibone hamikdosh, ir Tziyōn temalay,
V'shom noshir shir chodosh,
uvirnonoh na-aleh,
Horachamon hanikdosh, Yisborach v'yis-aleh,
Al kōs yayin molay, k'virkas Adōnoy.
    Tzur mishelō ochalnu, borchu emunay,
    Sovanu v'hōsarnu, k'dvar Adōnoy.

Sholom Zochor
Welcoming the Male

he *sholom zochor* is a unique celebration in Judaism. On the first Friday night after a Jewish boy is born, friends and family join the parents of the new-born child in wishing them *mazel tov* at their home or, alternatively, in a synagogue hall. "When a male, *zochor* comes to the world, *sholom*, peace comes to the world" (Talmud, *Niddah* 31a). This usually takes place after the Shabbos meal.

Light refreshments are served, accompanied by joyous song, celebration and words of Torah. It is held on Friday night because it is a time when most Jews are found at home (*Tur, Yorah Deah* 265:13). Although there is no meal held in conjunction with a *sholom zochor*, it is customary to serve *arbis*, cooked chickpeas.

These are traditionally served to a mourner. When the young boy was still developing in his mother's womb, his soul was taught the entire Torah. When he enters this world, an angel taps him above his mouth, and he forgets that which he has learned. We gather to bless him and comfort him for the loss of his Torah knowledge (*Taz, Yoreh Deah* 265:13).

The *midrash* says that one has to be granted permission from the queen before entering the palace. We come together on Friday night "to pass before the Shabbos Queen." Shabbos is called an *os*, a sign, as is circumcision. We are given a sign in the dimension of time, Shabbos, and circumcision, which is a sign of connectedness with God on the body of man.

Shown below are some songs appropriate for the sholom zochor:

UR-AY *vonim l'vonecho, sholōm al Yisro-ayl.*

וּרְאֵה בָנִים לְבָנֶיךָ שָׁלוֹם עַל יִשְׂרָאֵל

And you will live to see your children's children, and peace upon Israel.

ZAR-O CHA-YO *v'ka-yomo, Zar-o di lo yifsōk v'di lo yivtōl, mipisgomay ōraiso.*

זַרְעָא חַיָּא וְקַיְמָא זַרְעָא דִי לָא יִפְסוֹק וְדִי לָא יִבְטוֹל מִפִּתְגָּמֵי אוֹרַיְיתָא

[May we be blessed with] offspring who will neither interrupt nor cease from words of the Torah.

SIMON TŌV *umazol tōv y'hay lonu ulchol Yisro-ayl, omayn.*

סִימָן טוֹב וּמַזָּל טוֹב יְהֵא לָנוּ וּלְכָל יִשְׂרָאֵל אָמֵן

May we and all Israel have a good sign and good luck, Amen.

DOVID *melech Yisro-ayl chai v'ka-yom. Simon tōv umazol tōv y'hay lonu ulchol Yisro-ayl, omayn.*

דָּוִד מֶלֶךְ יִשְׂרָאֵל חַי וְקַיָּם. סִימָן טוֹב וּמַזָּל טוֹב יְהֵא לָנוּ וּלְכָל יִשְׂרָאֵל אָמֵן

David, King of Israel, lives forever. May we and all Israel have a good sign and good luck, amen.

Bircas Hamazon:
BLESSINGS AND APPRECIATION

Bircas Hamazon
Grace After Meals
Blessings and Appreciation

ircas Hamazon, Grace After Meals, (*bentching* in common parlance), is the only blessing, according to most commentaries, that is of Torah origin. "And you will eat and be satisfied and you will bless Hashem, your God" (*Devarim* 8:10). The Sustainer of all mankind gave us the gift of life and the provisions for living. We call out to God in thanks and in blessing, appreciating the nourishment that we have received. To recite a blessing before we eat is an expression of our dependence on God; to say *bentching* afterward, when one has already eaten his fill, is a deeper, more profound appreciation of His goodness.

Maharal of Prague (*Nesivos Olam*, chapter 18) analyzes the magnificent structure of the prayer, and how it enumerates our thanks for all of our deficiencies. The three blessings הזן, Who sustains us, על הארץ, for the land, and בונה ירושלים, rebuild Jerusalem, are of Torah origin; the fourth, הטוב והמטיב, was established by the Rabbis in Yavneh (Talmud, *Berachos* 48a).

Upon entry into the world, man, in contradistinction to animals, is totally dependent. His food, his personal care, shelter and clothing must always be provided by others. A life which is predicated on dependence of others should simultaneously focus on appreciation for those who always meet his needs. Parents, as the primary care-givers, and Hashem, as the Ultimate Provider, are deserving of constant thanks for their incessant provisions.

Each blessing touches on the wholesome beneficence that God has bestowed upon us. The first blessing, הזן, relates to Hashem's provision of our basic needs, those which help us to merely exist. "The One Who gave us life will give us food," and we express our appreciation to God for our simplest level of subsistence.

With the second blessing, על הארץ, we thank God for a higher level of His goodness to us. If a philanthropist would offer a needy person simple provisions to satisfy his hunger, how thankful the person would be! And if he would provide the indigent individual with non-essential items out of his love for him, how much more must he appreciate his benefactor's kindness? The gift of Israel, "the desirable, good and spacious land," takes us beyond the essential. God showers His love upon us, manifesting His particular love for His nation.

With the Temple, we were individually satisfied, nationally enabled and spiritually complete; without it we are a nation bereft of its physical and spiritual state of perfection.

Bircas Hamazon
Grace After Meals
Blessings and Appreciation

With the third blessing, beseeching God to rebuild Jerusalem and the Holy Temple, we point to the unique relationship we had with God in the spiritual dimension. The veils of nature part as we enter the portals of the *Bais Hamikdash,* the Holy Temple, repository on earth for the Divine Presence. Seemingly miraculous events were commonplace there, as when the Temple stood. It was the center locus where God's omnipresence could be most keenly felt. It was the conduit of Divine blessing for Israel, and indeed, for the entire world.

With the destruction of Jerusalem and the Holy Temple, the source of blessing was removed from the world (Talmud, *Sotah* 48a). With the Temple, we were individually satisfied, nationally enabled and spiritually complete; without it we are a nation bereft of its physical and spiritual state of perfection.

With the last blessing, the Rabbinic enactment of הטוב והמטיב, *the Good One who bestows goodness,* we complete the blessings of *bircas hamazon.* What prompted the Rabbis to initiate yet another opportunity of appreciation in our prayers after we ate? Fifty-two years after the destruction of the Temple, a small pocket of resistance still managed to exist in the Jewish camp. In Beitar, a final attempt at insurgency flickered against the Roman army, until it was brutally snuffed out. Thousands of dead were strewn about in Beitar, and the Jewish resistance was overwhelmingly decimated.

This was the early background against which the Rabbis etched these blessings into our collective souls. *HaTov,* the Good One, is exemplified with His Goodness, because miraculously the bodies did not decompose over such a long period of time.

VeHamaitiv, the Omnipresent, all-giving God bestowed yet another great kindness upon us, that these bodies were saved from further degradation and were allowed to be buried (Talmud, *Berachos* 48b).

Are *these* cause for blessing and celebration? *Maharal* offers a fascinating insight into God's workings in our world and our reaction to it. The destruction of the Holy Temple by God, through His Roman emissaries, defined a period of Divine justice to the Jews. The spiritual foundation of the Temple had long since eroded, and its physical collapse was soon to follow. In this time of Divine concealment, an exiled Jewish nation seemed almost devoid of all hope. Tens of thousands had died, and a bereaved nation seemingly had lost its position of prominence as God's Chosen People.

Bircas Hamazon
Grace After Meals
Blessings and Appreciation

Amidst the despair, God shone a ray of light. The massacred soldiers and civilians of Beitar are given a heavenly sign, a miraculous testimony to God's presence with them in their suffering. Their bodies remain intact, and ultimately, they return to the earth from which they came. Moses authored a blessing to thank God for manna from heaven, Joshua enacted his upon entering the land of Israel. Kings David and Solomon thanked God for the spiritual perfection of Jerusalem and the Holy Temple, yet these blessings of praise were offered in times of joy. God's Goodness to us, the penultimate goodness, is most manifest when He reveals His love for a people amidst such pain. The highest order of appreciation, one instituted by mortals, recognizes the embrace of the Creator even in times of concealment.

Our generations, those which followed the Holocaust, can certainly appreciate the words of *Maharal*. The millions who died sanctified God's Name, the cities that were destroyed, the religious institutions that were decimated, left the Jewish people broken and shattered. Could we even recapture the spiritual grandeur of Eastern Europe? Yet, a beleaguered nations begins the slow, arduous, painful task of rebuilding. Survivors built a homeland in Israel, America and beyond, and we began to see glimpses of hope and the rays through the darkness. Families are begun, children are born, and the rudiments of new communities began to form in what was once called a spiritual wasteland, America.

Our brethren in the Soviet Union yearned for religious freedom, and after years of persecution, suddenly the Communist regime and its ideology collapses. In the United States and world over, men and women who had never been privileged to experience their Jewish heritage, began to passionately lay claim to their rightful inheritance. Academies of learning, yeshivos, synagogues, charitable institutions and Jewish communal groups begin to proliferate at a rate not seen since the destruction of the Temple. So much more still needs to be done, so many more have to experience the joy and vibrancy of Judaism, but the process has begun. The pain still remains, but the glimmering of God's radiant Countenance peers out through the darkness. We recognize God in His concealment, and we pause to offer our humble blessings as we wait for the day when our exultant songs of praise and blessings will be uttered when all the world will see the Presence of God revealed.

The highest order of appreciation, one instituted by mortals, recognizes the embrace of the Creator even in times of concealment.

Bircas Hamazon/ Grace After Meals
In the Talmud and Midrash

A good guest (at a meal), what does he say? "How much effort did the master of the home do for me? How much meat, wine and baked goods did he set before me? All the effort that he expended was for my benefit!" A bad guest (at a meal), what does he say? "What effort did the master of the home do? I ate only one piece of bread, one slice, and drank only one cup. All the efforts that he expended were for his wife and children!" (Talmud, *Berachos* 58a). The *Gaon* of Vilna interprets this thought homiletically. Each person is a guest in God's world. A good guest will see all of the goodness, and will come away with a deep sense of appreciation, seeing it as a personal kindness. The unappreciative guest in this world sees God's kindness as general in nature. He fails to see that each of God's acts of kindness to the world impact on him directly.

The master of the home makes the blessing over the bread and a guest offers a blessing. What is his blessing? "May it be the will of God that this host not be ashamed in this world or in the World to Come. May he be successful in all his possessions, and may they and their parents be successful in raising God-fearing children" (Talmud, *Berachos* 46a).

The ministering angels come before the Heavenly tribunal and say, "Master of the World! In Your Torah You write: (God) Who does not show favoritism, yet You in fact do" ("God will turn His Countenance to you")? God answers the angels, "How can I *not* treat them favorably? I wrote in the Torah that one is obligated to recite Grace after Meals only if one is fully satisfied, and they are so exacting in the law to obligate themselves after eating only an olive-sized or egg-sized piece of bread?" (Talmud, *Berachos* 20b).

Moses established the first blessing of Grace after Meals, הזן, when manna fell from heaven; Joshua established the second blessing, על הארץ, when the Jewish nation entered Israel; Kings David and Solomon established the third blessing of בונה ירושלים (Talmud, *Berachos* 48b).

At the end of days, God will make a banquet for the righteous. The assembled will pass the cup (of wine) to Abraham to lead the blessings after the meal. "I cannot lead the grace," said Abraham, "because Yishmael descended from me." They will then ask Isaac to lead. "I cannot lead the *bentching*, because Esau descended from me." Yaakov will refuse because he married two sisters. Moses will not lead because he never entered the land of Israel, and Yehoshua will not be able to lead because he never had any sons. King David will then be given the cup. "I will *bentch*, and it is appropriate for me to *bentch*, as it says, "I lift up the cup of salvation and I call out in the Name of God" (Talmud, *Pesachim* 119b).

Food Blessings During the Meal

- In general, it is not necessary to recite blessings over other foods eaten during a bread meal, with certain exceptions:

- It is questionable whether fruit served as an appetizer requires a blessing. Preferably, one should either eat a piece of fruit before washing for bread and recite a blessing with the intention that it will cover all fruit eaten during the meal, or eat the fruit together with a piece of bread. One should recite a blessing over fruit served as a dessert. Wine drunk during the meal would not require a blessing if the person drank from the *kiddush* wine, and if wine is commonly served at the meal. If either one of these two conditions is not met, one must recite a blessing over the wine.

- A blessing should be recited on candy or chocolate eaten at any point during the meal.

- There is much discussion among halachic authorities as to whether one is required to recite a blessing over ice cream, various cakes and pies eaten during the meal. One should consult the appropriate *halachic* authority for guidance.

Grace after Meals

- After one has completed a meal and is satisfied, there is a Biblical obligation to give appropriate thanks to God by reciting the Grace after Meals, *bentching*. One should recite the grace while seated.

- There are three major differences between the grace recited during the week and grace recited on *Shabbos*.

   1) *r'tzay* is added before *uvnay Yerushalayim* 2) An extra *horachomon* is added. See page 96. 3) *migdol* replaces *magdil*. See page 96.

- If *r'tzay* is forgotten, one should repeat the entire Grace after Meals. However, if one forgot the other two additions, it is not repeated.

- If one is in doubt as to whether or not he recited *r'tzay,* he must assume he didn't and the entire grace is repeated.

- An exception to the above is at *shalosh seudos,* the third meal. Even if one is sure he forgot *r'tzay,* grace is not repeated.

- On Festivals and *Rosh Chodesh* we add *ya-aleh v'yovo* with an addition for each appropriate holiday. On holidays, if one forgets to recite *yaleh vyovo* or is in doubt, he must repeat it. On *Rosh Chodesh,* however, if *ya-aleh v'yovo* is forgotten, the grace is not repeated.

- On Chanukah and Purim the prayer of *al hanisim* is added before *v'al hakol.* If forgotten, one does not repeat the Grace after Meals.

Laws of Mayim Achronim
Washing Before Grace after Meals

- One washes his hands before reciting the Grace after Meals. This washing ritual is known as *mayim achronim*.

- There are various reasons why this washing is performed.

  1)Out of respect to Grace after Meals, one's hands should be clean and free of any food residue. 2)A caustic salt, called *melach Sedomis,* existed and possibly still exists, causing harm upon eye contact. We, therefore, wash after eating to remove any such salt. 3)Reasons explained in the *Zohar* (*Kabbalistic* or mystical teachings)

- Women are generally not accustomed to wash *mayim achronim*.

- The washing should be done into a vessel or sink, and not onto the floor.

- After washing is completed, the custom is to remove the water from the table or cover it before beginning the Grace after Meals.

- Many have the custom to wash the outer surface of their mouths with the *mayim achronim* after they wash their hands.

- The washing should be done until the second knuckle on one's fingers. Some follow the view that it is preferable to wash until the wrist. One should dry his hands after washing.

- Talking after washing *mayim achronim* should be avoided. If one speaks, he should rewash *mayim achronim*. Even the psalm *Shir Hama'alos*, which is customarily sung prior to the Grace after Meals, should be done so before washing *mayim achronim*.

Laws of Zimun: Invitation to Bentch

- When a minimum of three men over 13 years of age have eaten together, the *zimun*, a formal invitation for all present to *bentch*, is performed. If 10 men over 13 years of age are present they add the name of God in their response.

- The host either leads or designates one of the participants as the leader. The leader begins "*Rabosai n'voraych*" as found on page 80. All present respond "*Yihi shem...*"

- After completing the *zimun*, the leader should recite the entire first blessing aloud as the others follow along in an undertone.

  - At the end of the blessing, the participants should finish the blessing before the leader in order to answer "*amen*" to his blessing. If they both finish the blessing at the same time, the participants do not respond with "*amen*".

  - There are various customs regarding the use of wine as part of the *zimun*. Some use a cup of wine whenever the *zimun* is recited, others only do so when 10 or more men are present. Some only do so by festive occasions, such as a *sheva b'rachos*.

סדר ברכת המזון

PSALM 126 IS RECITED ON שבת AND יו"ט. IT DESCRIBES THE JOY OF THE FUTURE REDEMPTION

PSALM 137 IS RECITED ON WEEKDAYS TO REMEMBER THE TEMPLE'S DESTRUCTION

הַמַּעֲלוֹת בְּשׁוּב יְיָ אֶת
שִׁיבַת צִיּוֹן הָיִינוּ כְּחֹלְמִים: אָז
יִמָּלֵא שְׂחוֹק פִּינוּ וּלְשׁוֹנֵנוּ
רִנָּה: אָז יֹאמְרוּ בַגּוֹיִם
הִגְדִּיל יְיָ לַעֲשׂוֹת עִם אֵלֶּה:
הִגְדִּיל יְיָ לַעֲשׂוֹת עִמָּנוּ הָיִינוּ
שְׂמֵחִים: שׁוּבָה יְיָ אֶת שְׁבִיתֵנוּ
כַּאֲפִיקִים בַּנֶּגֶב: הַזֹּרְעִים
בְּדִמְעָה בְּרִנָּה יִקְצֹרוּ: הָלוֹךְ יֵלֵךְ
וּבָכֹה נֹשֵׂא מֶשֶׁךְ הַזָּרַע בֹּא
יָבֹא בְרִנָּה נֹשֵׂא אֲלֻמֹּתָיו:

יֵשׁ מוֹסִיפִים פְּסוּקִים אֵלוּ

תְּהִלַּת יְיָ יְדַבֶּר פִּי וִיבָרֵךְ
כָּל בָּשָׂר שֵׁם קָדְשׁוֹ לְעוֹלָם
וָעֶד: וַאֲנַחְנוּ נְבָרֵךְ יָהּ
מֵעַתָּה וְעַד עוֹלָם הַלְלוּיָהּ:
הוֹדוּ לַיְיָ כִּי טוֹב כִּי לְעוֹלָם
חַסְדּוֹ: מִי יְמַלֵּל גְּבוּרוֹת
יְיָ יַשְׁמִיעַ כָּל תְּהִלָּתוֹ:

נַהֲרוֹת בָּבֶל שָׁם יָשַׁבְנוּ
גַּם בָּכִינוּ בְּזָכְרֵנוּ אֶת צִיּוֹן:
עַל עֲרָבִים בְּתוֹכָהּ תָּלִינוּ
כִּנֹּרוֹתֵינוּ: כִּי שָׁם שְׁאֵלוּנוּ
שׁוֹבֵינוּ דִּבְרֵי שִׁיר וְתוֹלָלֵינוּ
שִׂמְחָה שִׁירוּ לָנוּ מִשִּׁיר
צִיּוֹן: אֵיךְ נָשִׁיר אֶת שִׁיר
יְיָ עַל אַדְמַת נֵכָר: אִם
אֶשְׁכָּחֵךְ יְרוּשָׁלָיִם תִּשְׁכַּח
יְמִינִי: תִּדְבַּק לְשׁוֹנִי לְחִכִּי
אִם לֹא אֶזְכְּרֵכִי אִם לֹא
אַעֲלֶה אֶת יְרוּשָׁלַיִם עַל רֹאשׁ
שִׂמְחָתִי: זְכֹר יְיָ לִבְנֵי
אֱדוֹם אֵת יוֹם יְרוּשָׁלָיִם:
הָאֹמְרִים עָרוּ עָרוּ עַד
הַיְסוֹד בָּהּ: בַּת בָּבֶל
הַשְּׁדוּדָה אַשְׁרֵי שֶׁיְּשַׁלֶּם
לָךְ אֶת גְּמוּלֵךְ שֶׁגָּמַלְתְּ
לָנוּ: אַשְׁרֵי שֶׁיֹּאחֵז וְנִפֵּץ
אֶת עֹלָלַיִךְ אֶל הַסָּלַע:

Psalms 137 is said on weekdays to remember the destruction of the Holy Temple

Psalm 126 is said on Shabbos and on Festivals, describing the joy of the future redemption

rivers of Babylon, there we sat and we also wept when we remembered Zion. Upon its willows in the midst we hung our lyres. For there our captors demanded song from us. From our instruments joyous melody. "Sing to us from the songs of Zion!" How can we sing the song of Hashem on foreign soil? If I forget thee, Jerusalem, let my right hand's skill be forgotten. Let my tongue cleave to my palate if I don't remember You. If I fail to elevate Jerusalem above my highest joy. Remember Hashem for the descendants of Edom, who say "Raze it, raze it to its very foundation." Daughter of Babylon who is laid to waste. Fortunate is he who repays you for what you have done to her. Fortunate is he who grasps and shatters your infants against the rock.

of ascents, When Hashem will return the captives of Zion we will have been like dreamers. Then our mouths will be filled with laughter and our tongues with mirth. Then it will be said among the nations, "Hashem has done great things for them." Hashem has done great things with us, and we will rejoice. Return, Hashem, our captives like streams in the desert. Those who sow with tears will reap in jubilation. He walks on, weeping, carrying a load of seed, but he will return with jubilation, carrying the sheaves.

Some add the following verses

Praise of Hashem my mouth will declare and all flesh will bless His holy Name forever and ever. And we will bless God from now until eternity, halleluyah. Thank Hashem for He is good, His kindness endures forever. Who will utter the strengths of Hashem, will make all of his praises heard?

AL NAHARŌS BOVEL *shom yoshavnu gam bochinu b'zochraynu es Tziyōn. Al arovim b'sochoh tolinu kinōrosaynu, ki shom sh'aylunu shōvainu divray shir v'sōlolaynu simchoh, shiru lonu mishir Tziyōn. Aych noshir es shir Adōnoy al admas naychor. Im eshkochaych Y'rusholoyim tishkach y'mini. Tidbak l'shōni l'chiki im lō ezk'raychi, im lō a-aleh es Y'rusholoyim al rōsh simchosi. Z'chor Adōnoy liv'nay Edōom ays yōm Y'rusholoyim, ho'omrim oru, oru ad hayesōd boh. Bas Bovel hashdudoh, ashray she-y'shalem loch es g'mulaych shegomalt lonu. Ashray sheyochayz v'nipaytz es ololayich el hasola.*

SHIR HAMA-ALŌS, *b'shuv Adōnoy es shivas Tziyōn ho-yinu k'chōl'mim. Ōz yimolay s'chōk pinu ulshōnaynu rino, oz yom'ru vagōyim, higdil Adōnoy la-asōs im ayle. Higdil Adōnoy la-asōs imonu ho-yinu s'maychim. Shuvo Adōnoy es sh'visaynu ka-afikim banegev. Hazōr'im b'dim-o b'rino yiktzōru. Holōch yaylaych uvochō nōsay meshech hazora, bō yovō v'rino, nōsay alumōsov. T'hilas Adonoy y'daber pi, vivoraych kol bosor shem kodshō l'ōlom vo-ed. Va-anachnu n'voraych Yōh, may-ato v'ad ōlam, hal'luyoh. Hōdu Ladonoy ki tov, ki l'ōlom chasdo. Mi y'malayl g'vurōs Adonoy, yashmi-a kol t'hilosō.*

Zimun/Invitation For A Regular Meal

If three or more males, aged thirteen or older, participate in a meal, a leader is
appointed to formally invite the others to join him in reciting of grace after meals.
If there are more than ten males present, add the word in parentheses

רַבּוֹתַי נְבָרֵךְ **-** LEADER ‎   GROUP **-** יְהִי שֵׁם יְיָ מְבֹרָךְ מֵעַתָּה וְעַד עוֹלָם

יְהִי שֵׁם יְיָ מְבֹרָךְ מֵעַתָּה וְעַד עוֹלָם: **-**LEADER

בִּרְשׁוּת מָרָנָן וְרַבָּנָן וְרַבּוֹתַי נְבָרֵךְ(אֱלֹהֵינוּ) שֶׁאָכַלְנוּ מִשֶּׁלּוֹ.

בָּרוּךְ (אֱלֹהֵינוּ) שֶׁאָכַלְנוּ מִשֶּׁלּוֹ וּבְטוּבוֹ חָיִינוּ. **-** GROUP

בָּרוּךְ(אֱלֹהֵינוּ) שֶׁאָכַלְנוּ מִשֶּׁלּוֹ וּבְטוּבוֹ חָיִינוּ. **-**LEADER

בָּרוּךְ הוּא וּבָרוּךְ שְׁמוֹ. **-** ALL quietly

Leader: Gentlemen, let us say the blessing.

Others: Blessed is the Name of Hashem from this time and forever!

Leader: Blessed is the Name of Hashem from this time and forever!

With the permission of the distinguished people present let us bless our God from Whom we have eaten.

Others: Blessed is our God in of Whose we have eaten and through Whose goodness we live.

Leader: Blessed is He and Blessed is His Name.

Leader: *Rabōsai n'voraych.*

Others: *Y'hi shaym Adōnoy m'vōroch may-ato v'ad ōlom.*

Leader: *Y'hi shaym Adōnoy m'vōroch may-ato v'ad ōlom.*

If ten men join in the zimun, the word in parentheses is added.

Bir-shus moronon v'rabonon v'rabōsai, n'voraych (Elōhaynu)
she- ochalnu mi-shelō.

Others: *Boruch (Elōhaynu)she-ochalnu mi-shelō uvtuvō cho-yinu.*

Those who have not eaten respond: Boruch (Elōhaynu) umvōroch sh'mo tomid l'ōlom vo-ed.

Leader: *Boruch (Elōhaynu) she-ochalnu mishelō uvtuvō cho-yinu.*

All: *Boruch hu uvoruch sh'mō.*

Zimun For A Wedding

At a wedding meal, the leader asks the group to join him in Bircas Hamazon

LEADER - רַבּוֹתַי נְבָרֵךְ — GROUP - יְהִי שֵׁם יְיָ מְבֹרָךְ מֵעַתָּה וְעַד עוֹלָם

LEADER - דְּוַי הָסֵר וְגַם חָרוֹן וְאָז אִלֵּם בְּשִׁיר יָרוֹן. נְחֵנוּ בְּמַעְגְּלֵי צֶדֶק שְׁעֵה בִרְכַּת (בְּנֵי יְשֻׁרוּן)

בְּנֵי אַהֲרֹן: בִּרְשׁוּת מָרָנָן וְרַבָּנָן וְרַבּוֹתַי נְבָרֵךְ אֱלֹהֵינוּ שֶׁהַשִּׂמְחָה בִּמְעוֹנוֹ וְשֶׁאָכַלְנוּ מִשֶּׁלּוֹ.

GROUP - בָּרוּךְ אֱלֹהֵינוּ שֶׁהַשִּׂמְחָה בִּמְעוֹנוֹ וְשֶׁאָכַלְנוּ מִשֶּׁלּוֹ וּבְטוּבוֹ חָיִינוּ.

LEADER - בָּרוּךְ אֱלֹהֵינוּ שֶׁהַשִּׂמְחָה בִּמְעוֹנוֹ וְשֶׁאָכַלְנוּ מִשֶּׁלּוֹ וּבְטוּבוֹ חָיִינוּ.

All quietly - בָּרוּךְ הוּא וּבָרוּךְ שְׁמוֹ.

Leader: Gentlemen, let us say the blessing.

Others: Blessed is the Name of Hashem from this time and forever!

Leader: Blessed is the Name of Hashem from this time and forever!
Banish pain and also anger, and then the mute will exult in song.
Guide us in paths of righteousness; heed the blessing of the
children of Aaron. With the permission of the distinguished people
present let us bless our God in Whose abode is this celebration,
from Whom we have eaten.

Others: Blessed is our God in Whose abode is this celebration,
from Whom we have eaten and through Whose goodness we live.

Leader: Blessed is our God in Whose abode is this celebration,
from Whom we have eaten, and through Whose goodness we live.
Blessed is He and Blessed is His Name.

Leader: Gentlemen let us bless.

Others: Blessed is the Name of Hashem from this time and forever!

Leader: Blessed is the Name of Hashem from this time and forever!

Others: Blessed is our God in Whose abode is this celebration,
from Whom we have eaten and throughWhose goodness we live.

Leader: Blessed is our God in Whose abode is this celebration, from
Whom we have eaten, and through Whose goodness we live.
Blessed is He and Blessed is His Name.

Leader: *Rabōsai n'voraych.*

Others: *Y'hi shaym Adōnoy m'vōroch may'atoh v'ad ōlom.*

Leader: *Y'hi shaym Adōnoy m'vōroch may'atoh v'ad ōlom.*

Leader: *D'vai hosayr v'gam chorōn, v'oz ilaym b'shir yorōn, n'chaynu b'maglay
tzedek, sh'ay birkas b'nay Aharōn. Birshus moronon v'rabonon v'rabōsai
n'voraych Elōhaynu shehasimchoh bim-ōnō v'she-ochalnu mishelō.*

Others: *Boruch Elōhaynu shehasimchoh bim-ōnō v'she-ochalnu mishelō
uvtuvō choyinu.*

Leader: *Boruch Elōhaynu shehasimchoh bim-ōnō v'she-ochalnu mishelō
uvtuvō choyinu.*

All say: *Boruch Hu uvoruch sh'mō.*

THE FIRST BLESSING of ברכת המזון WAS composed
BY MOSES. IT THANKS GOD FOR GIVING THE JEWS
MANNA TO SUSTAIN THEM WHILE IN THE WILDERNESS.

בָּרוּךְ אַתָּה יְיָ אֱלֹהֵינוּ מֶלֶךְ הָעוֹלָם הַזָּן אֶת הָעוֹלָם כֻּלּוֹ בְּטוּבוֹ בְּחֵן בְּחֶסֶד וּבְרַחֲמִים הוּא נֹתֵן לֶחֶם לְכָל בָּשָׂר כִּי לְעוֹלָם חַסְדּוֹ. וּבְטוּבוֹ הַגָּדוֹל תָּמִיד לֹא חָסַר לָנוּ וְאַל יֶחְסַר לָנוּ מָזוֹן לְעוֹלָם וָעֶד. בַּעֲבוּר שְׁמוֹ הַגָּדוֹל כִּי הוּא אֵל זָן וּמְפַרְנֵס לַכֹּל וּמֵטִיב לַכֹּל וּמֵכִין מָזוֹן לְכָל בְּרִיּוֹתָיו אֲשֶׁר בָּרָא. בָּרוּךְ אַתָּה יְיָ הַזָּן אֶת הַכֹּל:

THE SECOND BLESSING WAS COMPOSED BY JOSHUA
IN THANKS TO GOD FOR GIVING US THE LAND OF ISRAEL

נוֹדֶה לְּךָ יְיָ אֱלֹהֵינוּ עַל שֶׁהִנְחַלְתָּ לַאֲבוֹתֵינוּ אֶרֶץ חֶמְדָּה טוֹבָה וּרְחָבָה. וְעַל שֶׁהוֹצֵאתָנוּ יְיָ אֱלֹהֵינוּ מֵאֶרֶץ מִצְרַיִם וּפְדִיתָנוּ מִבֵּית עֲבָדִים וְעַל בְּרִיתְךָ שֶׁחָתַמְתָּ בִּבְשָׂרֵנוּ וְעַל תּוֹרָתְךָ שֶׁלִּמַּדְתָּנוּ וְעַל חֻקֶּיךָ שֶׁהוֹדַעְתָּנוּ וְעַל חַיִּים חֵן וָחֶסֶד שֶׁחוֹנַנְתָּנוּ וְעַל אֲכִילַת מָזוֹן שָׁאַתָּה זָן וּמְפַרְנֵס אוֹתָנוּ תָּמִיד בְּכָל יוֹם וּבְכָל עֵת וּבְכָל שָׁעָה:

JUST AS BREAD SUSTAINS THE PHYSICAL EXISTENCE OF MAN'S BODY, TORAH SUSTAINS THE SPIRITUAL EXISTENCE OF HIS SOUL

THE FIRST BLESSING OF GRACE AFTER MEALS WAS COMPOSED BY MOSES, THANKING HASHEM FOR SUSTAINING THE JEWS WITH MANNA IN THE WILDERNESS

BLESSED ARE YOU, Hashem, our God, King of the universe, who nourishes the entire world with His goodness, with favor, loving kindness and with mercy. He gives nourishment to all flesh, because His loving kindness is eternal, and through His abundant goodness we have never been lacking and may we never be lacking forever and ever. For the sake of His great name, because He is Almighty and provides food for all, and He benefits all and provides for the needs of all of his creatures which He has created. Blessed are You, Hashem, who sustains all.

WE GIVE thanks to You, Hashem, our God, that You have bequeathed to our forefathers a desirable, good and spacious land: and because You have brought us out, Hashem, our God, from the land of Egypt, and redeemed us from the house of bondage: and for Your convenant which You have sealed in our flesh and for Your Torah which You have taught us, and for Your statutes which You have made known to us; and for the life, grace and lovingkindness which You have favored us; and for the food which we have eaten through which You nourish and maintain us constantly, every day, in every season, and at any hour.

BORUCH *ato Adōnoy Elōhaynu melech ho-ōlom, hazon es ho-ōlom kulō, b'tuvō, b'chayn b'chesed uvrachamim hu nōsayn lechem l'chol bosor, ki l'ōlom chasdō. Uvtuvō hagodōl, tomid lō chosar lonu, v'al yechsar lonu mozōn l'ōlom vo-ed. ba-avur sh'mō hagodōl, ki hu Ayl zon umfarnays lakōl, u-maytiv lakōl, u-maychin mozōn l'chōl b'riyōsov asher boro. Boruch ato Adōnoy, hazon es hakōl.*(All present respond: *Omayn*)

NŌ-DE *l'cho, Adōnoy Elōhaynu, al shehinchalto la-avōsaynu eretz chemdo tōvo urchovo, V'al shehōtzaysonu Adōnoy Elōhaynu may- eretz Mitzra-yim, ufdisonu mibays avodim, v'al b'ris'cho shechosamto bivsoraynu, v'al tōros'cho shelimad-tonu, v'al chu-kecho shehōdatonu, v'al cha-yim chayn vo-chesed shechōnantonu, v'al achilas mozōn sho-ato zon umfarnays ōsonu tomid, b'chol yōm uv'chol ays uvchol sho-o.*

ON CHANUKAH על הנסים, A PRAYER OF THANKSGIVING IS ADDED, COMMEMORATING
THE MIRACULOUS VICTORY OF THE JEWS OVER ANTIOCHUS AND THE SYRIAN-GREEKS

עַל הַנִּסִּים וְעַל הַפֻּרְקָן וְעַל הַגְּבוּרוֹת וְעַל הַתְּשׁוּעוֹת וְעַל הַמִּלְחָמוֹת שֶׁעָשִׂיתָ לַאֲבוֹתֵינוּ בַּיָּמִים הָהֵם בַּזְּמָן הַזֶּה:

בִּימֵי מַתִּתְיָהוּ בֶּן יוֹחָנָן כֹּהֵן גָּדוֹל חַשְׁמוֹנָאִי וּבָנָיו כְּשֶׁעָמְדָה מַלְכוּת יָוָן הָרְשָׁעָה עַל עַמְּךָ יִשְׂרָאֵל לְהַשְׁכִּיחָם תּוֹרָתֶךָ וּלְהַעֲבִירָם מֵחֻקֵּי רְצוֹנֶךָ. וְאַתָּה בְּרַחֲמֶיךָ הָרַבִּים עָמַדְתָּ לָהֶם בְּעֵת צָרָתָם, רַבְתָּ אֶת רִיבָם, דַּנְתָּ אֶת דִּינָם, נָקַמְתָּ אֶת נִקְמָתָם, מָסַרְתָּ גִבּוֹרִים בְּיַד חַלָּשִׁים, וְרַבִּים בְּיַד מְעַטִּים, וּטְמֵאִים בְּיַד טְהוֹרִים, וּרְשָׁעִים בְּיַד צַדִּיקִים, וְזֵדִים בְּיַד עוֹסְקֵי תוֹרָתֶךָ. וּלְךָ עָשִׂיתָ שֵׁם גָּדוֹל וְקָדוֹשׁ בְּעוֹלָמֶךָ, וּלְעַמְּךָ יִשְׂרָאֵל עָשִׂיתָ תְּשׁוּעָה גְדוֹלָה וּפֻרְקָן כְּהַיּוֹם הַזֶּה. וְאַחַר כֵּן בָּאוּ בָנֶיךָ לִדְבִיר בֵּיתֶךָ וּפִנּוּ אֶת הֵיכָלֶךָ וְטִהֲרוּ אֶת מִקְדָּשֶׁךָ וְהִדְלִיקוּ נֵרוֹת בְּחַצְרוֹת קָדְשֶׁךָ וְקָבְעוּ שְׁמוֹנַת יְמֵי חֲנֻכָּה אֵלּוּ לְהוֹדוֹת וּלְהַלֵּל לְשִׁמְךָ הַגָּדוֹל:

On Chanukah על הניסים, a prayer of thanksgiving is added, commemorating the miraculous victory of the Jews over Antiochus and the Syrian-Greeks

FOR THE MIRACLES and for the redemption, and for the mighty deeds, and for the deliverances, and for the wars that you performed for our forefathers in those days at this time.

In the days of Matisyahu, the son of Yochanan, the High Priest, the Hashmonean and his sons, when the evil Greek empire rose up against Your nation, Israel, to make them forget Your Torah and to turn them from the statutes of Your will. And You, in Your great mercy, stood up for them in their time of distress. You fought their struggle, judged their judgment, avenged their wrong. You delivered the strong into the hands of the weak, the many into the hands of the few, the wicked into the hands of the righteous, the defiant sinners into the hands of those who study Your Torah. And for Yourself You made a great and holy Name, and for Your nation, Israel, You've wrought great salvation and redemption as this very day. And then Your children came into Your Holy of Holies and cleansed Your temple, purified Your sanctuary, kindled lights in Your holy courtyards, and designated these eight days of Chanukah, to give thanks and praise to Your holy Name.

AL HANISIM, *v'al hapurkon, v'al hag'vurōs, v'al hat'shu-ōs, v'al hamilchomōs, she-osiso la-avōsaynu ba-yomim hohaym baz'man ha-ze.*

nikmosom. Mosarto gibōrim b'yad chaloshim, v'rabim b'yad m'atim, utmay-im b'yad t'hōrim, ursho-im b'yad tzadikim v'zaydim b'yad ōs'kay sōrosecho. Ulcho osiso shaym godōl v'kodōsh b'ōlomecho, ul-am'cho Yisro-ayl osiso t'shu-o g'dōlo u-furkon k'ha-yōm ha-ze. V'achar kayn bo-u vonecho lidvir bay-secho, u-tinu es haycholecho, v'tiharu es mikdoshecho, v'hidliku nayrōs b'chatzrōs kod-shecho, v'kov'u sh'mōnas y'may Chanuko aylu, l'hōdōs ulhalayl l'shimcho hagodōl.

Bimay *Matisyohu ben Yōchonon kōhayn godōl chashmōno-i u-vonov, k'she-om'do malchus yovon hor'sho-o al am'cho Yisro-ayl, l'hashkichom tōrosecho, ulha-avirom maychukay r'tzōnecho. V'ato b'racha-mecho horabim, omadto lohem b'ays tzorosom, ravto es rivom, danto es dinom, nokamto es*

סֵדֶר בִּרְכַּת הַמָּזוֹן

ON PURIM עַל הַנִּסִּים, A PRAYER OF THANKSGIVING, IS RECITED. IT COMMEMORATES
ESTHER AND MORDECHAI'S ROLE IN HELPING SAVE THE JEWS FROM HAMAN'S PLOT.

עַל הַנִּסִּים וְעַל הַפֻּרְקָן
וְעַל הַגְּבוּרוֹת
וְעַל הַתְּשׁוּעוֹת וְעַל הַמִּלְחָמוֹת שֶׁעָשִׂיתָ
לַאֲבוֹתֵינוּ בַּיָּמִים הָהֵם בַּזְּמָן הַזֶּה:

בִּימֵי מָרְדְּכַי וְאֶסְתֵּר
בְּשׁוּשַׁן הַבִּירָה כְּשֶׁעָמַד
עֲלֵיהֶם הָמָן הָרָשָׁע בִּקֵּשׁ
לְהַשְׁמִיד לַהֲרֹג וּלְאַבֵּד
אֶת כָּל הַיְּהוּדִים מִנַּעַר
וְעַד זָקֵן טַף וְנָשִׁים בְּיוֹם
אֶחָד בִּשְׁלֹשָׁה עָשָׂר לְחֹדֶשׁ
שְׁנֵים עָשָׂר הוּא חֹדֶשׁ
אֲדָר וּשְׁלָלָם לָבוֹז וְאַתָּה
בְּרַחֲמֶיךָ הָרַבִּים הֵפַרְתָּ
אֶת עֲצָתוֹ וְקִלְקַלְתָּ אֶת
מַחֲשַׁבְתּוֹ וַהֲשֵׁבוֹתָ לּוֹ
גְּמוּלוֹ בְּרֹאשׁוֹ וְתָלוּ אוֹתוֹ
וְאֶת בָּנָיו עַל הָעֵץ.

לַיְּהוּדִים הָיְתָה אוֹרָה

וְשִׂמְחָה וְשָׂשׂוֹן וִיקָר

ON PURIM פורים על הנסים, A PRAYER OF THANKSGIVING IS RECITED. IT COMMEMORATES ESTHER AND MORDECHAI'S ROLE IN HELPING SAVE THE JEWS FROM HAMAN'S PLOT.

FOR THE MIRACLES AND FOR THE REDEMPTION, AND FOR THE MIGHTY DEEDS, AND FOR THE DELIVERANCES, AND FOR THE WARS THAT YOU PERFORMED FOR OUR FOREFATHERS IN THOSE DAYS AT THIS TIME:

IN THE DAYS OF MORDECHAI AND ESTHER IN SHUSHAN, THE CAPITAL, THE EVIL HAMAN ROSE UP AGAINST THEM AND TRIED TO DESTROY, KILL AND ANNIHILATE THE JEWS, YOUNG AND OLD, INFANTS AND WOMEN, ON ONE DAY, THE 13th DAY OF THE 12th MONTH, ADAR, AND THEIR WEALTH WOULD BE PLUNDERED. BUT YOU, IN YOUR ABUNDANT MERCY, THWARTED HIS PLAN AND FOILED HIS INTENTIONS AND BROUGHT JUST RETRIBUTION BACK UPON HIS OWN HEAD. AND HE AND HIS SONS WERE HANGED

AL HANISIM, *v'al hapurkon, v'al hag'vurōs, v'al hat'shu-ōs, v'al hamilchomōs, she-osiso la-avōsaynu ba-yomim hohaym baz'man ha-ze.*

BIMAY *Mord'chai v'Estayr b'Shushan habiroh k'she-omad alayhem Homon horosho, bikaysh l'hashmid laharōg ul-abayd es kol ha-Y'hudim mina-ar v'ad zokayn, taf v'noshim b'yōm echod, bishlōshoh osor l'chōdesh Ador, ushlolom lovōz. V'atoh b'rachamecho horabim hayfarto es atzosō v'kilkalto es machashavtō, vahashayvōso lō g'mulō b'rōshō, v'solu ōsō v'es bonov al ho-aytz.*

וְעַל הַכֹּל יְיָ אֱלֹהֵינוּ אֲנַחְנוּ מוֹדִים לָךְ וּמְבָרְכִים אוֹתָךְ יִתְבָּרַךְ שִׁמְךָ בְּפִי כָּל חַי תָּמִיד לְעוֹלָם וָעֶד. כַּכָּתוּב וְאָכַלְתָּ וְשָׂבָעְתָּ וּבֵרַכְתָּ אֶת יְיָ אֱלֹהֶיךָ עַל הָאָרֶץ הַטּוֹבָה אֲשֶׁר נָתַן לָךְ. בָּרוּךְ אַתָּה יְיָ עַל הָאָרֶץ וְעַל הַמָּזוֹן:

the third blessing was composed by king david as a prayer for Jerusalem, with a prayer for the בית המקדש later added by king solomon

רַחֵם (נא) יְיָ אֱלֹהֵינוּ

וְלִירוּשָׁלַיִם עִירְךָ בְּרַחֲמִים תָּשׁוּב

עַל יִשְׂרָאֵל עַמֶּךָ וְעַל יְרוּשָׁלַיִם עִירֶךָ וְעַל צִיּוֹן מִשְׁכַּן כְּבוֹדֶךָ וְעַל מַלְכוּת בֵּית דָּוִד מְשִׁיחֶךָ וְעַל הַבַּיִת הַגָּדוֹל וְהַקָּדוֹשׁ שֶׁנִּקְרָא שִׁמְךָ עָלָיו. אֱלֹהֵינוּ אָבִינוּ רְעֵנוּ זוּנֵנוּ פַּרְנְסֵנוּ וְכַלְכְּלֵנוּ וְהַרְוִיחֵנוּ וְהַרְוַח לָנוּ יְיָ אֱלֹהֵינוּ מְהֵרָה מִכָּל צָרוֹתֵינוּ. וְנָא אַל תַּצְרִיכֵנוּ יְיָ אֱלֹהֵינוּ לֹא לִידֵי מַתְּנַת בָּשָׂר וָדָם וְלֹא לִידֵי הַלְוָאָתָם כִּי אִם לְיָדְךָ הַמְּלֵאָה הַפְּתוּחָה הַקְּדוֹשָׁה וְהָרְחָבָה שֶׁלֹּא נֵבוֹשׁ וְלֹא נִכָּלֵם לְעוֹלָם וָעֶד:

AND FOR all things Hashem, our God, we thank and bless You. May Your Name be blessed in the mouth of all living things, always and forever. As it is written, "and you shall eat and be satisfied, and you shall bless Hashem, your God, for the good land and for the food.

the third blessing was composed by king david as a prayer for jerusalem, with a prayer for the בית המקדש later added by king solomon

PLEASE, HASHEM, our God, have compassion on Israel, Your nation and on Jerusalem, Your Holy City and on Zion, the sanctuary of Your Glory, and on the kingship of David, Your anointed, and on the great and holy house upon which Your Name is called. Our God, our Father, tend us, nourish us, sustain and maintain us, relieve us and grant us relief, Hashem, our God, speedily from all our distresses, and please, Hashem, our God, do not make us dependent on gifts from the hands of man, and not upon their loans, but only upon Your full, open, holy and bountiful hand that we may never be embarrassed or ashamed.

V'AL HAKŌL, Adōnoy Elōhaynu, anachnu mōdim loch, umvor'chim ōsoch, yisborach shimcho b'fi kol chai tomid l'ōlom vo-ed. Kakosuv: V'ochalto v'sovoto, u-vayrachto es Adōnoy Elōhecho, al ho-oretz hatōvo asher nosan loch. Boruch ato Adōnoy, al ho-oretz v'al hamozōn. (All present respond: Omayn)

RACHAYM (nah) Adōnoy Elōhaynu al Yisro-ayl amecho, v'al Y'rushola-yim i-recho, v'al Tziyōn mishkan k'vōdecho, v'al malchus bays Dovid m'shichecho, v'al haba-yis hagodōl v'hakodōsh shenikro shimcho olov. Elōhaynu ovinu, r'aynu, zunaynu, parn'saynu v'chalk'laynu v'harvichaynu, v'harvach lonu Adōnoy Elōhaynu m'hayro mikol tzorōsaynu. V'no al tatzrichaynu, Adōnoy Elōhaynu, lō liday mat'nas bosor vodom, v'lō liday halvo-osom, ki im l'yod'cho ham'lay-o hap'su-cho hak'dōsho v'hor'chovo, shelō nayvōsh v'lō nikolaym l'ōlom vo-ed.

סדר ברכת המזון

ON SHABBOS ADD THE FOLLOWING:

רְצֵה וְהַחֲלִיצֵנוּ

יְיָ אֱלֹהֵינוּ בְּמִצְוֹתֶיךָ וּבְמִצְוַת
יוֹם הַשְּׁבִיעִי הַשַּׁבָּת הַגָּדוֹל
וְהַקָּדוֹשׁ הַזֶּה כִּי יוֹם זֶה גָּדוֹל
וְקָדוֹשׁ הוּא לְפָנֶיךָ לִשְׁבָּת בּוֹ
וְלָנוּחַ בּוֹ בְּאַהֲבָה כְּמִצְוַת רְצוֹנֶךָ וּבִרְצוֹנְךָ הָנִיחַ לָנוּ יְיָ
אֱלֹהֵינוּ שֶׁלֹּא תְהֵא צָרָה וְיָגוֹן וַאֲנָחָה בְּיוֹם מְנוּחָתֵנוּ
וְהַרְאֵנוּ יְיָ אֱלֹהֵינוּ בְּנֶחָמַת צִיּוֹן עִירֶךָ וּבְבִנְיַן יְרוּשָׁלַיִם
עִיר קָדְשֶׁךָ כִּי אַתָּה הוּא בַּעַל הַיְשׁוּעוֹת וּבַעַל הַנֶּחָמוֹת:

ON ROSH CHODESH AND FESTIVALS ADD THE FOLLOWING,
INSERTING THE APPROPRIATE PHRASE

אֱלֹהֵינוּ וֵאלֹהֵי אֲבוֹתֵינוּ

יַעֲלֶה וְיָבֹא

וְיַגִּיעַ וְיֵרָאֶה וְיֵרָצֶה וְיִשָּׁמַע וְיִפָּקֵד
וְיִזָּכֵר זִכְרוֹנֵנוּ וּפִקְדוֹנֵנוּ וְזִכְרוֹן
אֲבוֹתֵינוּ וְזִכְרוֹן מָשִׁיחַ בֶּן דָּוִד עַבְדֶּךָ וְזִכְרוֹן יְרוּשָׁלַיִם
עִיר קָדְשֶׁךָ וְזִכְרוֹן כָּל עַמְּךָ בֵּית יִשְׂרָאֵל לְפָנֶיךָ לִפְלֵיטָה
לְטוֹבָה לְחֵן וּלְחֶסֶד וּלְרַחֲמִים לְחַיִּים וּלְשָׁלוֹם בְּיוֹם

shavuos	passover	rosh chodesh
חַג הַשָּׁבֻעוֹת	חַג הַמַּצּוֹת	רֹאשׁ הַחֹדֶשׁ

shmini atzeres/simchas torah	succos	rosh hashanah
הַשְּׁמִינִי חַג הָעֲצֶרֶת	חַג הַסֻּכּוֹת	הַזִּכָּרוֹן

הַזֶּה . זָכְרֵנוּ יְיָ אֱלֹהֵינוּ בּוֹ לְטוֹבָה . וּפָקְדֵנוּ בוֹ
לִבְרָכָה . וְהוֹשִׁיעֵנוּ בוֹ לְחַיִּים טוֹבִים . וּבִדְבַר
יְשׁוּעָה וְרַחֲמִים חוּס וְחָנֵּנוּ וְרַחֵם עָלֵינוּ וְהוֹשִׁיעֵנוּ
כִּי אֵלֶיךָ עֵינֵינוּ כִּי אֵל מֶלֶךְ חַנּוּן וְרַחוּם אָתָּה:

GRACE AFTER MEALS

on shabbos add the following:

AY IT PLEASE

You, Hashem, our God, and strengthen us in Your commandments, and in this great and holy Shabbos, for this day is great and holy before You, to refrain from work on it and rest on it with love according to Your Will. And with Your Will, grant us, Hashem, our God, that there shall be no distress, nor any anguish or sighing on the day of Your rest. And show us, Hashem, our God, the consolation of Zion, Your city, and in the rebuilding of Jerusalem, Your holy city, because You are the Master of Salvations and the Master of comforts.

on Rosh chodesh and festivals add the following, inserting the appropriate phrase

Our God and the God of our forefathers,

AY IT ASCEND,

and come, and appear, and be desired, and heard, and recalled, and remembered, our remembrance and designation, and remembrance of our forefathers, and that of Moshiach, the son of David, Your servant, and the remembrance of Your nation, Israel, before You for survival, goodness and lovingkindness, compassion, life and peace on this day of:

The New Moon / The Festival of Matzos / The Festival of Weeks / Remembrance / The Festival of Tabernacles / The Eighth Day Festival

Remember us, Hashem, our God, on it, on it for goodness, and recall us on it for a blessing, and save us on it for a good life. And with a promise of salvation and compassion. Please spare us and favor us and save us, because we turn our eyes to You, because You are the Almighty King, gracious and merciful.

---

on shabbos add the following:

R'TZAY *v'hachalitzaynu Adōnoy Elōhaynu b'mitzvōsecho, uvmitzvas yōm hash'vi-i ha-Shabbos hagodōl v'hakodōsh ha-ze, ki yōm ze godōl v'kodōsh hu l'fonecho, lishbos bō v'lonu-ach bō b'ahavo k'mitzvas r'tzōnecho. U-virtzōn'cho honi-ach lonu, Adōnoy Elōhaynu, shelō s'hay tzoro v'yogōn va-anocho b'yōm m'nuchosaynu. V'har-aynu Adōnoy Elōhaynu b'nechomas Tziyōn i- recho, uv'vinyan Y'rushola-yim ir kodshecho, ki ato hu ba-al hai- shu-ōs uva-al hanechomōs.*

on rosh chodesh and festivals add the following, inserting the appropriate phrase

ELŌHAYNU *Vaylōhay avōsaynu, ya-a-le v'yovō v'yagi-a v'yayro-e v'yayro-tze v'yi-shoma v'yipokayd v'yizochayr zichrōnaynu u- fikdōnaynu, v'zichrōn avōsaynu, v'zichrōn Moshi-ach ben Dovid avdecho, v'zichrōn Y'rushola-yim ir kod'shecho, v'zichrōn kol am'cho bays Yisro-ayl l'fonecho, lif-layto l'tōvo l'chayn ulchesed ulrachamim, l'cha-yim ulsholōm*

On Rosh Chodesh: *b'yōm rōsh hachōdesh ha-ze.* **On Pesach:** *b'yōm chag hamatzōs ha-ze.* **On Shavuos:** *b'yōm chag hashovu-ōs ha-ze.* **On Rosh Hashanah:** *hazikaron ha-ze.* **On Succos:** *b'yōm chag hasukōs ha-ze.* **On Shemini Atzeres / Simchas Torah:** *b'yōm hash'mini chag ho-atzeress ha-ze.*

zoch'raynu Adōnoy Elōhaynu bō l'tōvo, u-fokdaynu vō livrocho, v'hōshi- aynu vō l'cha-yim. U-vidvar y'shu-o v'rachamim, chus v'chonaynu v'rachaym olaynu v'hōshi-aynu, ki aylecho aynaynu, ki Ayl (melech) chanun v'rachum oto.

וּבְנֵה יְרוּשָׁלַיִם

עִיר הַקֹּדֶשׁ בִּמְהֵרָה בְיָמֵינוּ.

בָּרוּךְ אַתָּה יְיָ בּוֹנֵה בְרַחֲמָיו יְרוּשָׁלַיִם. אָמֵן:

בָּרוּךְ אַתָּה יְיָ אֱלֹהֵינוּ

THE FOURTH BLESSING WAS COMPOSED BY RABBAN GAMLIEL'S
COURT IN THANKS TO GOD FOR PRESERVING THE BODIES OF
BETAR'S VICTIMS AND ALLOWING THEM TO BE PROPERLY BURIED

מֶלֶךְ הָעוֹלָם הָאֵל אָבִינוּ מַלְכֵּנוּ אַדִּירֵנוּ בּוֹרְאֵנוּ
גּוֹאֲלֵנוּ יוֹצְרֵנוּ קְדוֹשֵׁנוּ קְדוֹשׁ יַעֲקֹב רוֹעֵנוּ רוֹעֵה
יִשְׂרָאֵל הַמֶּלֶךְ הַטּוֹב וְהַמֵּטִיב לַכֹּל שֶׁבְּכָל יוֹם
וָיוֹם הוּא הֵטִיב הוּא מֵטִיב הוּא יֵיטִיב לָנוּ.
הוּא גְמָלָנוּ הוּא גוֹמְלֵנוּ הוּא יִגְמְלֵנוּ לָעַד לְחֵן
וּלְחֶסֶד וּלְרַחֲמִים וּלְרֶוַח הַצָּלָה וְהַצְלָחָה
בְּרָכָה וִישׁוּעָה נֶחָמָה פַּרְנָסָה וְכַלְכָּלָה
וְרַחֲמִים וְחַיִּים וְשָׁלוֹם וְכָל טוֹב וּמִכָּל טוּב
לְעוֹלָם אַל יְחַסְּרֵנוּ:

הָרַחֲמָן הוּא יִמְלוֹךְ עָלֵינוּ לְעוֹלָם וָעֶד.
הָרַחֲמָן הוּא יִתְבָּרַךְ בַּשָּׁמַיִם וּבָאָרֶץ.
הָרַחֲמָן הוּא יִשְׁתַּבַּח לְדוֹר דּוֹרִים וְיִתְפָּאַר
בָּנוּ לָעַד וּלְנֵצַח נְצָחִים וְיִתְהַדַּר
בָּנוּ לָעַד וּלְעוֹלְמֵי עוֹלָמִים.

REBUILD JERUSALEM

the holy city, speedily in our days. Blessed are You, Hashem, who rebuilds Jerusalem in His compassion, amen.

BLESSED are You, Hashem, our God, King of the universe, the Almighty, our Father, our King, our Mighty One, our Creator, our Redeemer, our Maker, our Holy One, the Holy One of Jacob, our Shepherd, the shepherd of Israel, the good King, Who bestows goodness to all, for on every single day, He did good, He does good and will do good for us. He has benefited us, He benefits us, and will benefit us forever with favor, with lovingkindness, and with compassion, and with relief, rescue and success, blessing and salvation, comfort, sustenance and support and compassion, life and peace and all goodness. From all goodness may He never deprive us.

THE COMPASSIONATE ONE may He rule over us forever and ever.

THE COMPASSIONATE ONE may He be blessed in the heavens and on earth.

THE COMPASSIONATE ONE may He be praised for all generations, and may He be glorified through us for all the everlasting eternities, and may He be honored through us eternally.

UVNAY Y'rushola-yim ir hakōdesh bimhayro v'yomaynu. Boruch ato Adōnoy, bōnay (v'rachamov) Y'rusholo-yim. Omayn. (All present respond: Omayn)

BORUCH ato Adōnoy Blessed are You, Hashem, Elōhaynu melech ho- ōlom, ho-Ayl ovinu malkaynu adiraynu bōr'aynu gō-alaynu yōtz'raynu, k'dōshaynu k'dōsh Ya-akōv, rō-aynu rō-ay Yisro-ayl. Hamelech hatōv v'hamaytiv lakōl, sheb'chol yōm vo-yōm hu haytiv, hu maytiv, hu yaytiv lonu. Hu g'molonu, hu gōm'laynu, hu yigm'laynu lo-ad, l'chayn ulchesed ulrachamim ulre vach, hatzolo v'hatzlocho, b'rocho vi-shu-o, nechomo, parnoso v'chalkolo, v'rachamim v'cha-yim v'sholōm v'chol tōv, u-mikol tuv l'ōlom al y'chas'raynu. (All present respond: Omayn)

HORACHAMON, hu yimlōch olaynu l'ōlom vo-ed.

HORACHAMON, hu yisborach bashoma-yim uvo-oretz.

HORACHAMON, hu yishtabach l'dōr dōrim, v'yispo-ar bonu lo-ad ulnaytzach n'tzochim, v'yis-hadar bonu lo-ad ul-ōl'may ōlomim.

הָרַחֲמָן הוּא יְפַרְנְסֵנוּ בְּכָבוֹד.

הָרַחֲמָן הוּא יִשְׁבֹּר עֻלֵּנוּ מֵעַל צַוָּארֵנוּ וְהוּא יוֹלִיכֵנוּ קוֹמְמִיּוּת לְאַרְצֵנוּ.

הָרַחֲמָן הוּא יִשְׁלַח לָנוּ בְּרָכָה מְרֻבָּה בַּבַּיִת הַזֶּה וְעַל שֻׁלְחָן זֶה שֶׁאָכַלְנוּ עָלָיו.

הָרַחֲמָן הוּא יִשְׁלַח לָנוּ אֶת אֵלִיָּהוּ הַנָּבִיא זָכוּר לַטּוֹב וִיבַשֶּׂר לָנוּ בְּשׂוֹרוֹת טוֹבוֹת יְשׁוּעוֹת וְנֶחָמוֹת.

this blessing, found in the talmud (berachos 46a), is recited by a guest for his host.

יְהִי רָצוֹן שֶׁלֹּא יֵבוֹשׁ וְלֹא יִכָּלֵם בַּעַל הַבַּיִת הַזֶּה. לֹא בָּעוֹלָם הַזֶּה וְלֹא בָּעוֹלָם הַבָּא, וְיַצְלִיחַ בְּכָל נְכָסָיו, וְיִהְיוּ נְכָסָיו מֻצְלָחִים וּקְרוֹבִים לָעִיר, וְאַל יִשְׁלֹט שָׂטָן בְּמַעֲשֵׂה יָדָיו, וְאַל יִזְדַּקֵּק לְפָנָיו שׁוּם דְּבַר חֵטְא וְהִרְהוּר עָוֹן, מֵעַתָּה וְעַד עוֹלָם.

guests add the following phrases, and children at their parents' table add the words in parentheses.

הָרַחֲמָן הוּא יְבָרֵךְ

אֶת (אָבִי מוֹרִי) בַּעַל הַבַּיִת הַזֶּה וְאֶת (אִמִּי מוֹרָתִי) בַּעֲלַת הַבַּיִת הַזֶּה, אוֹתָם וְאֶת בֵּיתָם וְאֶת זַרְעָם וְאֶת כָּל אֲשֶׁר לָהֶם

those eating at their own table add the following words in parentheses as they apply

אוֹתִי (וְאֶת אִשְׁתִּי / בַּעְלִי / וְאֶת זַרְעִי) וְאֶת כָּל אֲשֶׁר לִי

all continue here

אוֹתָנוּ וְאֶת כָּל אֲשֶׁר לָנוּ כְּמוֹ שֶׁנִּתְבָּרְכוּ אֲבוֹתֵינוּ אַבְרָהָם יִצְחָק וְיַעֲקֹב בַּכֹּל מִכֹּל כֹּל כֵּן יְבָרֵךְ אוֹתָנוּ כֻּלָּנוּ יַחַד בִּבְרָכָה שְׁלֵמָה וְנֹאמַר אָמֵן:

בַּמָּרוֹם יְלַמְּדוּ עֲלֵיהֶם וְעָלֵינוּ זְכוּת שֶׁתְּהֵא לְמִשְׁמֶרֶת שָׁלוֹם. וְנִשָּׂא בְרָכָה מֵאֵת יְיָ וּצְדָקָה מֵאֱלֹהֵי יִשְׁעֵנוּ וְנִמְצָא חֵן וְשֵׂכֶל טוֹב בְּעֵינֵי אֱלֹהִים וְאָדָם:

בְּרִית מִילָה
At a
see page 104

The Compassionate One may He sustain us honorably.

The Compassionate One may He break the yoke from our necks, and may He lead us upright to our land.

The Compassionate One may He send us a bountiful blessing in this house and on this table from which we have eaten.

The Compassionate One may He send us Elijah the Prophet, his memory be blessed, that he may announce to us good tidings, salvations and comforts.

This blessing, found in the Talmud (Berachos 46a) is recited by a guest for his host. May it be Your will that the host of this house not be shamed or embarrassed, not in this world nor in the world to come. May he be successful in all his endeavors, and may his endeavors be successful and close to the city, and may no evil rule over the work of his hand, and may no object of sin or thought of iniquity be found before him now and forever.

Guests add the phrases shown: children at their parents' table add the words in parentheses. The Compassionate One, may He bless (my father, my teacher) the host of this house and (my mother, my teacher) the hostess of this house, them and their children and all that is theirs.

Those eating at their own table add the words in parentheses as they apply. Me (my wife/my husband/my children) and all that is mine.

All continue here. Us and all that is ours, just as our forefathers Abraham, Isaac and Jacob were blessed in all things, from everything, with everything, so shall He bless all of us together with a complete blessing and let us say, amen.

In the celestial heights, may there be a merit pleaded for them and for us, that it should be a protection of peace, and may we receive a blessing from Hashem and righteousness from our God of Salvation and may we find favor and beneficial understanding in the eyes of God and man.

Horachamon, *hu y'farn'saynu b'chovōd.*

Horachamon, *hu yishbōr ulaynu may-al tzavoraynu, v'hu yōli-chaynu kōm'miyus l'artzaynu.*

Horachamon, *hu yishlach lonu b'rocho m'rubo baba-yis ha-ze, v'al shulchon ze she-ochalnu olov.*

Horachamon, *hu yishlach lonu es Ayliyohu Hanovi zochur latōv, vivaser lonu b'sōrōs tōvōs y'shu-ōs v'nechomōs.*

This blessing, found in the Talmud (Berachos 46a) is recited by a guest for his host
Y'hi rotzon shelō yayvōsh v'lō yikolaym ba-al habayis hazeh, lō vo'ōlom hazeh v'lō vo'ōlom habo, v'yatzli'ach b'chol n'chosov, v'yihyu n'chosov mutzlochim u'krōvim lo'ir, v'al yishlōt soton b'ma-asay yodov, v'al yizdakayk l'fonov shum d'var chayt v'hirhur ovon, may-atoh v'ad ōlom.

At one's own table (include the applicable words in parentheses):
Horachamon, *hu y'voraych ōsi (v'es ishti/v'es bali. v'es zari) v'es kol asher li.*

Guests recite the following (children at their parents' table add the applicable words):
Horachamon, *hu y'voraych es (ovi mōri) ba-al haba-yis ha-ze, v'es (imi mōrosi) ba-alas haba-yis ha-ze,*

All continue: *ōsom v'es baysom v'es zar-om v'es kol asher lohem, ōsonu v'es kol asher lonu, k'mō shenisbor'chu avōsaynu Avrohom Yitzchok v'Ya- akōv bakōl mikōl kōl. Kayn y'voraych ōsonu kulonu yachad bivrocho sh'laymo. V'nōmar: Omayn.*

Bamorōm *y'lam'du alayhem v'olaynu z'chus, shet'hay l'mishmeres sholōm, V'niso v'rocho may-ays Adōnoy, utzdoko may-Elōhay yish-aynu, v'nimtzo chayn v'saychel tōv b'aynay Elōhim v'odom.*

At a Bris see page 104

סֵדֶר בִּרְכַּת הַמָּזוֹן

הָרַחֲמָן הוּא יַנְחִילֵנוּ יוֹם שֶׁכֻּלּוֹ שַׁבָּת וּמְנוּחָה לְחַיֵּי הָעוֹלָמִים:

הָרַחֲמָן הוּא יְחַדֵּשׁ עָלֵינוּ אֶת הַחֹדֶשׁ הַזֶּה לְטוֹבָה וְלִבְרָכָה:

הָרַחֲמָן הוּא יַנְחִילֵנוּ יוֹם שֶׁכֻּלּוֹ טוֹב:

הָרַחֲמָן הוּא יְחַדֵּשׁ עָלֵינוּ אֶת הַשָּׁנָה הַזֹּאת לְטוֹבָה וְלִבְרָכָה:

הָרַחֲמָן הוּא יָקִים לָנוּ אֶת סֻכַּת דָּוִד הַנּוֹפָלֶת:

on purim בִּימֵי מָרְדְּכַי or on chanukah בִּימֵי מַתִּתְיָהוּ was not said in its proper place, recite the following phrase and continue with עַל הַנִּסִּים IF (Pages 88, 90)

הָרַחֲמָן הוּא יַעֲשֶׂה לָנוּ נִסִּים וְנִפְלָאוֹת כַּאֲשֶׁר עָשָׂה לַאֲבוֹתֵינוּ בַּיָּמִים הָהֵם בַּזְּמַן הַזֶּה:

הָרַחֲמָן הוּא יְזַכֵּנוּ לִימוֹת הַמָּשִׁיחַ וּלְחַיֵּי הָעוֹלָם הַבָּא. (מַגְדִּל (on weekdays:

יְשׁוּעוֹת (on shabbos, festivals and rosh chodesh מַגְדּוֹל) מַלְכּוֹ וְעֹשֶׂה חֶסֶד לִמְשִׁיחוֹ לְדָוִד וּלְזַרְעוֹ עַד עוֹלָם. עֹשֶׂה שָׁלוֹם בִּמְרוֹמָיו הוּא יַעֲשֶׂה שָׁלוֹם עָלֵינוּ וְעַל כָּל יִשְׂרָאֵל. וְאִמְרוּ אָמֵן:

יְראוּ אֶת יְיָ קְדֹשָׁיו כִּי אֵין מַחְסוֹר לִירֵאָיו. כְּפִירִים רָשׁוּ וְרָעֵבוּ וְדֹרְשֵׁי יְיָ לֹא יַחְסְרוּ כָל טוֹב. הוֹדוּ לַיְיָ כִּי טוֹב כִּי לְעוֹלָם חַסְדּוֹ. פּוֹתֵחַ אֶת יָדֶךָ וּמַשְׂבִּיעַ לְכָל חַי רָצוֹן. בָּרוּךְ הַגֶּבֶר אֲשֶׁר יִבְטַח בַּיְיָ וְהָיָה יְיָ מִבְטַחוֹ. נַעַר הָיִיתִי גַּם זָקַנְתִּי וְלֹא רָאִיתִי צַדִּיק נֶעֱזָב וְזַרְעוֹ מְבַקֶּשׁ לָחֶם. יְיָ עֹז לְעַמּוֹ יִתֵּן יְיָ יְבָרֵךְ אֶת עַמּוֹ בַשָּׁלוֹם.

GRACE AFTER MEALS

On Shabbos: The Compassionate One, may He let us inherit a day that is all Shabbos and rest for eternal life. **On Rosh Chodesh:** The Compassionate One, may He renew for us this month for goodness and blessing. **On Festivals:** The Compassionate One, may He let us inherit a day that is all goodness. **On Rosh Hashanah:** The Compassionate One, may He renew the new year upon us for goodness and blessing. **On Succos:** The Compassionate One, may He erect for us the fallen tabernacle of David.

If "For the miracles" was not recited in its proper place, recite the following phrase and continue with "In the days of Matisyahu" (Chanukah, page 88) or "In the days of Mordechai" (Purim, page 90). The Compassionate One, may He perform miracles and wonders for us as He did for our forefathers in those days at this time.

THE COMPASSIONATE ONE, may He let us merit the days of Moshiach and life in the world to come (on weekdays: He makes great salvations for His king) (on Shabbos, New Moon, Festivals: He is a tower of deliverance for His king) and does kindness to David, His anointed, and his descendants forever. He who makes peace in His celestial heights may He make peace for us and for all Israel, and say amen.

REVERE Hashem, His holy ones, for there is never deprivation for those who revere Him. Young lions may be hungry and needy, but those who seek Hashem shall never be deprived of any goodness. Give thanks to Hashem for He is good, for His lovingkindness is everlasting. Open Your Hand, Hashem, and satiate the needs of all living things. Blessed is the man who trusts in God, and God will be his security. I once was youthful and I have also aged, and I have never seen a righteous person forsaken, that his children must seek bread. God will give might to His nation. God will bless His nation with peace.

On Shabbos add:
Horachamon, hu yanchilaynu yōm shekulō Shabbos umnucho l'cha-yay ho-ōlomim.

On Rosh Chodesh add:
Horachamon, hu y'chadaysh olaynu es hachōdesh ha-ze l'tōvo v'livrocho.

On Festivals add:
Horachamon, hu yanchilaynu yōm shekulō tōv.

On Succos add:
Horachamon, hu yokim lonu es sukas Dovid hanōfoles.

Horachamon, hu y'zakaynu limōs hamoshi-ach ulcha-yay ho-ōlom habo.

On the Sabbath, Festivals, Chol Hamoed, and Rosh Chodesh:
Migdōl

On weekdays: Magdil
y'shu-ōs malkō, v'ōse chesed limshichō l'Dovid ulzar-ō ad ōlom. Ō-se sholōm bimrōmov, hu ya-a-se sholōm olaynu v'al kol Yisro-ayl. V'imru: Omayn.

Y'RU es Adōnoy k'dōshov, ki ayn machsōr liray-ov. K'firim roshu v'ro-ayvu, v'dōr'shay Adōnoy lō yachs'ru chol tōv. Hōdu Ladōnoy ki tōv, ki l'ōlom chasdō. Pōsay-ach es yodecho, u-masbi-a l'chol chai rotzōn. Boruch hagever asher yivtach bAdōnoy, v'ho-yo Adōnoy miv tachō. Na-ar ho-yisi gam zokanti, v'lō ro-isi tzadik ne-ezov, v'zar-ō m'vakaysh lochem. Adōnoy ōz l'amō yitayn, Adōnoy y'voraych es amō va-sholōm.

- Moshe established the seven days of festivities for the *choson* and *kallah* (Talmud *Yerushalmi, Kesubos* 1:1). A Torah allusion to the seven days is found when Yaakov rejoiced with his wife, Leah, for seven days. Similarly, Shimshon spent seven days rejoicing after his marriage (*Yalkut Shoftim* 14 and *Pirkei d'Rabi Eliezer* chapter 16).

- Except for Shabbos, one should invite a new guest, a *ponim chadoshos*, to each *sheva berachos* meal. Preferably, it should be a person who would add to the *simcha* of the *choson* and *kallah* by his presence. On Shabbos, this requirement is waived, as Shabbos itself is considered the *ponim chadoshos*.

The Wedding Meal

here is no greater *seudas mitzvah* than that of the wedding, where we bless the *choson* and *kallah* with joy, jubilation and happiness. *(Minhag Yisroel Torah*, in the name of *Chavos Ya'ir*, chapter 20).

- The souls of the departed parents of the celebrants join in their *simcha*. Since there are three partners in the formation of a person, Hashem and one's father and mother, all three join the celebration of the *simcha* of their child.

- It is customary to dispense charity at the wedding meal. This applies to the guests, and all the more so to the celebrants themselves. Since the poor look forward to the wedding as a time when many guests gather together, one should take advantage of this opportunity for *tzedakah* (*Chasan Sofer*, Responsa, chapter 1).

- Often times it was customary for the *choson* or other rabbis to share words of Torah during the wedding meal. Gifts were given to the *choson* at the end of his Torah discourse. This was called *d'rasha geshank*. Since the groom is compared to a king, the discourse was his inaugural address, and the presents were comparable to those given to a person of stature (*Midrash Talpios*). It is said that G-d, too, gives a gift to the *choson* and *kallah* on the day of their wedding — the gift of forgiveness from their sins (In the name of Rav Gedalia Schorr, *zt"l*).

Rejoicing with the Choson and Kallah

av Shmuel bar Rav Yitzchak would juggle three myrtle branches in front of the bride and groom to gladden them at their wedding. Rav Zeira disapproved, saying that these actions were unbefitting a Rabbi of such stature. When Rav Shmuel passed away, a myrtle-shaped column of fire separated his grave from those around him. As this occurrence took place only once or twice in a generation, Rav Zeira said that Rav Shmuel had received a heavenly approbation of his wedding antics (Talmud, *Kesubos* 17a).

✎ It is a great *mitzvah* to dance before the bride and groom and make them happy. One sings the praises of the *kallah* כַּלָּה נָאָה וַחֲסוּדָה, a lovely and kindly bride, even if the accolades are not fully warranted (Talmud, *Kesubos* and *Tur*, chapter 65*).*

✎ One should not partake of the wedding meal of a groom and not gladden him. He can, however, fulfill his obligation by dancing and singing before him, with praises about aspects of his marriage, or with gifts (*Minhag Yisroel Torah* in the name of *Be'er Sheva*, chapter 50).

✎ **MITZVAH TANTZ** — At many Chassidic weddings a special dance called the *Mitzvah Tantz* is held after the grace after meals. Relatives of the bride and groom are called up by a *badchan*, or rhymester, to share in the *simcha* and dance with the *kallah*, holding a handkerchief or other item. Some attribute mystical significance to the dance, symbolic of one's desire to connect himself to the Shechinah, the Divine Presence. In the World to Come there will be a dance for the righteous, with the Divine Presence, as it were, in the center of the circle.

There are those who take issue with the practice, citing the phrase "How does one dance *in front of* the kallah?" (Talmud, *Kesubos* 17a) rather than *with* the kallah. (*Pischei Teshuvah* 560:2) *Maharshal* concludes that where it was accepted as a practice, it should be upheld, otherwise it is forbidden.

✎ **SHEVA BEROCHOS** — For seven days after the wedding the bride and groom have joyous feasts tendered in their honor by family and friends. Neither go to work during those days, but spend the time together as king and queen.

הֲרֵי אַתְּ מְקֻדֶּשֶׁת לִי

בָּרוּךְ

אַתָּה יְיָ אֱלֹהֵינוּ מֶלֶךְ הָעוֹלָם שֶׁהַכֹּל בָּרָא לִכְבוֹדוֹ:

בָּרוּךְ אַתָּה יְיָ אֱלֹהֵינוּ מֶלֶךְ הָעוֹלָם יוֹצֵר הָאָדָם:

בָּרוּךְ אַתָּה יְיָ אֱלֹהֵינוּ מֶלֶךְ הָעוֹלָם אֲשֶׁר יָצַר
אֶת הָאָדָם בְּצַלְמוֹ בְּצֶלֶם דְּמוּת תַּבְנִיתוֹ
וְהִתְקִין לוֹ מִמֶּנּוּ בִּנְיַן עֲדֵי עַד. בָּרוּךְ אַתָּה יְיָ יוֹצֵר הָאָדָם:

שׂוֹשׂ תָּשִׂישׂ וְתָגֵל הָעֲקָרָה בְּקִבּוּץ בָּנֶיהָ
לְתוֹכָהּ בְּשִׂמְחָה. בָּרוּךְ אַתָּה יְיָ מְשַׂמֵּחַ
צִיּוֹן בְּבָנֶיהָ:

שַׂמֵּחַ תְּשַׂמַּח רֵעִים הָאֲהוּבִים כְּשַׂמֵּחֲךָ יְצִירְךָ
בְּגַן עֵדֶן מִקֶּדֶם. בָּרוּךְ אַתָּה יְיָ
מְשַׂמֵּחַ חָתָן וְכַלָּה:

בָּרוּךְ אַתָּה יְיָ אֱלֹהֵינוּ מֶלֶךְ הָעוֹלָם אֲשֶׁר
בָּרָא שָׂשׂוֹן וְשִׂמְחָה חָתָן וְכַלָּה גִּילָה
רִנָּה דִּיצָה וְחֶדְוָה אַהֲבָה וְאַחֲוָה וְשָׁלוֹם
וְרֵעוּת מְהֵרָה יְיָ אֱלֹהֵינוּ יִשָּׁמַע בְּעָרֵי
יְהוּדָה וּבְחוּצוֹת יְרוּשָׁלַיִם קוֹל שָׂשׂוֹן וְקוֹל
שִׂמְחָה קוֹל חָתָן וְקוֹל כַּלָּה קוֹל מִצַּהֲלוֹת
חֲתָנִים מֵחֻפָּתָם וּנְעָרִים מִמִּשְׁתֵּה נְגִינָתָם.
בָּרוּךְ אַתָּה יְיָ מְשַׂמֵּחַ חָתָן עִם הַכַּלָּה:

בָּרוּךְ אַתָּה יְיָ אֱלֹהֵינוּ מֶלֶךְ הָעוֹלָם בּוֹרֵא
פְּרִי הַגָּפֶן:

ובמזל טוב   מַזָל טוֹב   בסימן טוב

SALVATION · SUSTENANCE · A GOOD HEART · NOURISHMENT · SWEETNESS · HELP FROM

1.BLESSED are You, Hashem, our God, King of the universe, Who created everything for His glory.

2.BLESSED are You, Hashem, our God, King of the universe, Who formed man.

3.BLESSED are You, Hashem, our God, King of the universe, Who formed man in His image, in the image of His likeness and fashioned for him out of his very being an eternal building. Blessed are You, Hashem, Who formed man.

4.MAY the barren woman rejoice and surely exult when her children are gathered into her midst with happiness. Blessed are You, Hashem, Who makes Zion happy through her children.

5.GRANT abundant happiness to the beloved friends just as You made Your creation happy in the Garden of Eden of old. Blessed are You, Hashem, Who makes the groom and bride happy.

1.BORUCH ato Adōnoy, Elōhaynu melech ho-ōlom, shehakōl boro lichvōdō.

2.BORUCH ato Adōnoy, Elōhaynu melech ho-olom, yotzayr ho-odom.

3.BORUCH ato Adōnoy, Elōhaynu melech ho-ōlom, asher yotzar es ho-odom b'tzalmō, b'tzelem d'mus tavnisō, v'hiskin lō mimenu binyan aday ad. Boruch atoh Adōnoy, yōtzayr ho-odom.

4.SŌS tosis v'sogayl ho-akoroh b'kibutz bōneho l'sōchoh b'simchoh. Boruch atoh Adōnoy, m'samayach Tziyon b'voneho.

5.SAMAYACH t'samach ray-im ho-ahuvim, k'samaychacho y'tzir'cho b'Gan Ayden mikedem. Boruch atoh Adonoy, m'samayach choson v'chaloh.

6.BORUCH atoh Adonoy, Elōhaynu melech ho-ōlom, asher boro sosōn v'simchoh, choson, v'chaloh, giloh, rinoh, ditzoh, v'chedvoh, ahavoh v'achvoh, v'sholōm v'rayus. M'hayroh Adōnoy Elōhaynu yishoma b'oray Y'hudoh u'vchutzōs Y'rusholayim, kōl soson v'kōl simchoh, kōl choson v'kōl kaloh, kōl mitzhalōs chasonim maychuposom, un-orim mimishtay n'ginosom. Boruch atoh Adōnoy, m'samayach choson im hakaloh.

7.BORUCH atoh Adonoy, Elohaynu melech ho-olom, boray p'ri hagefen.

6.BLESSED are You, Hashem, our God, King of the universe, Who created happiness and joy, groom and bride, exultation, joyous song, pleasure, delight, love and brotherhood, and peace and companionship. Soon, Hashem, our God, let there be heard in the cities of Judah and the outskirts of Jerusalem, the voice of happiness, the voice of joy, the voice of the groom, the voice of the bride, the voice of the grooms' jubilation from the chupah and youths from their of joyous song. Blessed are You, Hashem, Who gladdens the groom with the bride.

7.BLESSED are You, Hashem, our God, King of the universe, Who created the fruit of the vine.

ברכת המזון לברית מילה

WHEN A זמון IS PRESENT, the זמון IS SAID OVER A CUP OF WINE.

LEADER - רַבּוֹתַי נְבָרֵךְ.

GROUP - יְהִי שֵׁם יְיָ מְבֹרָךְ מֵעַתָּה וְעַד עוֹלָם.

LEADER - יְהִי שֵׁם יְיָ מְבֹרָךְ מֵעַתָּה וְעַד עוֹלָם.

נוֹדֶה לְשִׁמְךָ בְּתוֹךְ אֱמוּנַי, בְּרוּכִים
אַתֶּם לַיְיָ:

GROUP - נוֹדֶה לְשִׁמְךָ בְּתוֹךְ אֱמוּנַי, בְּרוּכִים
אַתֶּם לַיְיָ:

LEADER - בִּרְשׁוּת אֵל אָיוֹם וְנוֹרָא, מִשְׂגָּב
לְעִתּוֹת בַּצָּרָה, אֵל נֶאְזָר בִּגְבוּרָה,
אַדִּיר בַּמָּרוֹם יְיָ:

GROUP - נוֹדֶה לְשִׁמְךָ בְּתוֹךְ אֱמוּנַי, בְּרוּכִים
אַתֶּם לַיְיָ:

LEADER - בִּרְשׁוּת הַתּוֹרָה הַקְּדוֹשָׁה, הַטְּהוֹרָה הִיא וְגַם פְּרוּשָׁה, צִוָּה לָנוּ מוֹרָשָׁה,
GROUP - נוֹדֶה לְשִׁמְךָ בְּתוֹךְ אֱמוּנַי ...   מֹשֶׁה עֶבֶד יְיָ.

LEADER - בִּרְשׁוּת הַכֹּהֲנִים הַלְוִיִּם אֶקְרָא לֵאלֹהֵי הָעִבְרִים, אֲהוֹדֶנּוּ בְּכָל
GROUP - נוֹדֶה לְשִׁמְךָ בְּתוֹךְ אֱמוּנַי ...   אִיִּים, אֲבָרְכָה אֶת יְיָ.

LEADER - בִּרְשׁוּת מָרָנָן וְרַבָּנָן וְרַבּוֹתַי, אֶפְתְּחָה בְּשִׁיר פִּי וּשְׂפָתַי, וְתֹאמַרְנָה
GROUP - נוֹדֶה לְשִׁמְךָ בְּתוֹךְ אֱמוּנַי ...   עַצְמוֹתַי, בָּרוּךְ הַבָּא בְּשֵׁם יְיָ.

LEADER - בִּרְשׁוּת מָרָנָן וְרַבָּנָן וְרַבּוֹתַי, נְבָרֵךְ אֱלֹהֵינוּ שֶׁאָכַלְנוּ מִשֶּׁלּוֹ.

GROUP - בָּרוּךְ אֱלֹהֵינוּ שֶׁאָכַלְנוּ מִשֶּׁלּוֹ וּבְטוּבוֹ חָיִינוּ.

LEADER - בָּרוּךְ אֱלֹהֵינוּ שֶׁאָכַלְנוּ מִשֶּׁלּוֹ וּבְטוּבוֹ חָיִינוּ. בָּרוּךְ הוּא וּבָרוּךְ שְׁמוֹ.

AFTER RECITING ברכת המזון עד וְאָדָם וְנָשִׂים בְּעֵינֵי אֱלֹהִים, A DESIGNATED PERSON BEGINS HERE.

הָרַחֲמָן הוּא יְבָרֵךְ אֲבִי הַיֶּלֶד וְאִמּוֹ, וְיִזְכּוּ לְגַדְּלוֹ וּלְחַנְּכוֹ וּלְחַכְּמוֹ,
מִיּוֹם הַשְּׁמִינִי וָהָלְאָה יֵרָצֶה דָמוֹ, וִיהִי יְיָ אֱלֹהָיו עִמּוֹ.

הָרַחֲמָן הוּא יְבָרֵךְ בַּעַל בְּרִית הַמִּילָה, אֲשֶׁר שָׂשׂ לַעֲשׂוֹת צֶדֶק
בְּגִילָה, וִישַׁלֵּם פָּעֳלוֹ וּמַשְׂכֻּרְתּוֹ כְּפוּלָה, וְיִתְּנֵהוּ לְמַעְלָה לְמָעְלָה.

הָרַחֲמָן הוּא יְבָרֵךְ רַךְ הַנִּמּוֹל לִשְׁמוֹנָה, וְיִהְיוּ יָדָיו וְלִבּוֹ לָאֵל אֱמוּנָה,
וְיִזְכֶּה לִרְאוֹת פְּנֵי הַשְּׁכִינָה, שָׁלוֹשׁ פְּעָמִים בַּשָּׁנָה.

הָרַחֲמָן הוּא יְבָרֵךְ הַמָּל בְּשַׂר הָעָרְלָה, וּפָרַע וּמָצַץ דְּמֵי הַמִּילָה, אִישׁ
הַיָּרֵא וְרַךְ הַלֵּבָב עֲבוֹדָתוֹ פְּסוּלָה, וְאִם שְׁלָשׁ אֵלֶּה לֹא יַעֲשֶׂה לָהּ.

הָרַחֲמָן הוּא יִשְׁלַח מְשִׁיחוֹ הוֹלֵךְ תָּמִים, בִּזְכוּת חֲתַן לַמּוּלוֹת דָּמִים, לְבַשֵּׂר
בְּשׂוֹרוֹת טוֹבוֹת וְנִחוּמִים, לְעַם אֶחָד מְפֻזָּר וּמְפֹרָד בֵּין הָעַמִּים.

הָרַחֲמָן הוּא יִשְׁלַח לָנוּ כֹּהֵן צֶדֶק אֲשֶׁר לֻקַּח לְעֵילוֹם, עַד הוּכַן כִּסְאוֹ כַּשֶּׁמֶשׁ
וְיַהֲלוֹם, וַיָּלֶט פָּנָיו בְּאַדַּרְתּוֹ וַיִּגְלוֹם, בְּרִיתִי הָיְתָה אִתּוֹ הַחַיִּים וְהַשָּׁלוֹם.

CONTINUE WITH הָרַחֲמָן הוּא יְזַכֵּנוּ (FOR שבת AND יום טוב) OR THE APPROPRIATE הָרַחֲמָן (WEEKDAYS).

Zimun After The Meal
Following A Circumcision

Leader: Rabōsai n'voraych.

Group: Y'hi shaym Adōnoy m'vōroch may-atoh v'ad ōlom.

Leader: Y'hi shaym Adōnoy m'vōrach may-atoh v'ad ōlom.
Nōdeh l'shimchoh b'sōch emunoy, b'ruchim atem l'Adōnoy.

Group: Nōdeh l'shimcho b'sōch emunoy, b'ruchim atem l'Adōnoy.

Leader: Birshus Ayl oyōm v'nōro, misgov l'itōs batzoroh,
Ayl ne-zor bigvuroh, adir bamorōm Adonoy.

Group: Nōdeh l'shimcho b'sōch emunay, b'ruchim atem l'Adōnoy.

Leader: Birshus haTōrah hakdōshoh, t'hōroh hi v'gam p'rushoh, tzivoh lonu mōroshoh,
Mōshe eved Adōnoy.

Group: Nōdeh l'shimcho b'sōch emunoy, b'ruchim atem l'Adōnoy.

Leader: Birshus hakōhanim, halviyim, ekro l'Aylōhay ho-ivriyim, ahōdenu b'chol iyim,
avōrchoh es Adonoy.

Group: Nōdeh l'shimcho b'sōch emunoy, b'ruchim atem l'Adōnoy.

Leader: Birshus moronon v'rabonon v'rabōsai, eft'choh b'shir pi usfosai,
v'sōmarnoh atzmōsai, boruch habo b'shaym Adōnoy.

Group: Nōdeh l'shimcho b'sōch emunoy, b'ruchim atem l'Adōnoy.

Leader: Birshus moronon v'rabonon v'rabōsai, n'voraych Elōhaynu she'ochalnu mishelō.

Group: Boruch Elōhaynu she-ochalnu mishelō uvtuvō choyinu.

Leader: Boruch Elōhaynu she-ochalnu mishelō uvtuvō choyinu.

Group: Boruch hu, uvoruch sh'mō.

*(After reciting Birchas Hamozon until B'aynay Elohim v'adam,
a designated person begins here):*

HORACHAMON hu y'voraych avi hayeled v'imō, v'yizku l'gadlō ul'chanchō u'lchakmō,
miyōm hashmini vohol-oh yayrōtzeh domō, vihi Adōnoy Elōhov imō.

HORACHAMON hu y'vorach ba-al b'ris hamiloh, asher sos la'asōs tzedek b'giloh,
vishalaym po-olō umaskurtō k'fuloh, v'yitnayhu l'ma-loh l'mo-loh.

HORACHAMON hu y'voraych hanimōl lishmōnoh, v'yihyu yodov v'libō l'Ayl emunoh,
v'yizkeh lir-ōs p'nay haShechinoh, sholōsh p'omim bashonoh.

HORACHAMON hu y'voraych hamol b'sar orloh, ufora umotzatz d'may hamiloh, ish
hayoray v'rach halayvov avōdosō p'suloh, im sh'losh ayleh lō ya-aseh loh.

HORACHAMON hu yishlach lonu m'shichō hōlaych tomim, bizchus chasan lamulōs
domim, l'vasayr b'sorōs tōvōs v'nichumim, l'am echod m'fuzor um'fōrad bayn ho-amim.

HORACHAMON hu yishlach lonu kōhayn tzedek asher lukach l'aylōm, ad huchan
kis-ō kashemesh v'yohalōm, va-yolet ponov b'adartō va-yiglōm, b'risi hoysoh itō hacha-yim
v'hasholōm.

Continue with Horachamon, page 98

AFTER EATING FOODS FROM THE FIVE SPECIES
OF GRAINS, OR WINE, GRAPES, FIGS, OLIVES,
DATES OR POMEGRANATES, SAY THE FOLLOWING:

בָּרוּךְ אַתָּה יְיָ
אֱלֹהֵינוּ מֶלֶךְ
הָעוֹלָם עַל

AFTER FRUITS (FROM THE ABOVE)	AFTER WINE OR GRAPE JUICE	AFTER GRAIN PRODUCTS
הָעֵץ וְעַל פְּרִי הָעֵץ	הַגֶּפֶן וְעַל פְּרִי הַגֶּפֶן	הַמִּחְיָה וְעַל הַכַּלְכָּלָה

THE FIVE GRAINS ARE WHEAT, OATS, SPELT, BARLEY AND RYE

וְעַל תְּנוּבַת הַשָּׂדֶה, וְעַל אֶרֶץ חֶמְדָּה טוֹבָה וּרְחָבָה,
שֶׁרָצִיתָ וְהִנְחַלְתָּ לַאֲבוֹתֵינוּ, לֶאֱכוֹל מִפִּרְיָה וְלִשְׂבּוֹעַ
מִטּוּבָהּ. רַחֵם (נָא) יְיָ אֱלֹהֵינוּ עַל יִשְׂרָאֵל עַמֶּךָ, וְעַל
יְרוּשָׁלַיִם עִירֶךָ, וְעַל צִיּוֹן מִשְׁכַּן כְּבוֹדֶךָ, וְעַל מִזְבְּחֶךָ
וְעַל הֵיכָלֶךָ. וּבְנֵה יְרוּשָׁלַיִם עִיר הַקֹּדֶשׁ בִּמְהֵרָה
בְיָמֵינוּ, וְהַעֲלֵנוּ לְתוֹכָהּ, וְשַׂמְּחֵנוּ בְּבִנְיָנָהּ, וְנֹאכַל מִפִּרְיָהּ,
וְנִשְׂבַּע מִטּוּבָהּ, וּנְבָרֶכְךָ עָלֶיהָ בִּקְדוּשָׁה וּבְטָהֳרָה.

ON ROSH HASHANAH ADD:	ON ROSH CHODESH ADD:	ON SHABBOS ADD:
וּרְצֵה וְהַחֲלִיצֵנוּ	וְזָכְרֵנוּ (לְטוֹבָה) בְּיוֹם	וְזָכְרֵנוּ לְטוֹבָה
בְּיוֹם הַשַּׁבָּת הַזֶּה:	רֹאשׁ הַחֹדֶשׁ הַזֶּה:	בְּיוֹם הַזִּכָּרוֹן הַזֶּה:

ON FESTIVALS ADD:

וְשַׂמְּחֵנוּ בְּיוֹם

חַג הַמַּצּוֹת	חַג הַשָּׁבוּעוֹת	חַג הַסֻּכּוֹת	הַשְּׁמִינִי חַג
הַזֶּה:	הַזֶּה:	הַזֶּה:	הָעֲצֶרֶת הַזֶּה:

כִּי אַתָּה יְיָ טוֹב וּמֵטִיב לַכֹּל, וְנוֹדֶה לְךָ עַל הָאָרֶץ
וְעַל הַמִּחְיָה. וְעַל פְּרִי הַגֶּפֶן. וְעַל הַפֵּרוֹת.

בָּרוּךְ אַתָּה יְיָ עַל הָאָרֶץ

וְעַל הַמִּחְיָה:	וְעַל פְּרִי הַגֶּפֶן:	וְעַל הַפֵּרוֹת:

CONCLUDING BLESSING

After eating food from the five grains (wheat, oats, spelt, barley, rye) or wine, grapes, figs, olives, dates or pomegranates, say the following:

BLESSED ARE YOU,

Hashem, our God, King of the universe, for the

Grain products	Wine/grape juice	Fruits (as above)
nourishment and sustenance	vine and fruit of the vine	tree and fruit of the tree

WHEAT

BARLEY

GRAPES

FIGS

POMEGRANATES

OLIVES

and for the produce of the field and for the land which is desirable, good and spacious that You were pleased to bequeath to our fore-fathers, to eat from its fruit and be satisfied from its goodness. Please have mercy, Hashem, our God, on Israel, Your nation, and on Jerusalem, Your city, and on Zion, the dwelling place of Your Glory, and on Your altar, and upon Your Temple. And rebuild Jerusalem, the holy city, speedily, in our days, and bring us up to its midst. And let us rejoice in its rebuilding and let us eat from its fruit, and be satisfied from its goodness and we will bless You upon it in holiness and purity.

On Shabbos	On Rosh Chodesh	On Rosh Hashanah
and be pleased and let us rest on this Shabbos day	and remember us for goodness on this New Moon	and remember us for goodness on this New Year

On Festivals add: and gladden us on this

Matzos Festival | Shavuos Festival | Succos Festival | Eight day Festival

Blessed are You, Hashem, for the land and for the

Grain products	Wine/grape juice	Fruits (as above)
Nourishment	Fruit of the vine	Fruits

***BORUCH ATO** Adōnoy, Elōhaynu melech ho-ōlom,*

Grain products	Wine/grape juice	Fruits (as above)
al hamichyo v'al hakalkolo	al hagefen v'al p'ri hagefen	al ho-aytz v'al p'ri ho-aytz

v'al t'nuvas haso-de, v'al eretz chemdo tōva urchovo, sherotziso v'hinchalto la-avōsaynu, le-echōl mipiryoh v'lisbō-a mituvoh. Rachaym no Adōnoy Elōhaynu al Yisro-ayl amecho, v'al Y'rushola-yim i-recho, v'al Tzi-yōn mishkan k'vōdecho, v'al mizb'checho v'al haycholecho. Uvnay Y'rushola-yim ir hakōdesh bimhayro v'yomaynu, v'ha-alaynu l'sōchoh, v'samchaynu b'vinyonoh, v'nochal mipiryoh, v'nisba mituvoh, unvorech'cho oleho bikdusho uvtohoro.

On Shabbos	On Rosh Chodesh	On Rosh Hashanah
Urtzay v'ha-chalitzaynu b'yōm ha-Shabbos ha-ze	V'zochraynu l'tōvo b'yōm rōsh hachōdesh ha-ze	V'zochraynu l'tōvo b'yōm hazikarōn ha-ze

On Pesach	On Shavuos	On Succos
V'sam'chaynu b'yōm chag hamatzōs ha-ze	V'sam'chaynu b'yōm chag ha-shovu-ōs ha-ze	V'sam'chaynu b'yōm chag ha-sukōs ha-ze

On Shemini Atzeres and Simchas Torah:
*V'sam'chaynu b'yōm ha-shmini chag ho-atzeres ha-ze
Ki ato Adōnoy tōv u-maytiv lakōl, v'nō-de lecho al ho-oretz*

After grain products	After wine	After fruit
v'al hamichyo	v'al p'ri hagefen	v'al hapayrōs

Boruch ato Adōnoy, al ho-oretz

Grain: v'al hamichyo.   **Wine:** v'al p'ri hagefen.   **Fruit:** v'al ha payrōs.

DATES

Laws of Shabbos Day Kiddush
Sanctifying the Shabbos Day

- The required amount of wine necessary for the daytime Kiddush is 3.3 oz. One should drink a minimum of 1.65 oz.

- As with Friday night Kiddush, one should not eat or drink before reciting the Daytime Kiddush. However the obligation to recite Kiddush does not begin until after praying *Shachris*. Once one davens *Shachris* they should not eat or drink until reciting or hearing Kiddush.

- Before *Shachris* one technically can eat or drink. However as with every day it is improper to eat or drink before praying in the morning. Water, coffee, and tea can be drunk before praying in the morning.

- One who is weak or unwell may eat before davening. However, Kiddush should be recited before doing so.

- After reciting or listening to kiddush in shul or anywhere else, one is not required to repeat Kiddush when beginning the meal at home. However there are opinions that maintain that it is commendable to do so.

- Kiddush should be recited at the place where one plans to eat. Therefore one should not hear Kiddush in their shul and then eat unless they plan to eat a olive size piece of cake or drink 3.3 oz. of wine or grape juice. (See Laws for Friday Night Kiddush page 46)

- Kiddush may be recited on either wine or grape juice. One who is lacking or has difficulty drinking wine and grape juice can recite Kiddush on either beer or whiskey. Most halachic authorities rule that when whiskey is used one is nonetheless required to have 3.3 oz in the cup and drink a minimum of 1.65 oz.

- Even if one has fulfilled his own obligation for Kiddush, he may exempt someone else who has not. This is based on the principle of *arvus,* that each Jewish person is responsible for his fellow man.

Shabbos
Day of Delights

art of the *mitzvah* of *oneg Shabbos*, delighting the day, is to eat special foods in honor of theSshabbos. Even sleep on Shabbos, which is a very natural activity, can be included in *oneg Shabbos*, alluded to in the letters שבת. This stands for שֵׁינָה בְּשַׁבָּת תַּעֲנוּג, sleep on Shabbos is pleasurable. If one only delights in the body, however, he misses out on the opportunity to enhance the spiritual dimension of the day. Prayer and Torah study are especially important on Shabbos.

Rav Shraga Feivel Mendlowitz, head of Yeshiva Torah Vodaath, once met a group of his students engaged in seemingly insignificant chatter on a Shabbos afternoon. Concerned about their inappropriate use of the holy day of Shabbos, he gently rebuked them. "I understand that perhaps it may be difficult to spend the entire afternoon in Torah study. If so, there is another positive outlet, sleep. Our sages tell us שֵׁינָה בְּשַׁבָּת תַּעֲנוּג, Sleep on Shabbos is a delight. *That* would be an appropriate way to spend a Shabbos afternoon!"

One of Rav Shraga Feivel's students thought of a witticism that he hoped would answer his Rebbe's rebuke. "Perhaps there is another way one can interpret the letters שבת, "שִׂיחָה בְּשַׁבָּת תַּעֲנוּג," conversation on Shabbos is a delight. Rav Shraga Feivel mused, "Now I understand the verse (Ecclesiastes 10:2), לֵב חָכָם לִימִינוֹ וְלֵב כְּסִיל לִשְׂמֹאלוֹ, the heart of the wise is to the right, and the heart of the fool is to the left. What is the meaning of this verse? The letter a can be read as a שׁ, *shin*, if the dot is on the right, or as a שׂ (*sin*), if the dot is on the left. The wise person valuing the day of Shabbos, reads it as a שׁ, and his sleep on Shabbos honors the day. One who is not sensitive to the beauty of Shabbos, will unfortunately read the letter as a שׂ. The שִׂיחָה, idle conversation in which he engages won't allow him to fully benefit from the true delight of Shabbos.

It is told that the Emperor Napolean spent very little time sleeping. When asked about this unique habit, he told his questioner, "When I sleep, I am not Napolean!" The lesson we can glean from this story is that when we are involved in sleep, although we need to recharge our physical energies, it is a time when we are not fully productive. On Shabbos, when we can elevate the spiritual dimension of our soul, it is most important to use our time wisely.

אִם תָּשִׁיב מִשַּׁבָּת רַגְלֶךָ עֲשׂוֹת חֲפָצֶךָ בְּיוֹם קָדְשִׁי וְקָרָאתָ לַשַּׁבָּת עֹנֶג לִקְדוֹשׁ יְיָ מְכֻבָּד וְכִבַּדְתּוֹ מֵעֲשׂוֹת דְּרָכֶיךָ מִמְּצוֹא חֶפְצְךָ וְדַבֵּר דָּבָר: אָז תִּתְעַנַּג עַל יְיָ וְהִרְכַּבְתִּיךָ עַל בָּמֳתֵי אָרֶץ וְהַאֲכַלְתִּיךָ נַחֲלַת יַעֲקֹב אָבִיךָ כִּי פִי יְיָ דִּבֵּר:

וְשָׁמְרוּ בְנֵי יִשְׂרָאֵל אֶת הַשַּׁבָּת לַעֲשׂוֹת אֶת הַשַּׁבָּת לְדֹרֹתָם בְּרִית עוֹלָם: בֵּינִי וּבֵין בְּנֵי יִשְׂרָאֵל אוֹת הִוא לְעוֹלָם כִּי שֵׁשֶׁת יָמִים עָשָׂה יְיָ אֶת הַשָּׁמַיִם וְאֶת הָאָרֶץ וּבַיּוֹם הַשְּׁבִיעִי שָׁבַת וַיִּנָּפַשׁ:

זָכוֹר אֶת יוֹם הַשַּׁבָּת לְקַדְּשׁוֹ: שֵׁשֶׁת יָמִים תַּעֲבֹד וְעָשִׂיתָ כָּל מְלַאכְתֶּךָ: וְיוֹם הַשְּׁבִיעִי שַׁבָּת לַיְיָ אֱלֹהֶיךָ לֹא תַעֲשֶׂה כָל מְלָאכָה אַתָּה וּבִנְךָ וּבִתֶּךָ עַבְדְּךָ וַאֲמָתְךָ וּבְהֶמְתֶּךָ וְגֵרְךָ אֲשֶׁר בִּשְׁעָרֶיךָ: כִּי שֵׁשֶׁת יָמִים עָשָׂה יְיָ אֶת הַשָּׁמַיִם וְאֶת הָאָרֶץ אֶת הַיָּם וְאֶת כָּל אֲשֶׁר בָּם וַיָּנַח בַּיּוֹם הַשְּׁבִיעִי עַל כֵּן בֵּרַךְ יְיָ אֶת יוֹם הַשַּׁבָּת וַיְקַדְּשֵׁהוּ:

סַבְרִי מָרָנָן וְרַבָּנָן וְרַבּוֹתַי:

בָּרוּךְ אַתָּה יְיָ אֱלֹהֵינוּ מֶלֶךְ הָעוֹלָם בּוֹרֵא פְּרִי הַגָּפֶן:

Kiddush for Shabbos Day

IF YOU RESTRAIN, because of Shabbos, your feet, refrain from doing your personal desires on My holy day; if you call Shabbos 'a delight', the holy one of Hashem, 'honored one,' and you honor it by not doing your own ways, from seeking your personal desires and by not discussing forbidden matters, then shall you revel in pleasure with Hashem and I shall mount you upon the heights of the land, and I shall allow you to partake of the legacy given to Jacob, your father, for the mouth of Hashem has spoken.

AND THE CHILDREN of Israel guarded the Shabbos, to make the Shabbos for their generations as an eternal covenant. Between Me and the Children of Israel it is a sign forever, that in six days did Hashem make the heaven and the earth, and on the seventh day ceased to create and He rested.

REMEMBER the day of Shabbos to sanctify it. For six days you will labor and do all of your own work, but the seventh day is the Shabbos for to Hashem, Your God; you may do no work. You, your son your daughter, your slave and your maidservant, your animals, and the stranger who is in your gates. Because in six days Hashem made the heavens and the earth, the sea and all that is in them, and He rested on the seventh day.

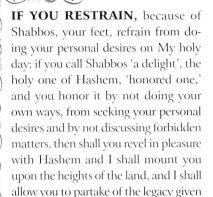

Therefore Hashem blessed the Shabbos day and made it holy.

BLESSED are You, Hashem, our God, King of the universe, Who creates the fruit of the vine.

IM TOSHIV miShabbos raglecho, asōs chafotzecho b'yōm kodshi, v'koroso laShabbos ōneg, likdōsh Adōnoy mechubod, v'chibad'to may-asōs d'rochecho, mimtzō chef-tzecho v'dabayr dovor: Oz tis-anag al Adōnoy, v'hirkavticho al bomosay oretz, veha-achalticho nachalas Ya-akōv ovicho, ki pi Adōnoy dibayr.

V'SHOM'RU v'nay Yisro-ayl es ha-Shabbos, la-asōs es ha-Shabbos l'dōrōsom b'ris ōlom. Bayni u-vayn b'nay Yisro-ayl ōs hi l'ōlom, ki shayshes yomim oso Adōnoy es ha-shoma-yim v'es ho-oretz, u-va-yōm hash'vi-i shovas va-yinofash.

ZOCHŌR es yōm ha-Shabbos l'kad'shō. Shayshes yomim ta-avōd v'osiso kol m'lachtecho. v'yōm hash'vi-i Shabbos lAdōnoy Elōhecho, lō sa-ase chol m'locho, ato u-vincho u-vitecho avd'cho va-amos'cho uvhemtecho, v'gayr'cho asher bish-orecho. Ki shayshes yomim oso Adōnoy es ha-shoma-yim v'es ho-oretz es ha-yom v'es kol asher bom, va-yonach ba-yōm hash'vi-i, al kayn bayrach Adōnoy es yōm ha-Shabbos vai-kad'shayhu.

Savri moronon v'rabonon v'rabōsai:

BORUCH ato Adōnoy Elōhaynu melech ho-ōlom, bōray p'ri hagofen.

All respond: Omayn

THIS SONG DESCRIBES THE REWARDS FOR ONE WHO OBSERVES SHABBOS PROPERLY. IT WAS
COMPOSED BY R' BARUCH BEN SHMUEL OF MAYENCE IN THE THIRTEENTH CENTURY.

בָּרוּךְ אֵל עֶלְיוֹן אֲשֶׁר נָתַן מְנוּחָה. לְנַפְשֵׁנוּ פִדְיוֹן
מִשֵּׁאת וַאֲנָחָה. וְהוּא יִדְרֹשׁ לְצִיּוֹן עִיר הַנִּדָּחָה. עַד
אָנָה תּוּגְיוֹן נֶפֶשׁ נֶאֱנָחָה. הַשּׁוֹמֵר שַׁבָּת הַבֵּן עִם הַבַּת
לָאֵל יֵרָצוּ כְּמִנְחָה עַל מַחֲבַת.

רוֹכֵב בָּעֲרָבוֹת מֶלֶךְ עוֹלָמִים. אֶת עַמּוֹ לִשְׁבּוֹת אִזֵּן
בַּנְּעִימִים. בְּמַאֲכָלֵי עֲרֵבוֹת בְּמִינֵי מַטְעַמִּים. בְּמַלְבּוּשֵׁי כָבוֹד
זֶבַח מִשְׁפָּחָה: הַשּׁוֹמֵר שַׁבָּת הַבֵּן עִם הַבַּת. לָאֵל יֵרָצוּ כְּמִנְחָה עַל מַחֲבַת.

וְאַשְׁרֵי כָּל חוֹכֶה לְתַשְׁלוּמֵי כֶפֶל. מֵאֵת כָּל סוֹכֶה שׁוֹכֵן
בָּעֲרָפֶל. נַחֲלָה לוֹ יִזְכֶּה בָּהָר וּבַשָּׁפֶל. נַחֲלָה וּמְנוּחָה
כַּשֶּׁמֶשׁ לוֹ זָרְחָה: הַשּׁוֹמֵר שַׁבָּת הַבֵּן עִם הַבַּת. לָאֵל יֵרָצוּ כְּמִנְחָה עַל מַחֲבַת.

כָּל שׁוֹמֵר שַׁבָּת כַּדָּת מֵחַלְּלוֹ. הֵן הֻכְשַׁר חִבַּת קֹדֶשׁ
גּוֹרָלוֹ. וְאִם יָצָא חוֹבַת הַיּוֹם אַשְׁרֵי לוֹ. אֶל אֵל אָדוֹן מְחוֹלְלוֹ
מִנְחָה הִיא שְׁלוּחָה: הַשּׁוֹמֵר שַׁבָּת הַבֵּן עִם הַבַּת. לָאֵל יֵרָצוּ כְּמִנְחָה עַל מַחֲבַת.

חֶמְדַּת הַיָּמִים קְרָאוֹ אֵלִי צוּר. וְאַשְׁרֵי לִתְמִימִים אִם יִהְיֶה
נָצוּר. כֶּתֶר הִלּוּמִים עַל רֹאשָׁם יָצוּר. צוּר הָעוֹלָמִים
רוּחוֹ בָּם נָחָה: הַשּׁוֹמֵר שַׁבָּת הַבֵּן עִם הַבַּת. לָאֵל יֵרָצוּ כְּמִנְחָה עַל מַחֲבַת.

זָכוֹר אֶת יוֹם הַשַּׁבָּת לְקַדְּשׁוֹ. קַרְנוֹ כִּי גָבְהָה נֵזֶר עַל
רֹאשׁוֹ. עַל כֵּן יִתֵּן הָאָדָם לְנַפְשׁוֹ. עֹנֶג וְגַם שִׂמְחָה
בָּהֶם לְמָשְׁחָה: הַשּׁוֹמֵר שַׁבָּת הַבֵּן עִם הַבַּת. לָאֵל יֵרָצוּ כְּמִנְחָה עַל מַחֲבַת.

קֹדֶשׁ הִיא לָכֶם שַׁבָּת הַמַּלְכָּה. אֶל תּוֹךְ בָּתֵּיכֶם לְהָנִיחַ בְּרָכָה.
בְּכָל מוֹשְׁבוֹתֵיכֶם לֹא תַעֲשׂוּ מְלָאכָה. בְּנֵיכֶם וּבְנוֹתֵיכֶם
עֶבֶד וְגַם שִׁפְחָה: הַשּׁוֹמֵר שַׁבָּת הַבֵּן עִם הַבַּת. לָאֵל יֵרָצוּ כְּמִנְחָה עַל מַחֲבַת.

This zemer is authored by Rabbi Boruch ben Shmuel in 13ᵗʰ century Mayence, whose name, Boruch Chazak is found in the acrostic. The song extols the virtue and outlines the reward awaiting those who fastidiously observe the Shabbos. Just as Shabbos offers respite from our personal suffering, we ask God to diminish the pain of our national tragedy with His return to Zion and Jerusalem.

BORUCH AYL ELYŌN,
asher nosan m'nuchoh,
L'nafshaynu fidyōn,
mishays va-anochoh.
V'hu yidrōsh l'Tzion, ir hanidochoh,
Ad onoh tugyōn nefesh ne'enochoh.

*Hashōmayr Shabbos habayn im habas,
Lo'Ayl yayrotzu k'minchoh al machavas.*

Rōchev bo'arovōs, melech ōlomim,
Es amō lishbōs izayn ban'imim.
B'ma-acholay arayvōs,
b'minay mat'amim,
B'malbushay chovōd
zevach mishpochoh.

*Hashōmayr Shabbos habayn im habas,
Lo'Ayl yayrotzu k'minchoh al machavas.*

V'ashray kol chōche,
l'sashlumay chayfel,
May'ays kōl socheh,
shōchayn bo'arofel,
Nachaloh lō yizkeh, bohor uvashofel,
Nachaloh u'menuchoh,
kashemesh lō zorchoh.

*Hashōmayr Shabbos habayn im habas,
Lo'Ayl yayrotzu k'minchoh al machavas.*

Kol shōmayr Shabbos
kados maychal'lō,
Hayn hechsher chibas kodesh gorolō,
V'im yotzo chōvas hayōm ashray lō,
El Ayl odōn m'chōl'lō
minchoh hi sh'luchoh.

*Hashōmayr Shabbos habayn im habas,
Lo'Ayl yayrotzu k'minchoh al machavas.*

Chemdas ha-yomim k'ro-ō Ayli tzur,
V'ashray lismimim im yihyeh notzur,
Keser hilumim al rōshom yotzur,
Tzur ho-ōlomim ruchō bom nochoh.

*Hashōmayr Shabbos habayn im habas,
Lo'Ayl yayrotzu k'minchoh al machavas.*

Zochōr es yom haShabbos l'kadshō,
Karnō ki govhoh nayzer al rōshō,
Al kayn yitayn ho-odom l'nafshō,
Ōneg v'gam simchoh bohem l'moshchoh.

*Hashōmayr Shabbos habayn im habas,
Lo'Ayl yayrotzu k'minchoh al machavas.*

Kōdesh hi lochem Shabbos hamalkoh,
El tōch botaychem l'honiyach b'rochoh,
B'chol mōshvōsaychem lo sa'asu m'lochoh,
B'naychem uvnōsaychem,
eved v'gam shifchoh.

*Hashōmayr Shabbos habayn im habas,
Lo'Ayl yayrotzu k'minchoh al machavas.*

THIS SONG IN HONOR OF SHABBOS WAS COMPOSED BY AN UNKNOWN
AUTHOR NAMED YISRAEL, WHOSE NAME FORMS AN ACROSTIC

יוֹם זֶה מְכֻבָּד מִכָּל יָמִים . כִּי בוֹ שָׁבַת צוּר עוֹלָמִים:

שֵׁשֶׁת יָמִים תַּעֲשֶׂה מְלַאכְתֶּךָ . וְיוֹם הַשְּׁבִיעִי לֵאלֹהֶיךָ . שַׁבָּת לֹא תַעֲשֶׂה בוֹ מְלָאכָה . כִּי כֹל עָשָׂה שֵׁשֶׁת יָמִים: יוֹם זֶה

רִאשׁוֹן הוּא לְמִקְרָאֵי קֹדֶשׁ . יוֹם שַׁבָּתוֹן יוֹם שַׁבַּת קֹדֶשׁ . עַל כֵּן כָּל אִישׁ בְּיֵינוֹ יְקַדֵּשׁ . עַל שְׁתֵּי לֶחֶם יִבְצְעוּ תְמִימִים: יוֹם זֶה

אֱכוֹל מַשְׁמַנִּים שְׁתֵה מַמְתַּקִּים . כִּי אֵל יִתֵּן לְכָל בּוֹ דְבֵקִים . בֶּגֶד לִלְבּוֹשׁ לֶחֶם חֻקִּים . בָּשָׂר וְדָגִים וְכָל מַטְעַמִּים: יוֹם זֶה

לֹא תֶחְסַר כֹּל בּוֹ . וְאָכַלְתָּ וְשָׂבָעְתָּ וּבֵרַכְתָּ אֶת יְיָ אֱלֹהֶיךָ אֲשֶׁר אָהַבְתָּ . כִּי בֵרַכְךָ מִכָּל הָעַמִּים: יוֹם זֶה

הַשָּׁמַיִם מְסַפְּרִים כְּבוֹדוֹ . וְגַם הָאָרֶץ מָלְאָה חַסְדּוֹ . רְאוּ כִּי כָל אֵלֶּה עָשְׂתָה יָדוֹ . כִּי הוּא הַצּוּר פָּעֳלוֹ תָמִים: יוֹם זֶה

R' YEHUDAH HALEVI, NOTED 11th CENTURY POET AND AUTHOR OF KUZARI COMPOSED
THIS SONG, DESCRIBING THE SHABBOS WHEN THE JEWS RECEIVED THE TORAH AT SINAI

יוֹם שַׁבָּתוֹן אֵין לִשְׁכּוֹחַ . זִכְרוֹ כְּרֵיחַ הַנִּיחֹחַ . יוֹנָה מָצְאָה בוֹ מָנוֹחַ . וְשָׁם יָנוּחוּ יְגִיעֵי כֹחַ:

הַיּוֹם נִכְבָּד לִבְנֵי אֱמוּנִים . זְהִירִים לְשָׁמְרוֹ אָבוֹת וּבָנִים . חָקוּק בִּשְׁנֵי לוּחוֹת אֲבָנִים . מֵרֹב אוֹנִים וְאַמִּיץ כֹּחַ: יוֹנָה מָצְאָה

וּבָאוּ כֻלָּם בִּבְרִית יַחַד . נַעֲשֶׂה וְנִשְׁמַע אָמְרוּ כְּאֶחָד . וּפָתְחוּ וְעָנוּ יְיָ אֶחָד . בָּרוּךְ הַנּוֹתֵן לַיָּעֵף כֹּחַ: יוֹנָה מָצְאָה

דִּבֶּר בְּקָדְשׁוֹ בְּהַר הַמּוֹר . יוֹם הַשְּׁבִיעִי זָכוֹר וְשָׁמוֹר . וְכָל פִּקּוּדָיו יַחַד לִגְמוֹר . חַזֵּק מָתְנַיִם וְאַמֵּץ כֹּחַ: יוֹנָה מָצְאָה

הָעָם אֲשֶׁר נָע כַּצֹּאן תָּעָה . יִזְכּוֹר לְפָקְדוֹ בְּרִית וּשְׁבוּעָה . לְבַל יַעֲבָר בָּם מִקְרֵה רָעָה . כַּאֲשֶׁר נִשְׁבַּעְתָּ עַל מֵי נֹחַ: יוֹנָה מָצְאָה

The honored quality of the Shabbos day is expressed in this zemer by an author known only as Yisrael. Man's six days of physical activity parallel the six days of Creation. On Shabbos, when God ceased activity, we refrain from physical pursuits and involve ourselves more in prayer, mitzvos and Torah study. The delicacies consumed on the Shabbos complement the spiritual nature of the day.

YŌM ZEH M'CHUBOD *mikol yomim,*
Ki vō shovas tzur ōlomim:

S*hayshes yomim ta-aseh m'lach'techo,*
V'yōm hash'vi-i l'Aylōhecho,
Shabbos lō sa-aseh vō m'lochoh,
Ki chōl oso shayshes yomim

> *Yōm zeh m'chubod mikol yomim,*
> *Ki vō shovas tzur ōlomim*

R*ishōn hu l'mikro-ay kōdesh,*
Yōm Shabboson, yōm Shabbos kōdesh,
Al kayn kol ish b'yaynō y'kadaysh,
Al shtay lechem yivtz'u s'mimim

> *Yōm zeh m'chubod mikol yomim,*
> *Ki vō shovas tzur ōlomim*

E*chōl mashmanim, sh'say mamtakim,*
Ki Ayl yitayn l'chōl bō d'vaykim,

Beged lilbōsh, lechem chukim,
Bosor v'dogim v'chol mat-amim

> *Yōm zeh m'chubod mikol yomim,*
> *Ki vō shovas tzur ōlomim*

L*ō sechsar kōl bō*
V'ochalto, v'sovoto,
U'vayrachto es Adōnoy Elōhecho asher ohavto,
Ki vayrach'cho mikol ho-amim

> *Yōm zeh m'chubod mikol yomim,*
> *Ki vō shovas tzur ōlomim*

H*ashomayim m'saprim k'vōdō,*
V'gam ho-oretz mol'oh chasdō,
R'eu ki chol ayleh os'soh yodō,
Ki hu hatzur po-olō somim.

> *Yōm zeh m'chubod mikol yomim,*
> *Ki vō shovas tzur ōlomim*

The famous 12th century composer Rabbi Yehuda Halevi, touches on a momentous Shabbos in the history of our nation—the Shabbos when the Jewish People received the Torah on Mount Sinai. The yonah, dove, that found rest on Shabbos refers to the one sent out of the ark by Noah, finding a resting place in the Garden of Eden (Midrash). Just as the dove found refuge there, so too, those who weary themselves in the teachings of Sinai will find their ultimate contentment in the Garden of Eden.

YŌM SHABBOSON *ayn lishkkōach,*
Zichrō k'rayach hanichōach.
> *Yōnoh motz-oh bō monōach,*
> *V'shom yonuchu y'gi-ay chōach.*

H*a-yōm nichbod livnay emunim,*
Z'hirim l'shomrō ovōs uvonim,
Chokuk bishnay luchōs avonim,
Mayrōv ōnim v'ameitz kōach.
> *Yōnoh motz-oh bō monōach,*
> *V'shom yonuchu y'gi-ay chōach.*

U*vo-u chulom bivris yachad,*
Na-aseh v'nishma omru k'echod,
Ufos-shu v'onu Adōnony echod,
Boruch hanosayn layo'ef koach.
> *Yōnoh motz-oh bō monōach,*
> *V'shom yonuchu y'gi-ay chōach.*

D*iber b'kodshō b'har hamōr,*
Yōm hashvi'i zochōr v'shomōr,
V'chol pikudov yachad ligmōr,
Chazayk mosnayim v'amaytz chōach.
> *Yōnoh motz-oh bō monōach,*
> *V'shom yonuchu y'gi-ay chōach.*

H*o'om asher no katzōn to-oh,*
Yizkōr l'fokdō b'ris ushvu-oh,
L'val ya-avor bom mikreh ro-oh,
Ka-asher nishbat-oh al may Nōach.
> *Yōnoh motz-oh bō monōach,*
> *V'shom yonuchu y'gi-ay chōach.*

THIS SONG ABOUT THE JOY OF SHABBOS AND ITS REWARDS WAS COMPOSED BY SHMUEL.

שַׁבָּת הַיּוֹם לַיְיָ: מְאֹד צַהֲלוּ בְרִנּוּנִי: וְגַם הַרְבּוּ מַעֲדַנֵּי: אוֹתוֹ לִשְׁמֹר כְּמִצְוַת יְיָ: שַׁבָּת הַיּוֹם לַיְיָ:

מֵעֲבֹר דֶּרֶךְ וּגְבוּלִים. מֵעֲשׂוֹת הַיּוֹם פְּעָלִים. לֶאֱכֹל וְלִשְׁתּוֹת בְּהִלּוּלִים. זֶה הַיּוֹם עָשָׂה יְיָ: שַׁבָּת הַיּוֹם לַיְיָ:

וְאִם תִּשְׁמְרֶנּוּ. יָהּ יִנְצָרְךָ כְּבָבַת. אַתָּה וּבִנְךָ וְגַם הַבַּת. וְקָרָאתָ עֹנֶג לַשַּׁבָּת. אָז תִּתְעַנַּג עַל יְיָ: שַׁבָּת הַיּוֹם לַיְיָ:

אֱכֹל מַשְׁמַנִּים וּמַעֲדַנִּים. וּמַטְעַמִּים הַרְבֵּה מִינִים. אֱגוֹזֵי פֶרֶךְ וְרִמּוֹנִים. וְאָכַלְתָּ וְשָׂבַעְתָּ וּבֵרַכְתָּ אֶת יְיָ: שַׁבָּת הַיּוֹם לַיְיָ:

לַעֲרֹךְ בַּשֻּׁלְחָן לֶחֶם חֲמוּדוֹת. לַעֲשׂוֹת הַיּוֹם שָׁלֹשׁ סְעוּדוֹת. אֶת הַשֵּׁם הַנִּכְבָּד לְבָרֵךְ וּלְהוֹדוֹת. שִׁקְדוּ וְשִׁמְרוּ וַעֲשׂוּ בָנַי: שַׁבָּת הַיּוֹם לַיְיָ:

THE 10th CENTURY POET DONASH BEN LABRAT OF FEZ COMPOSED THIS SONG. IT
ASKS GOD TO PROTECT ISRAEL AND DESTROY HER ENEMIES.

דְּרוֹר יִקְרָא לְבֵן עִם בַּת. וְיִנְצָרְכֶם כְּמוֹ בָבַת. נְעִים שִׁמְכֶם וְלֹא יֻשְׁבַּת. שְׁבוּ וְנוּחוּ בְּיוֹם שַׁבָּת: דְּרוֹשׁ נָוִי וְאוּלָמִי. וְאוֹת יֶשַׁע עֲשֵׂה עִמִּי: נְטַע שׂוֹרֵק בְּתוֹךְ כַּרְמִי. שְׁעֵה שַׁוְעַת בְּנֵי עַמִּי: דְּרוֹךְ פּוּרָה בְּתוֹךְ בָּצְרָה. וְגַם בָּבֶל אֲשֶׁר גָּבְרָה. נְתוֹץ צָרַי בְּאַף וְעֶבְרָה. שְׁמַע קוֹלִי בְּיוֹם אֶקְרָא: אֱלֹהִים תֵּן בַּמִּדְבָּר הַר. הֲדַס שִׁטָּה בְּרוֹשׁ תִּדְהָר. וְלַמַּזְהִיר וְלַנִּזְהָר. שְׁלוֹמִים תֵּן כְּמֵי נָהָר: הֲדוֹךְ קָמַי אֵל קַנָּא. בְּמוֹג לֵבָב וּבַמְּגִנָּה. וְנַרְחִיב פֶּה וּנְמַלְאֶנָּה. לְשׁוֹנֵנוּ לְךָ רִנָּה: דְּעֵה חָכְמָה לְנַפְשֶׁךָ. וְהִיא כֶתֶר לְרֹאשֶׁךָ. נְצוֹר מִצְוַת קְדוֹשֶׁךָ. שְׁמוֹר שַׁבַּת קָדְשֶׁךָ:

SHABBOS DAY

This zemer, composed by an unknown author, Shmuel, describes Shabbos as a day unto God. As is often the theme of many zemiros, physical delights and spiritual involvement complement each other, provided they are done in honor of the Shabbos. Being exacting in the laws of Shabbos and enjoying Shabbos delicacies are integral elements of declaring the day to be one consecrated for the Almighty.

SHABBOS HAYOM LA-ADŌNOY,
M'od tzahalu b'rinunay,
V'gam harbu ma'adonay,
Ōsō lishmor k'mitzvas Adōnoy,

       Shabbos hayom la-Adōnoy.

May'avōr derech u'gvulim,
May'asōs hayom p'olim,
Le-echol v'lishtōs b'hilulim,
Zeh hayom osoh Adonōy,

       Shabbos hayom la-Adōnoy.

V'im tishm'renu Yah yin'tzorcho k'vovas,
Atoh uvinhcho v'gam habas,
V'koroso oneg laShabbos,
Oz tisanag al Adonōy,

       Shabbos hayom la-Adōnoy.

Echōl mashmanim u-ma'adanim,
Umat'amim harbay minim,
Egōzay ferech v'rimōnim,
V'ochalto v'sovoto u-vayrachto es Adōnoy,

       Shabbos hayom la-Adōnoy.

La'arōch bashulchon lechem chamudōs,
La'asōs hayōm sholosh s'udōs,
Es HaShem hanichbod l'voraych u-l'hōdōs,
Shikdu v'shimru va'asu vonay,

       Shabbos hayom la-Adōnoy.

Dunash ibn Labrat of Baghdad, a renowned 10th century grammarian, was a relative of R' Saadiah Gaon. This zemer that he authored beseeches God to exact retribution from the nations of the world that oppress the Jews. Traditionally, reward is given to those who are exacting in the observance of Shabbos, and to those who assist others properly keeping its laws.

D'RŌR YIKRO, l'vayn im bas,
V'yintzorchem k'mō vovas,
N'im shimchem v'lō yushbas,
Sh'vu v'nuchu b'yōm Shabbos.

Drōsh novi v'ulomi,
V'ōs_yesha asay imi,
N'ta sōrek b'sōch karmi,
Sh'ay shav-as b'nay ami.

Drōch puroh b'sōch botzroh,
V'gam Bovel asher govroh,
N'sōtz tzorai b'af v'evroh,
Shma kōli b'yom ekro.

Elōhim tayn bamidbar har,
Hadas shitoh b'rōsh tidhor,
V'lamazhir v'lanizhor,
Shlōmim tayn k'may nohor.

Hadōch komay, Ayl kano,
B'mōg layvov uvamginoh,
V'narchiv peh u'nmal-enoh,
L'shōnaynu lecho rinoh.

D'ay chochmoh, l'nafshecho,
V'hi cheser l'rōshecho,
N'tzor mitzvas k'dōshecho,
Shmōr Shabbas kodshecho.

Shalosh Seudos
Time for Divine Favor

abbalistically, from the afternoon period on Shabbos, a time of Divine favor, רעוא דרעוין, *favor of favors,* descends upon the Jewish nation. In the *minchah* prayer on Shabbos afternoon, we recite the phrase לך ה' עת רצון, to You, Hashem it is a time of favor. It was at this time, according to the kabbalists, that the Almighty's desire to create the world, as it were, began. It was at this auspicious moment that the Divine beneficence to bestow His kindness on the world manifested itself. Each Shabbos at this time, this favorable inclination renews itself, asking that Hashem shower us with goodness. (*Taamei Minhagim*, from R' Menachem Mendel of Riminov).

The third Shabbos meal is generally called *shalosh seudos*, literally three meals. Grammatically, *seudah shelishis*, the third meal, would be more accurate, though this term is not common. In effect, the third meal indicates that *all* of one's meals were eaten to fulfill God's commandment to partake of the Shabbos meals. On Friday night, even though one delights in Shabbos, he eats to satisfy his hunger. At the second meal on Shabbos morning, one eats as well because he is hungry. At the third Shabbos meal, the individual is almost satisfied. Still, he fulfills the third Shabbos meal because God told us to do so. We reward him as if all three meals were eaten purely to fulfill God's command.

Shalosh seudos takes place as the last rays of Shabbos begin to fall beneath the horizon. It is a time when we can extend the holiness of the day through words of Torah and sing heartfelt songs that reflect the yearning of our souls to maintain the beautiful connection with our Creator that Shabbos afforded us. Additionally, the souls that were judged to go to *gehinnom* to be punished and purged of their transgressions, receive some respite on Shabbos. By prolonging the Shabbos in this way, we allow these souls some additional moments without spiritual pain. (*Taamei Minhagim*, in the name of *Ateres Zvi*).

Laws of Shalosh Seudos
The Third Shabbos Meal

- The third and final *Shabbos* meal should be eaten following one half hour past midday.

- One should preferably pray *minchah,* the afternoon service, before eating the third meal.

- Both men and women are obligated to eat the three *Shabbos* meals.

- When beginning the meal, the blessing of *hamotzi* should be recited over two covered whole loaves of *challah*

- One should begin eating before sundown. Once begun, he may continue eating the meal until the grace is recited. If one was unable to wash before sundown, one may wash until one half hour before nightfall. After the grace is recited, one must wait until after *havdalah* to eat again.

- If one finds it difficult to eat bread, one can fulfill the obligation for *shalosh seudos* with other foods in the following order of preference: 1) cake, cookies or *mezonos* foods 2) fish or meat 3) fruits.

The first paragraph, Askinu Seudoso, authored by the Arizal, introduces each of the Shabbos meals using Kabbalistic imagery. The World to Come is described in the Talmud (Berachos 17a) as a place where the righteous will sit with crowns of glory on their heads, enjoying the radiance of the Divine Presence. The Shabbos meal affords those who are worthy a microcosmic view of That next world's radiance, though it is filtered through the unclear vision of this world. The righteous yearns to see the diminutive radiance of the Divine Presence, as it were, and Shalosh Seudos, the third Shabbos meal, brings them closest to that vision. Kabbalistically, it is called רעוא דרעוין, the time of favor of favors. As the last rays of Shabbos fade and the darkness of the new week begins, God is favorably disposed to accept the supplications of His people.

אַתְקִינוּ סְעוּדָתָא דִמְהֵימְנוּתָא שְׁלֵימָתָא.
חֶדְוָתָא דְמַלְכָּא קַדִּישָׁא:
אַתְקִינוּ סְעוּדָתָא דְמַלְכָּא.דָּא הִיא סְעוּדָתָא דִזְעֵיר אַנְפִּין
וְעַתִּיקָא קַדִּישָׁא וַחֲקַל תַּפּוּחִין קַדִּישִׁין אַתְיָן לְסַעֲדָא בַּהֲדֵיהּ:

בְּנֵי הֵיכָלָא דְכְסִיפִין. לְמֶחֱזֵי זִיו דִזְעֵיר אַנְפִּין:
יְהוֹן הָכָא בְּהַאי תַּכָּא. דְּבֵהּ מַלְכָּא בְּגִלּוּפִין:
צְבוּ לַחֲדָא בְּהַאי וַעֲדָא. בְּגוֹ עִירִין וְכָל גַּדְפִּין:
חֲדוּ הַשְׁתָּא בְּהַאי שַׁעְתָּא.דְּבֵהּ רַעֲוָא וְלֵית זַעֲפִין:
קְרִיבוּ לִי חֲזוּ חֵילִי. דְּלֵית דִּינִין דִּתְקִיפִין:

לְבַר נַטְלִין וְלָא עָאלִין. הַנֵי כַּלְבִּין דַּחֲצִיפִין:
וְהָא אַזְמִין עַתִּיק יוֹמִין.לְמִנְחָה עֲדֵי יְהוֹן חָלְפִין:
רְעוּ דִּילֵהּ דְּגַלֵּי לֵהּ. לְבַטָּלָא בְּכָל קְלִיפִין:
יְשַׁוֵי לוֹן בְּנוּקְבֵּיהוֹן. וִיטַמְּרוּן בְּגוֹ כֵפִין:
אֲרֵי הַשְׁתָּא בְּמִנְחָתָא. בְּחֶדְוָתָא דִזְעֵיר אַנְפִּין:

ASKINU S'UDOSO *dimhaym'nuso sh'laymoso chedvoso d'malko kadisho:*
Askinu s'udoso d'malko, do hi s'udoso diz-ayr anpin v'atiko kadisho,
vachakal tapuchin kadishin asyon l'sa-ado bahaday.

B'nay haycholo dichsifin,
　　l'mechazay ziv diz-ayr anpin:

Y'hon hocho, b'hai tako,
　　d'vay malko b'gilufin:

Tz'vu lachado, b'hai va-ado,
　　b'gō irin v'chol gadfin:

Chadu hashto, b'hai sha-to,
　　d'vay ra-avo v'lays za-afin:

K'rivu li, chazu chayli,
　　d'lays dinin diskifin:

L'var natlin, v'lo olin,
　　hanay chalbin da-chatzifin:

V'ho azmin, atik yōmin,
　　l'minchoh aday y'hōn cholfin:

R'u dilay, d'galay lay,
　　l'vatolo b'chol k'lifin:

Y'shavay lōn, b'nōkvayhōn,
　　vitamrun b'gō chayfin:

Aray hashto, b'minchoso,
　　b'chedvoso diz-ayr anpin.

THIS PSALM (תהלים כג) EXPRESSES TO
GOD OUR LOVE FOR HIM AS OUR SHEPHERD.
IT IS USUALLY SUNG THREE TIMES.

מִזְמוֹר לְדָוִד

יְיָ רֹעִי לֹא אֶחְסָר:
בִּנְאוֹת דֶּשֶׁא יַרְבִּיצֵנִי עַל מֵי מְנֻחוֹת יְנַהֲלֵנִי:
נַפְשִׁי יְשׁוֹבֵב יַנְחֵנִי בְמַעְגְּלֵי צֶדֶק לְמַעַן שְׁמוֹ:
גַּם כִּי אֵלֵךְ בְּגֵיא צַלְמָוֶת לֹא אִירָא רָע כִּי
אַתָּה עִמָּדִי שִׁבְטְךָ וּמִשְׁעַנְתֶּךָ הֵמָּה יְנַחֲמֻנִי:
תַּעֲרֹךְ לְפָנַי שֻׁלְחָן נֶגֶד צֹרְרָי דִּשַּׁנְתָּ בַשֶּׁמֶן
רֹאשִׁי כּוֹסִי רְוָיָה: אַךְ טוֹב וָחֶסֶד יִרְדְּפוּנִי כָּל
יְמֵי חַיָּי וְשַׁבְתִּי בְּבֵית יְיָ לְאֹרֶךְ יָמִים:

OUR LOVE FOR GOD IS EXPRESSED IN THIS SONG BY THE KABBALIST R' ELIEZER AZIKRI.

יְדִיד נֶפֶשׁ אָב הָרַחֲמָן. מְשׁוֹךְ עַבְדְּךָ אֶל רְצוֹנֶךָ.
יָרוּץ עַבְדְּךָ כְּמוֹ אַיָּל. יִשְׁתַּחֲוֶה אֶל מוּל
הֲדָרֶךָ. יֶעֱרַב לוֹ יְדִידוֹתֶיךָ. מִנֹּפֶת צוּף וְכָל טָעַם:
הָדוּר נָאֶה זִיו הָעוֹלָם. נַפְשִׁי חוֹלַת אַהֲבָתֶךָ. אָנָּא אֵל נָא
רְפָא נָא לָהּ. בְּהַרְאוֹת לָהּ נֹעַם זִיוֶךְ. אָז תִּתְחַזֵּק
וְתִתְרַפֵּא. וְהָיְתָה לָהּ שִׂמְחַת עוֹלָם:
וָתִיק יֶהֱמוּ נָא רַחֲמֶיךָ. וְחוּסָה נָּא עַל בֵּן אֲהוּבָךְ. כִּי זֶה כַּמָּה
נִכְסוֹף נִכְסַפְתִּי לִרְאוֹת מְהֵרָה בְּתִפְאֶרֶת עֻזֶּךָ. אֵלֶּה חָמְדָה לִבִּי
וְחוּסָה נָּא וְאַל תִּתְעַלָּם:
הִגָּלֵה נָא וּפְרוֹשׂ חֲבִיבִי עָלַי אֶת סֻכַּת שְׁלוֹמֶךָ. תָּאִיר אֶרֶץ
מִכְּבוֹדֶךָ. נָגִילָה וְנִשְׂמְחָה בָךְ. מַהֵר אֱהֹב כִּי בָא מוֹעֵד.
וְחָנֵּנוּ כִּימֵי עוֹלָם:

Third Shabbos Meal

This psalm (תהלים כג) expresses to God our love for him as our shepherd. It is usually sung three times.

Hashem is my shepherd, I shall not lack. In lush meadows He lays me down, beside tranquil waters He leads me. He restores my soul. He leads me on paths of righteousness for His Name's sake. Though I walk in the valley overshadowed by death, I will fear no evil, for You are with me. Your rod and Your staff, they comfort me. You prepare a table before me in full view of my tormentors. You anointed my head with oil, my cup overflows. May only goodness and kindness pursue me all the days of my life, and I shall dwell in the House of Hashem for long days.

MIZMOR L'DOVID, Adōnoy rō'i lō echsor: Bin-ōs deshe yarbitzayni, al may m'nuchōs y'nahalayni: Nafshi y'shōvayv, yanchayni v'ma-g'lay tzedek l'ma-an sh'mō: Gam ki aylach b'gay tzalmoves lō iro ro, ki atoh imodi, shivt'cho umish-antecho, haymoh y'nachamuni: Ta-arōch l'fonai shulchon neged tzōr'roy, dishanto vashemen rōshi, kōsi r'voyo: Ach tov vochesed yird'funi kol y'may cha-yoy, v'shavti b'vays Adōnoy l'orech yomim.

R. Eliezer Azikri, 16th century author of this zemer and the classic work Sefer Charaidim, expressed the Jews' profound love for his Creator in Yedid Nefesh. While most acrostics allude to the author's name, the letters that g\begin each paragraph spell the name of God. God is referred to as "the beloved of my soul," underscoring the Jew's intense yearning to attain a spiritual relationship with Hashem.

Y'DID NEFESH, ov horachamon,
M'shōch avdecho el r'tzōnecho,
Yorutz avdecho k'mō ayol,
Yistachave el mul hadorecho,
Ye-erav lō y'didosecho,
Minōfes tzuf v'chol to-am.

Vosik yehemu no rachemecho,
V'chusoh no al bayn ahuvecho,
Ki zeh kamoh nichsōf nichsafti,
Lirōs b'siferes uzecho,
Ayleh chomdoh libi,
V'chusoh no v'al tis-alom.

> **H**odur no-eh, ziv ho-ōlom,
> Nafshi chōlas ahavosecho,
> Ono Ayl no r'fo no loh,
> B'harōs loh no-am zivecho,
> Oz tischazayk v'sisrapay,
> V'hoyso loh simchas ōlom.

> **H**igoleh no u'frōs chavivi olay,
> Es sukas sh'lōmecho,
> To'ir eretz mikvōdecho,
> Nogiloh v'nism'choh voch,
> Mahayr ehōv, ki vo mō'ayd,
> V'chonaynu kimay ōlom.

Laws of Havdalah
The conclusion of Shabbos

- *Havdalah* is recited after nightfall. There are various opinions as to when one marks the time of sundown – ranging from 45-72 minutes after sunset.

- One should not eat or drink (except for water) following the third meal until after *havdalah* is recited.

- One may perform work that is forbidden on *Shabbos* even before reciting *havdalah*. However an abbreviated form of *havdalah* must be recited before doing so, *"Baruch hamavdil bein kodesh l'chol."* – Blessed are You who separates between the holy and the profane. One should follow this recitation with the complete *havdalah* as soon as he is able.

- Wine or grape juice can be used for *havdalah*. If one has difficulty drinking wine or grape juice, beer may be used. One should use a cup with a minimum of 3.3 oz. A full cup, (preferably not a disposable one) should be used.

- The Talmud tells us that any home where wine is not poured like water lacks a sign of blessing. We therefore fill the cup so that it overflows when pouring the wine for *havdalah*.

- There are various customs as to whether one stands or sits while reciting *kiddush*. According to all opinions, one should sit while drinking the wine.

- The cup should be held in the right hand, (in the left hand for a left handed person) against the palm of the hand, with one's fingers around the cup.

- The leader recites the blessing *"Borei minai bisomim"* over the spices. All present respond *"omayn"* and the spices are passed around for all to smell.

- The leader recites the blessing of *"Borei m'orei ho-aish"* on the light from the candle. The candle should have two wicks. One may also hold single wick candles together or two matches together, so that a single flame is formed.

- All present should be close enough to derive benefit from the light. For this reason many have the custom to turn off any electric lights. After the blessing is recited the custom is for one to look at his fingernails using the light of the candle, first with the fingers bent in and then extended.

- While reciting the final blessing, one should look into the cup.

- After reciting the blessing of *"Borei pri hagafen"* one should drink a minimum of 1.65 oz. of the wine. It is preferable to drink the full 3.3 oz. in order to recite the after-blessing. It is customary that women do not drink from *havdalah*.

- There should be no talking until after the leader has finished drinking the required amount.

- The custom is to pour out some of the wine and use it to extinguish the flame.

Havdalah
In the Talmud and Midrash

❧ Three merit the World to Come: one who lives in Israel, one who raises his children for Torah study and one who makes *havdalah* at the conclusion of Shabbos (Talmud, *Pesachim* 113a)

❧ One who says *hamavdil* during *shemoneh esrei* should nonetheless say it in *havdalah*. (Talmud, *Pesachim* 109a)

❧ Whoever concludes (the blessing) with "He who sanctifies Israel" and "Who separates between the holy and the profane", his life is extended (Talmud, *Pesachim* 104a)

❧ Why does one make the blessing of *borei m'orei ha'aish,* the blessing of seeing the light of the *havdalah* candle on *motzei Shabbos,* at the conclusion of the Shabbos? That was when the light of the fire was created (*Midrash Rabbah: Bereishis* 11:2)

❧ He (Adam) saw a column of fire and was glad in his heart. He said, "Now I know that God is with me – he opened his hands to the light of the fire and he made the blessing *borei m'orei ha'aish*. Now I know that the holy day of Shabbos is separated from the days of the week and one is forbidden to kindle a light on Shabbos." He then said, " Blessed is He who separates between the holy and the profane(*Pirkei d'Rabbi Eliezer,* chapter 20)

❧ God prepared for Adam two stones. He banged them against each other, and a fire emerged. He then said *havdalah* (*Midrash Shochar Tov* Psalms 92)

❧ Whoever fails to say *havdalah* on wine at the conclusion of Shabbos, or doesn't hear *havdalah* from someone who recites it will never see a sign of blessing. Whoever does hear *havdalah* from another, or does so himself on wine, God takes him in as a treasured possession (*Pirkei d'Rabbi Eliezer,* chapter 20)

havdallah distinguishes between the holy and the profane. it is made on wine, on נשׂמה spices, to revive us after losing our יתירה, and on a candle with two wicks, as Adam discovered fire on motzoei shabbos

הִנֵּה אֵל יְשׁוּעָתִי אֶבְטַח וְלֹא אֶפְחָד, כִּי עָזִּי וְזִמְרָת יָהּ יְיָ וַיְהִי לִי לִישׁוּעָה: וּשְׁאַבְתֶּם מַיִם בְּשָׂשׂוֹן, מִמַּעַיְנֵי הַיְשׁוּעָה: לַיְיָ הַיְשׁוּעָה, עַל עַמְּךָ בִרְכָתֶךָ סֶּלָה: יְיָ צְבָאוֹת עִמָּנוּ, מִשְׂגָּב לָנוּ אֱלֹהֵי יַעֲקֹב סֶלָה: יְיָ צְבָאוֹת אַשְׁרֵי אָדָם בֹּטֵחַ בָּךְ: יְיָ הוֹשִׁיעָה הַמֶּלֶךְ יַעֲנֵנוּ בְיוֹם קָרְאֵנוּ: לַיְּהוּדִים הָיְתָה אוֹרָה וְשִׂמְחָה וְשָׂשׂוֹן וִיקָר. כֵּן תִּהְיֶה לָּנוּ: כּוֹס יְשׁוּעוֹת אֶשָּׂא, וּבְשֵׁם יְיָ אֶקְרָא:

בָּרוּךְ אַתָּה יְיָ אֱלֹהֵינוּ מֶלֶךְ הָעוֹלָם בּוֹרֵא פְּרִי הַגָּפֶן:

בָּרוּךְ אַתָּה יְיָ אֱלֹהֵינוּ מֶלֶךְ הָעוֹלָם בּוֹרֵא מִינֵי בְשָׂמִים:

בָּרוּךְ אַתָּה יְיָ אֱלֹהֵינוּ מֶלֶךְ הָעוֹלָם בּוֹרֵא מְאוֹרֵי הָאֵשׁ:

בָּרוּךְ אַתָּה יְיָ אֱלֹהֵינוּ מֶלֶךְ הָעוֹלָם הַמַּבְדִּיל בֵּין קֹדֶשׁ לְחוֹל בֵּין אוֹר לְחֹשֶׁךְ בֵּין יִשְׂרָאֵל לָעַמִּים, בֵּין יוֹם הַשְּׁבִיעִי לְשֵׁשֶׁת יְמֵי הַמַּעֲשֶׂה. בָּרוּךְ אַתָּה יְיָ הַמַּבְדִּיל בֵּין קֹדֶשׁ לְחוֹל:

BEHOLD!

God is my salvation, I shall trust and not fear — for God is my might and my praise — Hashem — and He was a salvation for me. You can draw water with joy, from the springs of salvation. Salvation is Hashem's, upon Your people is Your blessing, Selah. Hashem, Master of legions, is with us, a stronghold for us is the God of Jacob, Selah. Hashem, Master of legions, praised is the man who trusts in You. Hashem save! May the King answer us on the day we call. For the Jews there was light, gladness, joy, and honor — So may it be for us. I will raise the cup of salvations, and I shall invoke the Name of Hashem.

By your leave, my masters and teachers:
BLESSED are You, Hashem, our God, King of the universe, Who creates the fruit of the vine.

After this blessing, smell the spices:
BLESSED are You, Hashem, our God, King of the universe, Who creates species of fragrance.

After the following blessing hold fingers up to the flame to see the reflected light:
BLESSED are You, Hashem, our God, King of the universe, Who creates the illuminations of the fire.

BLESSED are You, Hashem, our God, King of the universe, Who separates between holy and secular, between light and darkness, between Israel and the nations, between the seventh day and the six days of labor. Blessed are You, Hashem, Who separates between the holy and secular.

At the conclusion of the Sabbath begin:

HINAY *Ayl y'shu-osi, evtach v'lō efchod ki ozi v'zimros Yoh Adônoy, vai-hi li lishu-o. Ush-avtem ma-yim b'soson, mima-ainay hai-shu-o.*
LaAdōnoy hai-shu-o, al am'cho virchosecho selo. Adōnoy Tz'vo-ōs imonu, misgov lonu Elōhay ya-akōv selo. Adōnoy Tz'vo-ōs, ashray odom bōtay-ach boch. Adōnoy hōshi-o, hamelech ya-anaynu v'yôm kor-aynu. La-y'hudim hoy'so ōro v'simcho, v'soso⁻n vikor. kayn tih-ye lonu. Kōs y'shu-ōs eso, uvshaym Adōnoy ekro.
Savri moronon v'rabonon v'rabōsai:

BORUCH *ato Adōnoy, Elōhaynu melech ho-ōlom, bōray p'ri hagofen.*

All present respond: Omayn

After the following blessing smell the spices.
BORUCH *ato Adōnoy, Elōhaynu melech ho-ōlom, bōray minay v'somim.*
All present respond: Omayn

After the following blessing hold your fingers up to the flame to see the reflected light:

BORUCH *ato Adōnoy, Elōhaynu melech ho-ōlom, bōray m'ōray ho-aysh.*
All present respond: Omayn

BORUCH *ato Adōnoy, Elōhaynu melech ho-ōlom, hamavdil bayn kōdesh l'chōl, bayn ōr l'chōshech, bayn yisro-ayl lo-amim, bayn yōm hash'vi-i l'shayshes y'may hama-ase. Boruch ato Adōnoy, hamavdil bayn kōdesh l'chōl.*

All present respond: Omayn

dimension which was a semblance of the World to Come. The physical constraints that weigh down upon us, the petty, mundane activities that engage man will once again become part of us. On Shabbos, body and soul existed harmoniously, and that beloved spiritual union which existed for a twenty-four hour period will now end. Shabbos is a world where the spiritual dominates over the physical, and where the aspects of the physical are elevated to a more exalted level.

As Shabbos exits, we take leave of our *neshama yesairah*, our additional soul. The Talmud (*Beitzah* 16a) relates that on Shabbos we receive an expansiveness of heart to allow the coarse, physical body of man to accept the rarified blessings of Shabbos. We inhale the fragrant spices at the *havdalah* service, and on some level restore the sense of equilibrium to our lives. We recognize the gifts of the spiritual dimension, and we attempt to incorporate it into our lives on a day-to-day basis.

As we bid farewell with the *havdalah* lights, we are reaffirming the spiritual value system that our Sages have established for us. We elevate our senses and refine our priorities as we go through Shabbos, and hopefully allow Shabbos to permeate our being. Strengthened by our enriched sense of self and sense of purpose, we are ready to take on the week once more.

On Shabbos, body and soul existed harmoniously, and that beloved spiritual union which existed for a twenty-four hour period will now end.

Laws of Melava Malka
Escorting the Shabbos Queen

- *Melava malka*, literally, "to accompany the queen", is a meal eaten after the cessation of *Shabbos* as a way of bidding a respectful farewell to *Shabbos*.

- Both men and women should partake in *melava malka*

- Preferably, the meal should begin with bread. If this is difficult, one can fulfill his obligation with cake or even fruit. If this, too, is exceedingly difficult, coffee or tea may be drunk *(Shemiras Shabbos K'hilchoso)*

- It is preferable to eat *melava malka* as soon as possible after *havdalah*.

- The latest time for *melava malka* is midnight.

- Some have the custom of lighting candles in honor of *melava malka*.

- If possible one should avoid changing out of his *Shabbos* garments until after eating *melava malka*.

Havdalah
Elevating the Senses

s the last rays of Shabbos fade and the darkness that begins the new week descends upon us, we attempt to imbue the weekdays with the holiness of Shabbos. *Havdalah* is the prayer that was instituted to separate the holy and profane, light and darkness, Israel and the nations of the world and between Shabbos and the six days of the week. Sometimes, these distinctions are obvious; often, the nuances are subtle and need a keen eye and tremendous perception.

Havdalah speaks of four distinctions, and four blessings were instituted as part of the *havdalah* prayer. The order designated by our sages is יבנה, to build, a reference to the first letter of each of the blessings. יין = י, the blessing on wine; בשמים = ב, that of the spices; נר = נ, the blessing on the light; and הבדלה = ה, the blessing which outlines the four separations.

Kaf Hachaim, in the name of *Rashbatz*, discusses the particular order of the blessings and their significance. The various parts of man's head are employed in the *havdalah* ceremony. We begin with the mouth, the lowest orifice on the head. The drinking of the wine, which is preceded by the first blessing, enters the body through the mouth. Contact is at its most base level, as one cannot eat or drink unless there is actual engagement between his food and the mouth. The second blessing is on the spices. As we move up to the nose, the contact with that organ is one step removed. A smell can waft from one end of the room to the other and there is no physical contact with the nose.

The third blessing, made on the flame of the candle, moves one yet higher in the hierarchy of the senses. We hold our hand to the glow of the candle to discern its light. The visual process is even more refined than the other two contacts with the senses. One can see for miles, even up to the heavens, and there need be no actual physical contact at all with the eye. The last blessing takes us beyond the physical to the realm of the mind. We are unlimited in our thought processes. Wisdom, knowledge, imagination, discernment are the subject of the blessing wherein we differentiate between the holy and the profane. We are unencumbered by any physical contact, as we can engage with objects and concepts totally removed from the arena of the physical.

The order of the four blessings follows the pattern of the parts of the head that were engaged in the experience of Shabbos, a

THIS PRAYER, ATTRIBUTED TO R' LEVI YITZCHOK OF BERDITCHEV, BESEECHES GOD FOR SUCCESS, GOOD FORTUNE AND GOOD HEALTH AS WE BEGIN A NEW WEEK.

גאָט פון אברהם און פון יצחק, און פון יעקב, באהיט

דיין פאלק ישראל פון אלעם בייזין אין דיינם לויב
אז דער ליבער שבת קדש גייט אוועק, אז די וואך
זאל אונז קומען צו אמונה צו שלמה, צו אמונת חכמים,
צו אהבת ודבוק חברים טובים, צו דביקות הבורא ברוך הוא,
מאמין צו זיין בשלשה עשר עיקרים שלך ובגאולה שלמה
וקרובה במהרה בימינו ובתחיית המתים, ונבואת משה רבינו
ע"ה. רבונו של עולם, דו ביסט דאך הנותן ליעף כח, גיב דיינע
ליבע אידישע קינדערליך אויך דיר צו לויבין, און דיך צו
דיענען און ווייטער קיינעם נישט. און די וואך זאל אונז
קומען צו חסד, און צו מזל, און צו ברכה, און צו
הצלחה, און צו גזונט, און צו עושר וכבוד, און צו בני
חיי, ומזוני רויחי לנו ולכל ישראל, אמן:

THIS PRAYER FOR FORGIVENESS WAS COMPOSED BY YITZCHOK BEN CHAYATT OF THE 11th CENTURY. THE ACROSTIC SPELLS יצחק הקטן

המבדיל בין קדש לחול חטאתינו הוא

ימחל. זרענו וכספנו ירבה כחול
וככוכבים בלילה: יום פנה כצל תמר אקרא לאל עלי גמר. אמר
שומר אתא בקר וגם לילה: צדקתך כהר תבור על חטאי עבור
תעבור. כיום אתמול כי יעבר ואשמירה בלילה: חלפה עונת
מנחתי. מי יתן מנוחתי. יגעתי באנחתי אשחה בכל לילה: קולי
בל יוטל. פתח לי שער המנטל. שראשי נמלא טל קוצותי רסיסי
לילה: העתר נורא ואיום אשוע תנה פדיום. בנשף בערב יום
באישון לילה: קראתיך יה הושיעני אורח חיים תודיעני. מדלה תבצעני
מיום ועד לילה: טהר טנוף מעשי פן יאמרו מכעיסי. איה נא אלוה
עשי נותן זמירות בלילה: נחנו בידך כחמר סלח נא על
קל וחמר. יום ליום יביע אמר ולילה ללילה: המבדיל בין
קדש לחול חטאתינו הוא ימחל. זרענו וכספנו ירבה כחול
וככוכבים בלילה:

CONCLUSION OF SHABBOS

This prayer, attributed to R' Levi Yitzchok of Berditchov, beseeches God for success, good fortune and good health, as we begin a new week. It was composed in Yiddish, the language common to Eastern Europe, and is often recited by women before havdalah.

GOD OF ABRAHAM and of Isaac and of Jacob, protect your people, Israel, from all evil in Your praise — as the beloved, Holy Sabbath takes leave — that the coming week may arrive to bring perfect faith, faith in scholars, love of and association with good friends, attachment to the Creator, Blessed is He, to have faith in Your Thirteen Principles, and in the complete and imminent redemption, speedily in our days, in the revival of the dead and in the prophecy of our teacher, Moses, may peace be upon him.

Master of the universe, since You are the One Who gives strength to the weary, give Your beloved Jewish children the strength to praise You, and to serve only You and no other.

May this week arrive for lovingkindness, for good fortune, for blessing, for success, for good health, for wealth and honor, and for children, life and sustenance, for us and for all Israel. Amen.

The author, Yitzchok Hakoton, composed this zemer, recited after havdalah at the conclusion of Shabbos. As we leave the rarified atmosphere of Shabbos, and begin the week anew, we ask God to forgive our transgressions.

HAMAVDIL bayn kōdesh l'chōl,
Chatōsaynu hu yimchōl,
Zar-aynu v'chaspaynu yarbeh kachol,
V'chakōchovim baloyloh.

  Yōm ponoh k'tzayl tōmer,
  Ekro lo-Ayl olai gōmayr,
  Omar shōmayr,
  Oso vōker v'gam loyloh.

Tzidkos-cho k'har tovōr,
Al chato-ai ovor ta'avōr,
K'yōm esmol ki ya-avōr,
V'ashmuroh valoyloh.

  Cholfoh ōnas minchosi,
  Mi yitayn m'nuchosi,
  Yoga-ti v'anchosi,
  As-cheh v'chol loyloh.

Kōli bal yuntal,
P'sach li sha-ar hamnutol,
Sherōshi nimlo tol,
K'vutzosai r'sisay loyloh.

Hay-osayr nōro v'oyōm,
Ashavay-a t'noh fidyōm,
B'neshef b'erev yōm,
B'ishōn loyloh.

  K'rosicho Yoh hōshi-ayni,
  Ōrach chaim tōdi-ayni,
  Midaloh s'vatz-ayni,
  Miyōm v'ad loyloh.

Tahayr tinuf ma-asai,
Pen yōm'ru mach-isai,
Ayay no Elōha ōsōy,
Nōsayn z'mirōs baloyloh.

  Nachnu v'yodcho kachōmer,
  S'lach no al kal vochōmer,
  Yōm l'yōm yabi-a ōmer,
  V'lailoh l'loyloh.

Hamavdil bayn kōdesh l'chōl,
Chatōsaynu hu yimchōl,
Zar-aynu v'chaspaynu yarbeh kachōl,
V'chakōchovim baloyloh.

סדר קידוש לבנה

The blessing of Kiddush Levana is generally said outdoors, preferably with a minyan, usually on Motzoei Shabbos. One may begin saying it from 72 hours after the molad of the new moon through the fifteenth of the month.

הַלְלוּיָהּ הַלְלוּ אֶת יְיָ מִן הַשָּׁמַיִם. הַלְלוּהוּ בַּמְּרוֹמִים. הַלְלוּהוּ כָל מַלְאָכָיו, הַלְלוּהוּ כָּל צְבָאָיו. הַלְלוּהוּ שֶׁמֶשׁ וְיָרֵחַ, הַלְלוּהוּ כָּל כּוֹכְבֵי אוֹר. הַלְלוּהוּ שְׁמֵי הַשָּׁמַיִם וְהַמַּיִם אֲשֶׁר מֵעַל הַשָּׁמַיִם. יְהַלְלוּ אֶת שֵׁם יְיָ, כִּי הוּא צִוָּה וְנִבְרָאוּ. וַיַּעֲמִידֵם לָעַד לְעוֹלָם, חָק נָתַן וְלֹא יַעֲבוֹר.

One should look at the moon, then recite this blessing

בָּרוּךְ אַתָּה יְיָ אֱלֹהֵינוּ מֶלֶךְ הָעוֹלָם, אֲשֶׁר בְּמַאֲמָרוֹ בָּרָא שְׁחָקִים וּבְרוּחַ פִּיו כָּל צְבָאָם. חָק וּזְמַן נָתַן לָהֶם שֶׁלֹּא יְשַׁנּוּ אֶת תַּפְקִידָם. שָׂשִׂים וּשְׂמֵחִים לַעֲשׂוֹת רְצוֹן קוֹנָם, פּוֹעֵל אֱמֶת שֶׁפְּעֻלָּתוֹ אֱמֶת. וְלַלְּבָנָה אָמַר שֶׁתִּתְחַדֵּשׁ עֲטֶרֶת תִּפְאֶרֶת לַעֲמוּסֵי בָטֶן שֶׁהֵם עֲתִידִים לְהִתְחַדֵּשׁ כְּמוֹתָהּ, וּלְפָאֵר לְיוֹצְרָם עַל שֵׁם כְּבוֹד מַלְכוּתוֹ. בָּרוּךְ אַתָּה יְיָ מְחַדֵּשׁ חֳדָשִׁים.

Each of the following verses through אמן...סימן טוב is repeated three times.

בָּרוּךְ יוֹצְרֵךְ בָּרוּךְ עוֹשֵׂךְ בָּרוּךְ קוֹנֵךְ בָּרוּךְ בּוֹרְאֵךְ.

כְּשֵׁם שֶׁאֲנִי רוֹקֵד כְּנֶגְדֵּךְ וְאֵינִי יָכוֹל לִנְגֹּעַ בָּךְ כָּךְ לֹא יוּכְלוּ כָּל אוֹיְבַי לִנְגֹּעַ בִּי לְרָעָה.

תִּפּוֹל עֲלֵיהֶם אֵימָתָה וָפַחַד בִּגְדֹל זְרוֹעֲךָ יִדְּמוּ כָּאָבֶן.

כָּאָבֶן יִדְּמוּ זְרוֹעֲךָ בִּגְדֹל וָפַחַד אֵימָתָה עֲלֵיהֶם תִּפּוֹל.

דָּוִד מֶלֶךְ יִשְׂרָאֵל חַי וְקַיָּם.

The greeting שלום עליכם is said to three different people, and the three people respond. —עֲלֵיכֶם שָׁלוֹם.

שָׁלוֹם עֲלֵיכֶם.

סִימָן טוֹב וּמַזָּל טוֹב יְהֵא לָנוּ וּלְכָל יִשְׂרָאֵל. אָמֵן. קוֹל דּוֹדִי הִנֵּה זֶה בָּא מְדַלֵּג עַל הֶהָרִים מְקַפֵּץ עַל הַגְּבָעוֹת. דּוֹמֶה דּוֹדִי

שִׁיר לַמַּעֲלוֹת לִצְבִי אוֹ לְעֹפֶר הָאַיָּלִים הִנֵּה זֶה עוֹמֵד אַחַר כָּתְלֵנוּ, מַשְׁגִּיחַ מִן הַחַלֹּנוֹת, מֵצִיץ מִן הַחֲרַכִּים.

אֶשָּׂא עֵינַי אֶל הֶהָרִים מֵאַיִן יָבֹא עֶזְרִי. עֶזְרִי מֵעִם יְיָ עֹשֵׂה שָׁמַיִם וָאָרֶץ. אַל יִתֵּן לַמּוֹט רַגְלֶךָ אַל יָנוּם שֹׁמְרֶךָ. הִנֵּה לֹא יָנוּם וְלֹא יִישָׁן שׁוֹמֵר יִשְׂרָאֵל. יְיָ שֹׁמְרֶךָ, יְיָ צִלְּךָ עַל יַד יְמִינֶךָ. יוֹמָם הַשֶּׁמֶשׁ לֹא יַכֶּכָּה וְיָרֵחַ בַּלָּיְלָה. יְיָ יִשְׁמָרְךָ מִכָּל רָע יִשְׁמֹר אֶת נַפְשֶׁךָ. יְיָ יִשְׁמָר צֵאתְךָ וּבוֹאֶךָ מֵעַתָּה וְעַד עוֹלָם.

Kiddush Levanah / Blessing for the Moon

The Jewish calendar is based on the lunar cycle of 354 days to the year, and a twenty-nine day month. We sanctify the moon each month with the blessing of Kiddush Levana, as it is compared to greeting the Divine Presence (Talmud, Sanhedrin 42a). The history of the Jewish people parallels the cycle of the moon. Our national destiny rose for fifteen generations, from Abraham, who illuminated the world with his teachings about God, to King Solomon, who built the Holy Temple. With the reign of King Zidkiyahu and the destruction of the Temple, the spiritual climax achieved by Solomon began to wane. Kiddush levana expresses our fervent hope that "the Jewish people renew themselves like the moon," when it one day will radiate like the sun.

HALLELUYAH! Praise Hashem from the heavens; praise Him in the heights. Praise Him, all His angels; praise Him, all His legions. Praise Him, sun and moon; praise Him, all bright stars. Praise Him, the most exalted of the heavens and the waters that are above the heavens. Let them praise the Name of Hashem, for He commanded and they were created. And He established them forever and ever, He issued a decree that will not change.

Behold I am prepared and ready to perform the commandment to sanctify the moon. For the sake of the unification of the Holy One, Blessed is He, and His Presence, through Him Who is hidden and inscrutable - (I pray) in the name of all Israel.

One should look at the moon before reciting this blessing:

BLESSED are You, Hashem, our God, King of the Universe, Who with His utterance created the heavens, and with the breath of His mouth all their legion. A decree and a schedule did He give them that they not alter their assigned task. They are joyous and glad to perform the will of their Owner - the Worker of truth Whose work is truth. To the moon He said that it should renew itself as a crown of .splendor for those borne [by Him] from the womb, those who are destined to renew themselves like it, and to glorify their Molder for the name of His glorious kingdom. Blessed are You, Hashem, Who renews the months.

Recite the following phrases three times each: Blessed is your Molder; blessed is your Maker; blessed is your Owner; blessed is your Creator.

Upon reciting the next verse, rise on the toes as if in dance: Just as I dance toward you but cannot touch you, may none of my enemies be able to touch me for evil.

Let fall upon them fear and terror; at the greatness of Your arm, let them be still as stone. As stone let them be still, at Your arm's greatness; terror and fear, upon them let fall. David, King of Israel, is alive and enduring.

Extend greetings to three different people:
Peace upon you — *who respond*: Upon you, peace.

Recite three times: May there be a good sign and a good fortune for us and for all Israel. Amen.

הַלְלוּיָהּ הַלְלוּ אֵל בְּקָדְשׁוֹ, הַלְלוּהוּ בִּרְקִיעַ עֻזּוֹ. הַלְלוּהוּ כְרֹב גֻּדְלוֹ. הַלְלוּהוּ בְּתֵקַע שׁוֹפָר, הַלְלוּהוּ בְּנֵבֶל וְכִנּוֹר. הַלְלוּהוּ בְּתֹף וּמָחוֹל, הַלְלוּהוּ בְּמִנִּים וְעֻגָב. הַלְלוּהוּ בְצִלְצְלֵי שָׁמַע, הַלְלוּהוּ בְּצִלְצְלֵי תְרוּעָה. כֹּל הַנְּשָׁמָה תְּהַלֵּל יָהּ, הַלְלוּיָהּ.

תָּנָא דְּבֵי רַבִּי יִשְׁמָעֵאל: אִלְמָלֵי לֹא זָכוּ יִשְׂרָאֵל אֶלָּא לְהַקְבִּיל פְּנֵי אֲבִיהֶם שֶׁבַּשָּׁמַיִם פַּעַם אַחַת בַּחֹדֶשׁ, דַּיָּם. אָמַר אַבַּיֵי: הִלְכָּךְ צָרִיךְ לְמֵימְרָא מְעֻמָּד. מִי זֹאת עֹלָה מִן הַמִּדְבָּר מִתְרַפֶּקֶת עַל דּוֹדָהּ.

וִיהִי רָצוֹן מִלְּפָנֶיךָ יְיָ אֱלֹהַי וֵאלֹהֵי אֲבוֹתַי לְמַלֹּאת פְּגִימַת הַלְּבָנָה וְלֹא יִהְיֶה בָהּ שׁוּם מִעוּט, וְיִהְיֶה אוֹר הַלְּבָנָה כְּאוֹר הַחַמָּה, וּכְאוֹר שִׁבְעַת יְמֵי בְרֵאשִׁית כְּמוֹ שֶׁהָיְתָה קוֹדֶם מִעוּטָהּ, שֶׁנֶּאֱמַר: אֶת שְׁנֵי הַמְּאֹרֹת הַגְּדֹלִים. וְיִתְקַיֵּם בָּנוּ מִקְרָא שֶׁכָּתוּב: וּבִקְּשׁוּ אֶת יְיָ אֱלֹהֵיהֶם וְאֵת דָּוִיד מַלְכָּם. אָמֵן.

לַמְנַצֵּחַ בִּנְגִינֹת מִזְמוֹר שִׁיר. אֱלֹהִים יְחָנֵּנוּ וִיבָרְכֵנוּ, יָאֵר פָּנָיו אִתָּנוּ סֶלָה. לָדַעַת בָּאָרֶץ דַּרְכֶּךָ, בְּכָל גּוֹיִם יְשׁוּעָתֶךָ. יוֹדוּךָ עַמִּים אֱלֹהִים, יוֹדוּךָ עַמִּים כֻּלָּם. יִשְׂמְחוּ וִירַנְּנוּ לְאֻמִּים, כִּי תִשְׁפֹּט עַמִּים מִישֹׁר וּלְאֻמִּים בָּאָרֶץ תַּנְחֵם סֶלָה. יוֹדוּךָ עַמִּים אֱלֹהִים, יוֹדוּךָ עַמִּים כֻּלָּם. אֶרֶץ נָתְנָה יְבוּלָהּ, יְבָרְכֵנוּ אֱלֹהִים אֱלֹהֵינוּ. יְבָרְכֵנוּ אֱלֹהִים, וְיִירְאוּ אוֹתוֹ כָּל אַפְסֵי אָרֶץ.

ALENU IS SAID AFTER KIDDUSH LEVANA

Kiddush Levanah / Blessing for the Moon

The voice of my beloved – Behold! It came suddenly, leaping over mountains, skipping over hills. My beloved is like a gazelle or a young hart. Behold! He was standing behind our wall, observing through the windows, peering through the lattices.

A SONG TO THE ASCENTS. I raise my eyes to the mountains; whence will come my help? My help is from Hashem, Maker of heaven and earth. He will not allow your foot to falter; your Guardian will not slumber. Behold, He neither slumbers nor sleeps - the Guardian of Israel. Hashem is your Guardian; Hashem is your Shade at your right hand. By day the sun will not harm you, nor the moon by night. Hashem will protect you from every evil; He will guard your .soul. Hashem will guard your departure and your arrival, from this time and forever.

HALLELUYAH! Praise God in His Sanctuary; praise Him in the firmament of His power. Praise Him for His mighty acts; praise Him as befits His abundant greatness. Praise Him with the blast of the shofar; praise Him with lyre and harp. Praise Him with drum and dance; praise Him with organ and flute. Praise Him with clanging cymbals; praise him with resonant trumpets. Let all souls praise God, Halleluyah!

THE ACADEMY of Rabbi Yishmael taught: Had Israel not been privileged to greet the countenance of their Father in Heaven except for once a month - it would have sufficed them. Abaye said: Therefore one must recite it while standing. Who is this who rises from the desert clinging to her Beloved!

MAY IT BE Your will, Hashem, my God and the God of my forefathers, to fill the flaw of the moon that there be no diminution in it. May the light of the moon be like the light of the sun and like the light of the seven days of creation, as it was before it was diminished, as it is said: 'The two great luminaries. And may there be fulfilled upon us the verse that is written: They shall seek Hashem, their God, and David, their king. Amen.

FOR THE CONDUCTOR, upon Neginos, a psalm, a song. May God favor us and bless us, may He illuminate His countenance with us, Selah. To make known Your way on earth, among all the nations Your salvation. The peoples will acknowledge You, O God, the peoples will acknowledge You, all of them. Nations will be glad and sing for joy, because You will judge the peoples fairly and guide the nations on earth, Selah. Then peoples will acknowledge You, O God, the peoples will acknowledge You, all of them. The earth has yielded its produce, may God, our own God, bless us. May God bless us and may all the ends of the earth fear Him.

קִדּוּשׁ לְשָׁלֹשׁ רְגָלִים

IF THE FESTIVAL BEGINS ON FRIDAY NIGHT, BEGIN HERE:

(בלחש)וַיְהִי עֶרֶב וַיְהִי בֹקֶר : יוֹם הַשִּׁשִּׁי . וַיְכֻלּוּ
הַשָּׁמַיִם וְהָאָרֶץ וְכָל צְבָאָם . וַיְכַל אֱלֹהִים בַּיּוֹם
הַשְּׁבִיעִי מְלַאכְתּוֹ אֲשֶׁר עָשָׂה . וַיִּשְׁבֹּת בַּיּוֹם הַשְּׁבִיעִי
מִכָּל מְלַאכְתּוֹ אֲשֶׁר עָשָׂה . וַיְבָרֶךְ אֱלֹהִים אֶת יוֹם הַשְּׁבִיעִי
וַיְקַדֵּשׁ אֹתוֹ.כִּי בוֹ שָׁבַת מִכָּל מְלַאכְתּוֹ אֲשֶׁר בָּרָא אֱלֹהִים לַעֲשׂוֹת:

IF THE FESTIVAL FALLS ON A WEEKNIGHT, BEGIN:

סַבְרִי מָרָנָן וְרַבּוֹתַי: בָּרוּךְ אַתָּה יְיָ אֱלֹהֵינוּ מֶלֶךְ הָעוֹלָם
בּוֹרֵא פְּרִי הַגָּפֶן: בָּרוּךְ אַתָּה יְיָ אֱלֹהֵינוּ מֶלֶךְ
הָעוֹלָם אֲשֶׁר בָּחַר בָּנוּ מִכָּל עָם וְרוֹמְמָנוּ
מִכָּל לָשׁוֹן וְקִדְּשָׁנוּ בְּמִצְוֹתָיו . וַתִּתֶּן לָנוּ יְיָ
אֱלֹהֵינוּ בְּאַהֲבָה (on shabbos שַׁבָּתוֹת לִמְנוּחָה וּ)
מוֹעֲדִים לְשִׂמְחָה . חַגִּים וּזְמַנִּים לְשָׂשׂוֹן
אֶת יוֹם (on shabbos הַשַּׁבָּת הַזֶּה וְאֶת יוֹם)

SHMINI ATZERES	SUCCOS	SHAVUOS	PESACH)
חַג	חַג הַשָּׁבוּעוֹת	חַג הַסֻּכּוֹת	הַשְּׁמִינִי חַג
הַמַּצּוֹת	הַזֶּה . זְמַן	הַזֶּה.זְמַן	הָעֲצֶרֶת הַזֶּה.
הַזֶּה.זְמַן חֵרוּתֵנוּ	מַתַּן תּוֹרָתֵנוּ	שִׂמְחָתֵנוּ	זְמַן שִׂמְחָתֵנוּ

(on shabbos בְּאַהֲבָה) מִקְרָא קֹדֶשׁ זֵכֶר לִיצִיאַת מִצְרָיִם. כִּי בָנוּ
בָחַרְתָּ וְאוֹתָנוּ קִדַּשְׁתָּ מִכָּל הָעַמִּים.(on shabbos וְשַׁבָּת)וּמוֹעֲדֵי
קָדְשֶׁךָ(on shabbos בְּאַהֲבָה וּבְרָצוֹן) בְּשִׂמְחָה וּבְשָׂשׂוֹן הִנְחַלְתָּנוּ.
בָּרוּךְ אַתָּה יְיָ מְקַדֵּשׁ(on shabbos הַשַּׁבָּת וְ)יִשְׂרָאֵל וְהַזְּמַנִּים.

ON THE FIRST NIGHT OF SUCCOS, RECITE THE בְרכה בסוכה OF לישב BEFORE THE שהחיינו.

בָּרוּךְ אַתָּה יְיָ אֱלֹהֵינוּ מֶלֶךְ הָעוֹלָם אֲשֶׁר קִדְּשָׁנוּ בְּמִצְוֹתָיו וְצִוָּנוּ לֵישֵׁב
בַּסֻּכָּה: THE שהחיינו IS OMITTED ON THE LAST TWO NIGHTS OF PASSOVER. בָּרוּךְ אַתָּה יְיָ
אֱלֹהֵינוּ מֶלֶךְ הָעוֹלָם שֶׁהֶחֱיָנוּ וְקִיְּמָנוּ וְהִגִּיעָנוּ לַזְּמַן הַזֶּה: IF THE FESTIVAL
שהחיינו OF ברכה OCCURS ON SATURDAY NIGHT, RECITE THE FOLLOWING TWO BLESSINGS BEFORE THE

בָּרוּךְ אַתָּה יְיָ אֱלֹהֵינוּ מֶלֶךְ הָעוֹלָם בּוֹרֵא מְאוֹרֵי הָאֵשׁ:בָּרוּךְ אַתָּה
יְיָ אֱלֹהֵינוּ מֶלֶךְ הָעוֹלָם הַמַּבְדִּיל בֵּין קֹדֶשׁ לְחוֹל בֵּין אוֹר
לְחֹשֶׁךְ בֵּין יִשְׂרָאֵל לָעַמִּים . בֵּין יוֹם הַשְּׁבִיעִי לְשֵׁשֶׁת יְמֵי הַמַּעֲשֶׂה
בֵּין קְדֻשַּׁת שַׁבָּת לִקְדֻשַּׁת יוֹם טוֹב הִבְדַּלְתָּ . וְאֶת יוֹם
הַשְּׁבִיעִי מִשֵּׁשֶׁת יְמֵי הַמַּעֲשֶׂה קִדַּשְׁתָּ.הִבְדַּלְתָּ וְקִדַּשְׁתָּ
אֶת עַמְּךָ יִשְׂרָאֵל בִּקְדֻשָּׁתֶךָ . בָּרוּךְ אַתָּה יְיָ
הַמַּבְדִּיל בֵּין קֹדֶשׁ לְקֹדֶשׁ:

Kiddush for the Festivals

On Friday night begin here; on other nights begin below.
(Vaihi erev vaihi vōker) **YŌM HA-SHISHI**.
Vaichulu ha-shoma-yim v'ho-oretz v'chol tz'vo-om. Vaichal
Elōhim ba-yōm hash'vi-i m'lachtō asher oso, va-yishbōs ba-yōm
hash'vi-i mikol m'lachtō asher oso. Vaivorech Elōhim es yōm hash'vi i
vaika daysh ōsō, ki vō shovas miko'l m'lachtō asher boro Elōhim la-asōs.

On all nights continue here: Savri moronon v'rabonon v'rabōsai:
BORUCH ato Adōnoy Elōhaynu melech ho-ōlom, bōray p'ri hagofen.

All present respond: Omayn
BORUCH ato Adōnoy Elōhaynu melech ho-ōlom, asher bochar bonu mikol
om v'rōm'monu mikol loshōn, v'kid'shonu b'mitzvōsov. Vatiten lonu Adōnoy
Elōhaynu b'ahavo, *(Shabbos) shabosōs limnucho u* ... mō-adim l'simcho,
chagim uz'manim l'sosōn, *(Shabbos) es yōm ha-shabos ha-ze v'* ...

Passover	Shavuos
es yōm chag hamatzōs ha-ze z'man chayrusaynu,	es yōm chag hashovu-ōs ha-ze, z'man matan tōrosaynu,
Succos	**Shemini Atzeres/Simchas Torah**
es yōm chag hasukōs ha-ze z'man simchosaynu	es yōm hash'mini chag ho-atzeres ha-ze, z'man simchosaynu

Shabbos: b'ahavo mikro kōdesh, zaycher litzi-as Mitzro-yim.
Ki vonu vocharto, v'ōsonu kidashto mikol ho-amim, *(Shabbos: v'Shabbos)*
u-mō-aday kod'shecho *(Shabbos: b'ahavo)* uvrotzōn b'simcho uvsosōn
hinchaltonu: Boruch ato Adōnoy, m'kadaysh
(Shabbos: hashabos v') ... yisro-ayl v'haz'manim. *All respond:* Omayn

*On Saturday night, two candles with flames touching are held and the follow ing blessings are recited.
After the first blessing, hold the fingers up to the flames to see the reflected light.*
BORUCH ato Adōnoy Elōhaynu melech ho-ōlom, bōray m'ōray ho-aysh.

All respond: Omayn
BORUCH ato Adōnoy, Elōhaynu melech ho-ōlom, hamavdil bayn kōdesh l'chōl, bayn
ōr l'chōshech, bayn Yisro-ayl lo-amim, bayn yōm hash'vi-i, l'shayshes y'may hama-ase,
bayn k'dushas Shabbos lik dushas yōm tōv hivdalto, v'es yōm hash'vi-i mi-shayshes
y'may hama-ase kidashto, hivdalto v'kidashto es am'cho yisro-ayl bik dushosecho.
Boruch ato Adōnoy hamavdil bayn kōdesh l'kōdesh.
All respond: Omayn

On Succos the following blessing is recited in the succah.
BORUCH ato Adōnoy Elōhaynu melech ho-ōlom, asher kid'shonu b'mitzvōsov
v'tzivonu layshayv basuko. *All respond:* Omayn

The following blessing is omitted on the last two nights of Pesach.
BORUCH ato Adōnoy Elōhaynu melech ho-ōlom, shehecheyonu
v'ki-y'monu v'higi-onu laz'man ha-ze.
All respond: Omayn

Jewish Music – Window Of The Soul

he Psalms of King David, the sweet singer of Israel, reach down to the depths of man's soul, touching a chord that runs the gamut of emotion. Reflecting the ecstasy of a festive occasion, the sorrow of a melancholy moment, and the yearning for salvation in times of despair, the song stirs the innermost recesses of our being.

The Talmud *(Pesachim 117a)* tells us, "sometimes we find the phrase מזמור לדוד, there is a song to David, while at other times the verse is stated as לדוד מזמור, to David there is a song." The change in text is not mere poetic license by the master of Jewish song. The interpretation given is that לדוד מזמור is the Divine presence resting on King David, and from that oneness with God, a song bursts forth. מזמור לדוד is the song composed by the Psalmist, and through that song the Divine Ppresence rested upon him.

The festive tune for the reading of the *megillah,* the despondent lament for the reading of איכה, do more than help us express the mood of the day; through song they hope to bring us closer to the Divine Presence. The medieval lyricist sings of לכל שיריך אני כנור. "For all your songs I am a harp". God plays upon the soul of man and hopefully we can play to the tune he has set out for us. But King David tells us of how much more we can do in helping create the music, the mood and even write the lyrics. ואני תפלתי, I am the essence of prayer, the ultimate expression of thanks, of sorrow, of pathos and of joy. All of these are found in my soul and can be released to play their tune — if we will but let them. Each one of us can create a מזמור לדוד, using song as the means to bring us close to God.

The *chassidic* masters of past eras left us a legacy of the *"chassidic nigun,"* an exultant march, a joyful refrain, a soulful chant which seems to virtually carry us to a higher plane. For them words can only inhibit, not allowing the pristine emotion that was welling within to come to the fore. What would we give to hear a *nigun* that was sung in the *Bais Hamikdash,* imbued with sanctity, truly a heavenly emanation that was rechanneled in his service?!

When King Solomon wrote כבד את ה מהונך, honor God with your wealth, our Sages, in a play on the word מהונך read it as מגרונך, from your voice. A pleasant voice can be a vessel used in the service of Hashem no less than the vessels used in the *Bais Hamikdash* which were consecrated for Divine service. Jewish song, in its pure untainted form can elevate and inspire, rejuvenate and uplift. Many people see listening to music as a passive experience, taking in the sounds around us, delighting in a harmonious blend of voices and instruments. For Jews, song is another tool fashioned to bring glory to His name, and we are the key players. Just as the angels above sing praises to Hashem, man can exalt his Creator through the songs of his soul.

For Jews, song is another tool fashioned to bring glory to His name, and we are the key players.

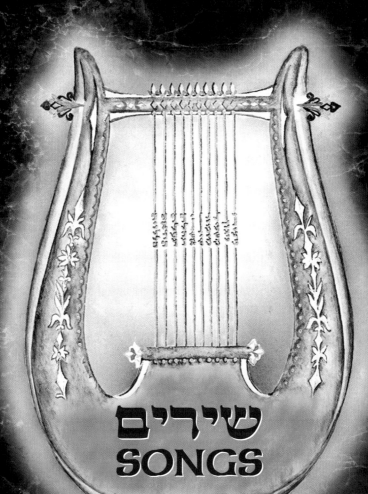

שירים
SONGS

Wedding Songs
שירי חתונה

1. ŌD YISHOMA *b'oray Yehudoh u'vchutzōs Y'rusholoyim kōl sosōn v'kōl simchoh kōl choson v'kōl kaloh.*

עוֹד יִשָּׁמַע **עוֹד יִשָּׁמַע** בְּעָרֵי יְהוּדָה וּבְחֻצוֹת יְרוּשָׁלַיִם קוֹל שָׂשׂוֹן וְקוֹל שִׂמְחָה קוֹל חָתָן וְקוֹל כַּלָה

May there still be heard in the cities of Judah and the outskirts of Jerusalem the words of gladness, the voice of joy, the voice of the bridegroom, the voice of the bride.

2. ASHER BORO *sosōn v'simchoh, choson v'chaloh, giloh, rinoh, ditzoh, v'chedvoh, ahavoh, v'achavoh, v'sholōm v'rayus. M'hayroh Hashem Elōkaynu yishoma b'oray Y'hudoh, uvchutzōs Y'rushola-yim, kōl sosōn v'kōl simchoh, kōl choson v'kōl kaloh.*

אֲשֶׁר בָּרָא **אֲשֶׁר בָּרָא** שָׂשׂוֹן וְשִׂמְחָה חָתָן וְכַלָה גִּילָה רִנָה דִּיצָה וְחֶדְוָה אַהֲבָה וְאַחֲוָה וְשָׁלוֹם וְרֵעוּת. מְהֵרָה ה' אֱלֹקֵינוּ יִשָּׁמַע בְּעָרֵי יְהוּדָה וּבְחֻצוֹת יְרוּשָׁלַיִם קוֹל שָׂשׂוֹן וְקוֹל שִׂמְחָה קוֹל חָתָן וְקוֹל כַּלָה

[Blessed is He] Who created joy and gladnesss, groom and bride, mirth, glad song, pleasure, delight, love, brotherhood, peace and friendship. May there soon be heard, Hashem our God, in the cities of Judah and the streets of Jerusalem, the sound of joy and sound of gladness, the voice of the groom and the voice of the bride.

3. KAYTZAD M'RAKDIM *lifnay hakaloh, kaloh no-oh vachasudoh.*

כֵּיצַד מְרַקְּדִין **כֵּיצַד מְרַקְּדִין** לִפְנֵי הַכַּלָה. כַּלָה נָאָה וַחֲסוּדָה

How do we dance before the bride? [We say] a beautiful and righteous bride.

4. VAIHI *vishurun melech b'his-asayf roshay om, yachad shivtay Yisro-ayl. Ōd yishoma b'oray Y'hudoh, uvchutzōs Y'rusholoyim, kōl sosōn, v'kōl simchoh, kōl choson v'kōl kaloh.*

וַיְהִי בִישׁוּרוּן **וַיְהִי בִישׁוּרוּן** מֶלֶךְ בְּהִתְאַסֵּף רָאשֵׁי עָם יַחַד שִׁבְטֵי יִשְׂרָאֵל עוֹד יִשָּׁמַע בְּעָרֵי יְהוּדָה וּבְחֻצוֹת יְרוּשָׁלַיִם קוֹל שָׂשׂוֹן וְקוֹל שִׂמְחָה קוֹל חָתָן וְקוֹל כַּלָה

He became King over Jeshurun when the numbers of the nation gathered, together the tribes of Israel. There will yet be heard in the cities of Jerusalem and in the streets of Jerusalem, the sound of joy and the sound of gladness, the voice of the groom and the voice of the bride.

5. SIMON TŌV *umazol tōv y'hay lonu ulchol Yisro-ayl, omayn.*

סִימָן טוֹב **סִימָן טוֹב** וּמַזָל טוֹב יְהֵא לָנוּ וּלְכָל יִשְׂרָאֵל אָמֵן

May we and all Israel have a good sign and good luck, Amen.

6. YOSIS *ola-yich Elokoyich, kimsōs choson al kaloh.*

יָשִׂישׂ עָלַיִךְ **יָשִׂישׂ עָלַיִךְ** אֱלֹקַיִךְ כִּמְשׂוֹשׂ חָתָן עַל כַּלָה

May God rejoice over you as a groom rejoices over a bride.

לא איש ולא אשה
ולא איש לא אשה

Man is incomplete without woman
and woman is incomplete without man

ולא שניהם ולא שכינה

And both are incomplete
without the divine presence

midrash rabbah-bereishis 8:9

Songs of Jerusalem

שִׁירֵי יְרוּשָׁלַיִם

7. YIBONEH hamikdosh,
ir Tziyon t'malay, v'shom noshir
shir chodosh, uvirnonoh na-aleh.

יִבָּנֶה הַמִּקְדָּשׁ עִיר צִיּוֹן תְּמַלֵּא וְשָׁם נָשִׁיר שִׁיר חָדָשׁ וּבִרְנָנָה נַעֲלֶה

May the Temple be rebuilt, may Zion be fulfilled, and there we shall sing a new song, and go up in jubilation.

8. U'VO'U ho-ōvdim b'eretz Ashur,
v'hanidochim b'eretz Mitzrayim,
v'hishtachavu la'Hashem
b'har hakōdesh bi'Y'rusholoyim

וּבָאוּ הָאֹבְדִים בְּאֶרֶץ אַשּׁוּר וְהַנִּדָּחִים בְּאֶרֶץ מִצְרָיִם וְהִשְׁתַּחֲווּ לַה' בְּהַר הַקֹּדֶשׁ בִּירוּשָׁלָיִם

And those who are lost in the land of Assyria and those cast away in the land of Egypt will come together and ill bow down to Hashem on the holy mountain of Jerusalem.

9. RACHAYM no Hashem Elōkaynu,
al Yisro-ayl amecho, v'al Y'rusholoyim
irecho, v'al Tziyōn mishkan k'vōdecho,
v'al malchus bays Dovid m'shichecho,
v'al habayis hagodōl v'hakodōsh.

רַחֵם נָא ה' אֱלֹקֵינוּ עַל יִשְׂרָאֵל עַמֶּךָ וְעַל יְרוּשָׁלַיִם עִירֶךָ וְעַל צִיּוֹן מִשְׁכַּן כְּבוֹדֶךָ וְעַל מַלְכוּת בֵּית דָּוִד מְשִׁיחֶךָ וְעַל הַבַּיִת הַגָּדוֹל וְהַקָּדוֹשׁ

Please have mercy, Hashem our God, on Israel Your nation, and on Jerusalem Your city, and on Zion the sanctuary of Your glory, and on the kingdom of the house of David Your annointed one, and on the great and holy Temple.

10. V'LIRUSHOLA-YIM ircho
b'rachamim toshuv v'siskōn b'sōchoh
ka-asher dibarto, uv'nay ōsoh b'korōv,
b'yomaynu binyan ōlom, v'chisay Dovid
avd'cho, ma'hayroh l'sōchoh tochin.

וְלִירוּשָׁלַיִם עִירֶךָ בְּרַחֲמִים תָּשׁוּב וְתִשְׁכּוֹן בְּתוֹכָהּ כַּאֲשֶׁר דִּבַּרְתָּ וּבְנֵה אוֹתָהּ בְּקָרוֹב בְּיָמֵינוּ בִּנְיַן עוֹלָם וְכִסֵּא דָוִד מְהֵרָה לְתוֹכָהּ תָּכִין

Return, out of compassion, to Jerusalem Your city, and reside in it as You spoke, and build it soon, in our days, an eternal structure, and establish the throne of David Your servant there swiftly.

11. IM ESHKOCHAYCH
Y'rusholoyim tishkach y'mini. Tidbak l'shō
ni l'chiki im lō ezk'raychi, im lō
a-aleh es Y'rusholoyim al rōsh simchosi.

אִם אֶשְׁכָּחֵךְ יְרוּשָׁלַיִם תִּשְׁכַּח יְמִינִי. תִּדְבַּק לְשׁוֹנִי לְחִכִּי אִם לֹא אֶזְכְּרֵכִי אִם לֹא אַעֲלֶה אֶת יְרוּשָׁלַיִם עַל רֹאשׁ שִׂמְחָתִי

If I forget thee, Jerusalem, let my right hand's skill be forgotten. Let my tongue cleave to my palate if I don't remember You. If I fail to elevate Jerusalem above my highest joy.

12. L'SHONO HABO-OH
bYerushalayim hab'nuyo

לְשָׁנָה הַבָּאָה בִּירוּשָׁלַיִם הַבְּנוּיָה

Next year in the rebuilt Jerusalem

13. OVINU MALKAYNU

p'sach sha-aray shomayim lis'filosaynu.

אָבִינוּ מַלְכֵּנוּ! אָבִינוּ מַלְכֵּנוּ
פְּתַח שַׁעֲרֵי שָׁמַיִם לִתְפִלָּתֵנוּ

Our Father, our King, open the gates of Heaven to our prayers.

14. AHAVAS ŌLOM tovi lohem,
u'vris ovōs labonim tizkōr.

אַהֲבַת עוֹלָם אַהֲבַת עוֹלָם
תָּבִיא לָהֶם וּבְרִית אָבוֹת לַבָּנִים תִּזְכּוֹר

Bring them eternal love, and remember the covenant of the forefathers for the sons.

15. ACHAS SHO-ALTI may-ays
Hashem, ōsoh avakaysh. Shivti b'vays
Hashem, kol y'may cha-yai, lachazōs
b'nō-am Hashem ulvakayr b'haycholō.

אַחַת שָׁאַלְתִּי אַחַת שָׁאַלְתִּי
מֵאֵת ה' אוֹתָהּ אֲבַקֵּשׁ שִׁבְתִּי בְּבֵית
ה' כָּל יְמֵי חַיַּי לַחֲזוֹת בְּנֹעַם ה' וּלְבַקֵּר
בְּהֵיכָלוֹ

One thing I request of God, only that will I seek: to dwell in the house of God all the days of my life,
to behold the pleasantness of God and to meditate in His Sanctuary.

16. ACHAYNU kol bays Yisro-ayl,
han'sunim b'tzoroh uv'shivyoh,
ho-ōmdim bayn ba-yom uvayn
ba-yaboshoh, haMakōm y'rachaym
alayhem v'yōtzi-aym mitzoroh lirvochoh,
umay-afayloh l'ōroh, umishibud lig'ulah,
hashto ba-agolo u-vizman koriv v'nōmar omayn.

אַחֵינוּ אַחֵינוּ כָּל בֵּית
יִשְׂרָאֵל הַנְּתוּנִים בְּצָרָה וּבַשִּׁבְיָה
הָעוֹמְדִים בֵּין בַּיָּם וּבֵין בַּיַּבָּשָׁה הַמָּקוֹם
יְרַחֵם עֲלֵיהֶם וְיוֹצִיאֵם מִצָּרָה לִרְוָחָה
וּמֵאֲפֵלָה לְאוֹרָה וּמִשִּׁעְבּוּד לִגְאֻלָּה
הַשְׁתָּא בַּעֲגָלָא וּבִזְמַן קָרִיב וְנֹאמַר אָמֵן

If any of our brothers, from the entire house of Israel, find themselves in trouble or in captivity, whether
they are at sea or on dry land, may God have mercy on them and deliver them from trouble to well being,
from darkness to light, from captivity to redemption, speedily, swiftly, and soon, and let us say amen.

17. AYN KAYLŌKAYNU,
ayn kadōnaynu, ayn k'malkaynu,
ayn k'mōshi-aynu; mi chaylōkaynu,
mi chadōnaynu, mi ch'malkaynu,
mi ch'mōshi-aynu.

אֵין כֵּאלֹקֵינוּ אֵין כֵּאלֹקֵינוּ
אֵין כַּאדוֹנֵינוּ אֵין כְּמַלְכֵּנוּ אֵין
כְּמוֹשִׁיעֵנוּ. מִי כֵאלֹקֵינוּ מִי כַאדוֹנֵינוּ
מִי כְמַלְכֵּנוּ מִי כְמוֹשִׁיעֵנוּ

There is none like our God, there is none like our Master, there is none like our King, there is none like our Savior.

18. AYN ARŌCH *l'cho Hashem Elōkaynu bo-ōlom hazeh, v'ayn zuloscho malkaynu l'chayay ho'ōlom habo, efes bilt'cho gō'alaynu limōs hamoshiach, v'ayn dōmeh lecho mōshiaynu lischiyas hamaysim.*

אֵין עֲרוֹךְ לְךָ
ה' אֱלֹקֵינוּ בָּעוֹלָם הַזֶּה וְאֵין זוּלָתְךָ
מַלְכֵּנוּ לְחַיֵּי הָעוֹלָם הַבָּא אֶפֶס בִּלְתְּךָ
גּוֹאֲלֵנוּ לִימוֹת הַמָּשִׁיחַ. וְאֵין דּוֹמֶה לְךָ
מוֹשִׁיעֵנוּ לִתְחִיַּת הַמֵּתִים

There is no comparison to You, Hashem our God in this world; and there will be nothing except for You, our King, in the life of the World to Come; there will be nothing without You, our Redeemer, in the Messianic days; and there will be none like You, our Savior, at the Resuscitation of the Dead.

19. AYLECHO *Hashem ekro, v'el Hashem eschanon. Sh'ma Hashem v'chonayni, Hashem he-yay ōzer li.*

אֵלֶיךָ ה' אֶקְרָא
וְאֶל ה' אֶתְחַנָּן. שְׁמַע ה' וְחָנֵּנִי ה' הֱיֵה
עֹזֵר לִי

I call out to You, God, and to God I beseech. Hearken God and be good to me; God, be my helper.

20. ELŌKIM *tz'vokōs shuv no, habayt mishomayim u'ray u'fkōd gefen zōs v'chano asher not'oh y'minecho v'al bayn imatztoh loch.*

אֱלֹקִים צְבָקוֹת
שׁוּב נָא הַבֵּט מִשָּׁמַיִם וּרְאֵה וּפְקֹד גֶּפֶן
זֹאת וְכַנָּה אֲשֶׁר־נָטְעָה יְמִינֶךָ וְעַל־בֵּן
אִמַּצְתָּה לָּךְ

God of Hosts, return, we beseech You. Look down from heaven and see, and be mindful of this vine, and of the foundation which Your right hand has planted, and upon the son whom You strengthened for Yourself.

21. ANI MA-AMIN *b'emunoh sh'laymoh b'vi-as hamoshi-ach, v'af al pi sheyismamay-ah, im kol zeh achakeh lō b'chol yōm she-yovō.*

אֲנִי מַאֲמִין
בֶּאֱמוּנָה שְׁלֵמָה בְּבִיאַת הַמָּשִׁיחַ וְאַף
עַל פִּי שֶׁיִּתְמַהְמֵהַּ עִם כָּל זֶה אֲחַכֶּה
לוֹ בְּכָל יוֹם שֶׁיָּבוֹא

I believe with perfect faith that the Messiah will come; and even though he tarries, nevertheless I will expect his arrival every day.

22. ANI MA-AMIN *b'emunoh sh'laymoh, shehabōray yisborach shmō hu bōray u'manhig l'chol hab'ru-im, v'hu l'vadō osoh v'ōseh, v'ya-aseh l'chol hama-asim.*

אֲנִי מַאֲמִין
בֶּאֱמוּנָה שְׁלֵמָה שֶׁהַבּוֹרֵא יִתְבָּרַךְ שְׁמוֹ
הוּא בּוֹרֵא וּמַנְהִיג לְכָל הַבְּרוּאִים וְהוּא
לְבַדּוֹ עָשָׂה וְעוֹשֶׂה וְיַעֲשֶׂה לְכָל הַמַּעֲשִׂים.

I believe with complete faith that the Creator, blessed is His Name, creates and guides all creatures, and that He alone made, makes and will make everything.

23. ANI HASHEM *Elokaychem emes*

אֲנִי ה' אֱלֹקֵיכֶם: אֱמֶת אֲנִי ה'

I am Hashem, your God, it is true

24. ONO HASHEM, *chi ani avd'cho, ani avd'cho ben amosecho, pitachto l'mosayroy.*

אָנָּה ה' כִּי אֲנִי אָנָּה ה'
עַבְדֶּךָ אֲנִי עַבְדְּךָ בֶּן אֲמָתֶךָ פִּתַּחְתָּ
לְמוֹסֵרָי

Please, Hashem, for I am Your servant, I am Your servant, the son of Your handmaid, You have released my bonds.

25. ESO EINAI *el hehorim, may'ayin yovō ezri? Ezri mayim Hashem, ōseh shomayim vo'oretz.*

אֶשָּׂא עֵינַי אֶל אֶשָּׂא עֵינַי
הֶהָרִים מֵאַיִן יָבוֹא עֶזְרִי: עֶזְרִי מֵעִם ה'
עֹשֵׂה שָׁמַיִם וָאָרֶץ: הִנֵּה לֹא יָנוּם וְלֹא
יִישָׁן שׁוֹמֵר יִשְׂרָאֵל

I will life my eyes to the mountains, from where will my help come? My help will come from God, Who makes heaven and earth.

26. ATOH TOKUM, *t'rachaym Tziyon, ki ays l'chen'no ki vo mo'ayd.*

אַתָּה תָקוּם אַתָּה תָקוּם
תְּרַחֵם צִיּוֹן כִּי עֵת לְחֶנְנָהּ כִּי בָא מוֹעֵד

You will arise, and have mercy on Zion, for it is time to be gracious to her, for the appointed time has come.

27. BILVOVI *mishkon evneh, l'hadar k'vodo, uvamishkon mizbayach osim, l'karnay hodo. Ul'nayr tomid ekach li, es aysh ho-akaydoh, ulkorbon akriv lo es nafshi ha-y'chidoh.*

בְּלִבָּבִי מִשְׁכָּן בִּלְבָבִי
אֶבְנֶה לַהֲדַר כְּבוֹדוֹ. וּבַמִּשְׁכָּן מִזְבֵּחַ
אָשִׂים לְקַרְנֵי הוֹדוֹ. וּלְנֵר תָּמִיד אֶקַּח לִי
אֵת אֵשׁ הָעֲקֵדָה וּלְקָרְבָּן אַקְרִיב לוֹ
אֵת נַפְשִׁי הַיְחִדָה.

I will erect a sanctuary in my heart to glorify His honor, and I will place an altar in the sanctuary to the glories of His splendor. For the eternal light I will take the fire of the Akeda, and for a sacrifice I will offer my soul, my unique soul.

28. BORUCH *Elōkaynu shebro-onu lichvōdō, v'hivdilonu min hatō-im, v'nosan lonu Toras emes, v'cha-yay ōlom nota b'sōchaynu.*

בָּרוּךְ אֱלֹקֵינוּ בָּרוּךְ אֱלֹקֵינוּ
שֶׁבְּרָאָנוּ לִכְבוֹדוֹ וְהִבְדִּילָנוּ מִן הַתּוֹעִים
וְנָתַן לָנוּ תּוֹרַת אֱמֶת וְחַיֵּי עוֹלָם נָטַע
בְּתוֹכֵנוּ

Blessed is G-d, Who created us for His glory, and set us apart from those who are misled, and gave us the Torah of truth, and planted eternal life in our midst.

29. DOVID melech Yisro-ayl chai v'ka-yom. Simon tōv umazol tōv y'hay lonu ulchol Yisro-ayl, omayn.

דָּוִד מֶלֶךְ יִשְׂרָאֵל חַי וְקַיָּם. סִימָן טוֹב וּמַזָּל טוֹב יְהֵא לָנוּ וּלְכָל יִשְׂרָאֵל אָמֵן

David, King of Israel, lives forever. May we and all Israel have a good sign and good luck, amen.

30. HASHEM Elōkay Yisro-ayl, shuv maycharōn apecho, v'hinochem al ho'ro-oh l'amecho.

ה' אֱלֹקֵי יִשְׂרָאֵל שׁוּב מֵחֲרוֹן אַפֶּךָ וְהִנָּחֵם עַל הָרָעָה לְעַמֶּךָ:

Hashem, God of Israel, relent from Your wrath, and reconsider regarding the bad decree against Your people.

31. HAKŌL yōducho, v'hakōl y'shabchucho, v'hakōl yōmru ayn kodōsh kaHashem; hakōl y'rom'mucho seloh, yōtzayr hakōl.

הַכֹּל יוֹדוּךָ וְהַכֹּל יְשַׁבְּחוּךָ וְהַכֹּל יֹאמְרוּ אֵין קָדוֹשׁ כַּה': הַכֹּל יְרוֹמְמוּךָ סֶלָה יוֹצֵר הַכֹּל

All shall thank You, and all shall praise You, and all shall say, there is none holy like God; all shall exalt You, sela, Creator of all.

32. HINAY onōchi shōlayach lochem, ays Eliyohu hanovi, lifnay bō yom Hashem hagodōl v'hanōro. V'hayshiv layv ovōs al bonim v'layv bonim al avōsom.

הִנֵּה אָנֹכִי שֹׁלֵחַ לָכֶם אֶת אֵלִיָּהוּ הַנָּבִיא לִפְנֵי בּוֹא יוֹם ה' הַגָּדוֹל וְהַנּוֹרָא. וְהֵשִׁיב לֵב-אָבוֹת עַל-בָּנִים וְלֵב בָּנִים עַל-אֲבוֹתָם

Behold I will send you Elijah the prophet, before the coming of the great and awesome day. And he shall return the hearts of the fathers to the sons, and the hearts of the sons to the fathers.

33. HINAY lō yonum v'lō yishon shōmer Yisro-ayl.

הִנֵּה לֹא יָנוּם וְלֹא יִישָׁן שׁוֹמֵר יִשְׂרָאֵל

Behold the Guardian of Israel does not slumber and does not sleep.

34. HINAY yomim bo-im, v'hishlachti ro-ov bo-oretz, lō ro-ov lalechem v'lō tzomo lama-yim, ki im lishmō-a ays divray Hashem.

הִנֵּה יָמִים בָּאִים וְהִשְׁלַחְתִּי רָעָב בָּאָרֶץ ... לֹא רָעָב לַלֶּחֶם וְלֹא צָמָא לְמַיִם כִּי אִם לִשְׁמֹעַ אֶת דְּבַר ה'

Behold, days are coming, and I will send a famine in the land; not a famine for bread, nor a thirst for water, but for learning the words of God.

35. HAMALOCH hagō-ayl ōsi mikol ro, y'voraych es han'orim, v'yikoray vohem sh'mi, v'shaym avōsai Avrohom v'Yitzchok, v'yidgu lorōv b'kerev ho-oretz.

הַמַּלְאָךְ הַגֹּאֵל אֹתִי מִכָּל רָע יְבָרֵךְ אֶת הַנְּעָרִים וְיִקָּרֵא בָהֶם שְׁמִי וְשֵׁם אֲבֹתַי אַבְרָהָם וְיִצְחָק וְיִדְגּוּ לָרֹב בְּקֶרֶב הָאָרֶץ:

May the angel who protects me from all evil bless the lads, and may my name be declared upon them, and the names of my forefathers, Abraham and Isaac, and may they proliferate abundantly within the land.

36. HINAY MAH TŌV u'mah no-im sheves achim gam yochad.

הִנֵּה מַה טּוֹב וּמַה נָּעִים שֶׁבֶת אַחִים גַּם־יָחַד

How good and how pleasant it is for brothers to dwell together in unity.

37. HAKODŌSH Boruch Hu, anachnu ōhavim oscho.

הַקָּדוֹשׁ בָּרוּךְ הוּא אֲנַחְנוּ אוֹהֲבִים אוֹתְךָ

God, we love, You!

38. HORACHAMON hu yanchilaynu yōm shekulō Shabbos um'nuchoh l'chayay ho-ōlomim.

הָרַחֲמָן הוּא יַנְחִילֵנוּ יוֹם שֶׁכֻּלּוֹ שַׁבָּת וּמְנוּחָה לְחַיֵּי הָעוֹלָמִים

The Merciful One will give us as an inheritance a day that is wholly a Sabbath and rest, for all eternity.

39. HAL'LU es Hashem kol gōyim, shab'chuhu kol ho-umim. Ki govar olaynu chasdō, v'emes Hashem l'ōlom, hal'luyoh.

הַלְלוּ אֶת ה' כָּל גּוֹיִם שַׁבְּחוּהוּ כָּל הָאֻמִּים. כִּי גָבַר עָלֵינוּ חַסְדּוֹ וֶאֱמֶת ה' לְעוֹלָם הַלְלוּיָהּ

Praise God, all the nations; praise Him all the peoples; for His kindness has overwhelmed us, and the truth of God is eternal, Halleluyah!

40. UVO l'Tziyōn gō'ayl

וּבָא לְצִיּוֹן גּוֹאֵל

And a redeemer will come to Zion.

41. VA-HAVI-ŌSIM el har kodshi, v'simachtim b'vays t'filosi, ōlosayhem v'zivchayhem l'rotzōn al mizb'chi, ki vaysi bays t'filoh yikoray, l'chol ho-amim.

וַהֲבִיאוֹתִים אֶל הַר קָדְשִׁי וְשִׂמַּחְתִּים בְּבֵית תְּפִלָּתִי עוֹלֹתֵיהֶם וְזִבְחֵיהֶם לְרָצוֹן עַל־מִזְבְּחִי כִּי בֵיתִי בֵּית תְּפִלָּה יִקָּרֵא לְכָל הָעַמִּים

And I will bring them to My holy mountain, and I will gladden them in My house of prayer, their elevation offerings and their feast offerings will find favor on My altar, for My House will be called a house of prayer for all peoples.

42. V'YAYD'U ki atoh shimchoh
Hashem l'vadechoh, elyōn al kol ho-oretz.

וְיֵדְעוּ כִּי־אַתָּה שְׁמְךָ ה' לְבַדֶּךָ עֶלְיוֹן עַל־כָּל־הָאָרֶץ

And all shall know that Your Name is alone, most high over all the earth.

43. V'HO-AYR aynaynu v'sōrosecho,
v'dabayk libaynu b'mitzvōsecho,
v'yachayd l'vovaynu l'ahavoh ulyir-oh
es sh'mecho, shelō nayvōsh, v'lō nikolaym
v'lo nikoshayl l'ōlom vo-ed.

וְהָאֵר עֵינֵינוּ בְּתוֹרָתֶךָ וְדַבֵּק לִבֵּנוּ בְּמִצְוֹתֶיךָ וְיַחֵד לְבָבֵנוּ לְאַהֲבָה וּלְיִרְאָה אֶת שְׁמֶךָ וְלֹא נֵבוֹשׁ לְעוֹלָם וָעֶד

Enlighten our eyes in Your Torah, attach our hearts to Your commandments, and unify our hearts to love and to fear Your Name, so that we should not feel shame, nor humiliation, nor stumble, for all eternity.

44. V'KORAYV p'zuraynu mibayn
hagōyim, unfutzōsaynu kanays
miyark'say oretz.

וְקָרֵב פְּזוּרֵינוּ מִבֵּין הַגּוֹיִם. וּנְפוּצוֹתֵינוּ כַּנֵּס מִיַּרְכְּתֵי אָרֶץ

Assemble our scattered people from among the nations, and gather our dispersed from the ends of the earth. And bring us to Zion, Your city, and to Jerusalem, Your Sanctuary, with eternal joy.

45. V'HARAYNU Hashem Elōkaynu
b'nechomas Tziyōn irecho, uv'vinyon
Y'rusholoyim ir kodshecho, ki atoh hu
ba'al hayeshu'ōs u'va'al hanechomōs.

וְהַרְאֵנוּ ה' אֱלֹקֵינוּ בְּנֶחָמַת צִיּוֹן עִירֶךָ וּבְבִנְיַן יְרוּשָׁלַיִם עִיר קָדְשֶׁךָ כִּי אַתָּה הוּא בַּעַל הַיְשׁוּעוֹת וּבַעַל הַנֶּחָמוֹת

And show us, Hashem, our God, the consolation of Zion, Your city, and the rebuilding of Jerusalem, city of Your holiness, for You are the Master of salvations and Master of consolations.

46. V'NISGOV Hashem l'vadō
vayōm hahu. Vayivosayr Ya'akov l'vadō,
vayay'ovayk ish imō, ad alos hashochar.

וְנִשְׂגָּב ה' לְבַדּוֹ בַּיּוֹם הַהוּא וַיִּוָּתֵר יַעֲקֹב לְבַדּוֹ וַיֵּאָבֵק אִישׁ עִמּוֹ עַד עֲלוֹת הַשָּׁחַר

And God alone will be exalted on that day. And Jacob remained alone, and a man wrestled with him until the break of dawn.

47. V'YA-AZOR v'yogayn
v'yōshi-a l'chōl hachōsim bō.

וַיַּעְזֹר וַיָּגֵן וְיוֹשִׁיעַ לְכֹל הַחוֹסִים בּוֹ

May He help, shield, and save all who take refuge in Him.

48. TOV l'hōdōs La'Hashem ul'zamayr
l'shimcho elyōn. L'hagid babōker
chasdecho, ve-emunoscho balaylōs.

טוֹב לְהֹדוֹת לַה' וּלְזַמֵּר לְשִׁמְךָ עֶלְיוֹן. לְהַגִּיד בַּבֹּקֶר חַסְדֶּךָ וֶאֱמוּנָתְךָ בַּלֵּילוֹת

It is good to give thanks to God, to sing praises to Your name, Exalted One; to tell of Your kindness in the morning, and of Your steadfastness by night.

49. *Yisro-ayl b'tach ba'Hashem, ezrom umoginom hu.*
ANACHNU MA-AMINIM *b'nay ma-aminim v'ayn lonu al mi l'hisho'ayn elo al ovinu she'bashomayim.*

יִשְׂרָאֵל בְּטַח בַּה׳ עֶזְרָם וּמָגִנָּם הוּא. אֲנַחְנוּ מַאֲמִינִים בְּנֵי מַאֲמִינִים וְאֵין לָנוּ עַל מִי לְהִשָּׁעֵן אֶלָּא עַל אָבִינוּ שֶׁבַּשָּׁמַיִם

Israel, have faith in God, He is their help and their shield. We are believers, the sons of believers, and we have no one on whom to depend, except our Father in Heaven.

50. YACHAD *kulom k'dushoh l'cho y'shalayshu ...v'koro zeh el zeh, v'omar.*

יַחַד כֻּלָּם קְדוּשָׁה לְךָ יְשַׁלֵּשׁוּ ... וְקָרָא זֶה אֶל זֶה וְאָמַר

Together, all of them [the angels] thrice recite ... and one will call another and say.

51. YOMIM *al yemay melech tōsif, sh'nōsov k'mo dor vodor.*

יָמִים עַל יְמֵי מֶלֶךְ תּוֹסִיף שְׁנוֹתָיו כְּמוֹ־דֹר וָדֹר

May You add days to the days of the king, may the length of his years be as generation after generation.

52. KŌ OMAR *Hashem zocharti loch chesed n'urayich, ahavas k'lulosayich, lechtaych acharay bamidbar b'eretz lō z'ru'oh.*

כֹּה אָמַר ה׳ זָכַרְתִּי לָךְ חֶסֶד נְעוּרַיִךְ אַהֲבַת כְּלוּלֹתָיִךְ לֶכְתֵּךְ אַחֲרַי בַּמִּדְבָּר בְּאֶרֶץ לֹא זְרוּעָה

Thus says God, I recall for you the kindness of your youth, the love of your nuptials, your following Me in the wilderness, into an unsown land.

53. KI ATOH *hu melech malchay ham'lochim, malchuscho netzach, nōrōsov sicho, sapru uzō pa'aru tzvo-ov, kadshuhu, romemuhu rōn shir voshevach tōkef t'hilōs tif'artō.*

כִּי אַתָּה הוּא מֶלֶךְ מַלְכֵי הַמְּלָכִים מַלְכוּתְךָ נֶצַח נוֹרְאוֹתָיו שְׂחוּ סַפְּרוּ עִזּוֹ פָּאֲרוּ צְבָאָיו קַדְּשׁוּהוּ רוֹן שִׁיר וְשֶׁבַח תּוֹקֶף תְּהִלּוֹת תִּפְאַרְתּוֹ

For You are the Supreme King of kings, Your kingship is eternal. He reveals Himself through His awesome prophecy, tell of His might, sanctify Him, exalt Him, happiness song and praise: we give power to the praise of His glory.

54. KI HAYM *cha-yaynu v'ōrech yomaynu, uvohem nehgeh yōmom voloyloh. V'ahavoscho al tosir mimenu l'ōlomim.*

כִּי הֵם חַיֵּינוּ וְאֹרֶךְ יָמֵינוּ וּבָהֶם נֶהְגֶּה יוֹמָם וָלַיְלָה וְאַהֲבָתְךָ אַל תָּסִיר מִמֶּנּוּ לְעוֹלָמִים

For they [the words of the Torah] are our lives, and the length of our days, and we will study them day and night. And Your love please do not remove from us forever.

55. KOL HO-ŌLOM *kulō gesher*
tzar m'ōd, v'ho'ikor lō l'fachayd k'lol.

כָּל הָעוֹלָם כֻּלּוֹ
גֶּשֶׁר צַר מְאֹד וְהָעִיקָר לֹא לְפַחֵד כְּלָל

All the world is a very narrow bridge, and the main thing is not to fear at all.

56. LAYV TOHŌR *b'ro li Elōkim,*
v'ruach nochōn chadaysh b'kirbi.
Al tashlichayni milfonecho
v'ruach kodsh'cho al tikach mimeni.

לֵב טָהוֹר
בְּרָא־לִי אֱלֹקִים וְרוּחַ נָכוֹן חַדֵּשׁ בְּקִרְבִּי.
אַל תַּשְׁלִיכֵנִי מִלְּפָנֶיךָ וְרוּחַ קָדְשְׁךָ עַל
תִּקַּח מִמֶּנִּי

Create in me, O God, a pure heart, and restore the proper spirit within me.
Do not reject me from before You, and do not take Your Divine spirit away from me.

57. LULAY TŌROSCHOH
sha-a-shu-ai, oz ovad'ti v'onyi.

לוּלֵי תוֹרָתֶךָ
שַׁעֲשֻׁעָי אָז אָבַדְתִּי בְעָנְיִי

Were it not for Your Torah in which I was engrossed, I would have perished in my affliction.

58. L'MA-AN ACHAI *v'ray-oy*
adabroh no sholōm boch. L'ma-an bays
Hashem Elōkaynu avakshoh tōv loch.
Hashem ōz l'amō yitayn,
Hashem y'voraych es amō vasholōm.

לְמַעַן אַחַי
וְרֵעָי אֲדַבְּרָה נָּא שָׁלוֹם בָּךְ. לְמַעַן בֵּית
ה' אֱלֹקֵינוּ אֲבַקְשָׁה טוֹב לָךְ. ה' עֹז
לְעַמּוֹ יִתֵּן ה' יְבָרֵךְ אֶת עַמּוֹ בַשָּׁלוֹם.

For the sake of my brothers and friends, let me now speak of peace. For the sake of the House of Hashem, our
God, I seek good for you. Hashem will give strength to His people, Hashem will bless His people with peace.

59. L'FONOV NA-AVŌD
b'yir'oh vofachad, v'nōdeh lishmo
b'chol yōm tomid.

לְפָנָיו נַעֲבוֹד
בְּיִרְאָה וָפַחַד וְנוֹדֶה לִשְׁמוֹ בְּכָל יוֹם
תָּמִיד

Before Him we shall worship with awe and with fear, and thank His name every day, always.

60. MŌDEH ANI *l'fonecho melech*
chai v'ka-yom, shehechezarto bi nishmosi
b'chemloh, raboh emunosecho.

מוֹדֶה אֲנִי
לְפָנֶיךָ מֶלֶךְ חַי וְקַיָּם שֶׁהֶחֱזַרְתָּ בִּי נִשְׁמָתִי
בְּחֶמְלָה רַבָּה אֱמוּנָתֶךָ

I acknowledge before You, King Who is eternal and everlasting,
that You have restored my soul to me in mercy; Your faithfulness is unbounded.

61. MIZMŌR *shir l'yōm haShabbos,* מִזְמוֹר שִׁיר
tōv l'hōdōs la'Hashem u'lzamayr לְיוֹם הַשַּׁבָּת: טוֹב לְהֹדוֹת לַה' וּלְזַמֵּר
l'shimchoh elyōn. לְשִׁמְךָ עֶלְיוֹן

A psalm, a song for the Sabbath day, It is good to praise God and to sing praise to Your Name.

62. MI HO-ISH *hechofaytz chayim,* מִי הָאִישׁ
ōhayv yomim lir'ōs tōv; n'tzōr l'shōnchoh הֶחָפֵץ חַיִּים אֹהֵב יָמִים לִרְאוֹת טוֹב:
mayro u'sfosecho midabayr mirmoh. נְצֹר לְשׁוֹנְךָ מֵרָע וּשְׂפָתֶיךָ מִדַּבֵּר מִרְמָה:
Sur mayro va-asay tōv, סוּר מֵרָע וַעֲשֵׂה טוֹב בַּקֵּשׁ שָׁלוֹם וְרָדְפֵהוּ
bakaysh sholōm,v'rodfayhu.

Who is the man who desires life, who loves days that he may see good? Guard your tongue from evil, and your lips from speaking deceitfully. Turn from evil and do good, seek peace and pursue it.

63. MIN HAMAYTZAR מִן הַמֵּצַר
korosi Koh, ononi vamerchov Koh. קָרָאתִי יָּהּ עָנָנִי בַמֶּרְחָב יָהּ

I called You from the straits, O God; God answered me with expansiveness.

64. MŌDIM *anachnu loch.* מוֹדִים אֲנַחְנוּ לָךְ

We thank You.

65. MIMKŌMCHO *malkaynu sōfi-a,* מִמְּקוֹמְךָ
v'simloch olaynu ki m'chakim anachnu מַלְכֵּנוּ תוֹפִיעַ וְתִמְלֹךְ עָלֵינוּ כִּי מְחַכִּים
loch. Mosai timlōch b'Tziyon, b'korōv אֲנַחְנוּ לָךְ. מָתַי תִּמְלֹךְ בְּצִיּוֹן בְּקָרוֹב
b'yomaynu, l'ōlom vo'ed tishkōn. Tisgadal בְּיָמֵינוּ לְעוֹלָם וָעֶד תִּשְׁכּוֹן. תִּתְגַּדַּל
v'siskadash b'sōch Yerusholoyim ircho, וְתִתְקַדַּשׁ בְּתוֹךְ יְרוּשָׁלַיִם עִירְךָ לְדוֹר
l'dōr vodōr ul'naytzach netzochim. וָדוֹר וּלְנֵצַח נְצָחִים. וְעֵינֵינוּ תִרְאֶינָה
V'aynaynu sir'enoh malchusecho, kadovor מַלְכוּתֶךָ כַּדָּבָר הָאָמוּר בְּשִׁירֵי עֻזֶּךָ עַל
ho-omur b'shiray u'zecho, al y'day Dovid יְדֵי דָוִד מְשִׁיחַ צִדְקֶךָ
m'shiach tzidkecho.

From Your place, our King, You will appear and reign over us, for we await You.When will You reign in Zion? Soon, in our days; forever and ever, may You dwell there. May You be exalted and sanctified within Jerusalem, Your city, from generation to generation and for all eternity. May our eyes see Your kindom, as it is expressed in the songs of Your might, written by David, Your righteous anointed.

66. M'KIMI *may-ofor dol.* מְקִימִי מֵעָפָר דָּל

He raises the needy from the dust.

67. NA-AR HO-YISI *gam zokanti* נַעַר הָיִיתִי גַם
v'lō ro-isi tzakik ne-ezov v'zar'ō m'vakesh זָקַנְתִּי וְלֹא רָאִיתִי צַדִּיק נֶעֱזָב וְזַרְעוֹ
lochem. Hashem ōz l'amō yitayn, Hashem מְבַקֶּשׁ לָחֶם: ה' עֹז לְעַמּוֹ יִתֵּן ה' יְבָרֵךְ
y'voraych es amō vasholōm. אֶת עַמּוֹ בַשָּׁלוֹם:

I was a youth, and I also aged, and I never saw a righteous person forsaken, with his children
begging for bread. Hashem will give might to His people. Hashem will bless His people with peace.

68. MALCHUSCHO *malchus kol* מַלְכוּתְךָ מַלְכוּת
ōlomim, u-memshalt'cho b'chol dōr vodōr. כָּל עֹלָמִים וּמֶמְשַׁלְתְּךָ בְּכָל דּוֹר וָדֹר

Your kingship is eternal, and Your sovereignty is from generation to generation.

69. ŌSEH SHOLŌM *bimrōmov,* עֹשֶׂה שָׁלוֹם
hu ya-aseh sholōm olaynu, בִּמְרוֹמָיו הוּא יַעֲשֶׂה שָׁלוֹם עָלֵינוּ וְעַל
v'al kol Yisro-ayl, v'imru omayn. כָּל יִשְׂרָאֵל וְאִמְרוּ: אָמֵן.

He Who makes peace in His exalted places, may He make peace for us, and for all Israel, and say Amen.

70. IVDU *es Hashem b'simchoh,* עִבְדוּ אֶת ה'
bō-u l'fonov birnonoh. בְּשִׂמְחָה בֹּאוּ לְפָנָיו בִּרְנָנָה

Worship God in joy, come before Him with happy singing.

71. AYTZ CHA-YIM *hi lamachazikim* עֵץ חַיִּים הִיא
boh, v'sōmcheho m'ushor. D'rocheho לַמַּחֲזִיקִים בָּהּ וְתֹמְכֶיהָ מְאֻשָּׁר. דְּרָכֶיהָ
darchay nō-am, v'chol n'sivosheho sholōm. דַרְכֵי נֹעַם וְכָל נְתִיבוֹתֶיהָ שָׁלוֹם

It is a Tree of Life to those who hold fast to it, and its supporters are happy.
Its ways are pleasant and all its path are peaceful.

72. PIS-CHU *li sha-aray tzedek,* פִּתְחוּ לִי שַׁעֲרֵי
ovō vom ōdeh Koh. Zeh hasha-ar צֶדֶק אָבֹא בָם אוֹדֶה קָהּ. זֶה הַשַּׁעַר
la'Hashem tzadikim yovo-u vō. לַה' צַדִּיקִים יָבֹאוּ בוֹ.

Open the gates of righteousness for me; I will go in and praise God.
This is the gateway to God, through which the righteous may enter.

73. KAVAY el Hashem, chazak
v'ya-amaytz libecho, v'kavay el Hashem.

קַוֵּה אֶל ה'
חֲזַק וְיַאֲמֵץ לִבֶּךָ וְקַוֵּה אֶל ה':

Hope in God, be strong and He will give you courage, and hope in God.

74. KAYL HAHŌDO-ŌS,
adōn hasholōm, m'kadaysh haShabbos
umvoraych sh'vi-i, umayniyach bikdushoh
l'am m'dushnay oneg, zaycher
l'ma-asay v'rayshis.

קֵל הַהוֹדָאוֹת
אֲדוֹן הַשָּׁלוֹם מְקַדֵּשׁ הַשַּׁבָּת וּמְבָרֵךְ
שְׁבִיעִי וּמֵנִיחַ בִּקְדֻשָּׁה לְעַם מְדֻשְּׁנֵי
עֹנֶג זֵכֶר לְמַעֲשֵׂה בְרֵאשִׁית

God of grateful praise, Master of peace, Who sanctifies the Sabbath and blesses the seventh day,
and gives rest in holiness to a people saturated in delight, in memory of the work of Creation.

75. K'CHU imochem d'vorim
v'shuvu el Hashem.

קְחוּ עִמָּכֶם
דְּבָרִים וְשׁוּבוּ אֶל ה'

Take words with you and return to Hashem.

76. KŌL DŌDI hinay zeh bo,
medalayg al herorim, m'kapaytz al
hagvo'ōs, v'kōl hatōr nishma b'artzaynu.

קוֹל דּוֹדִי הִנֵּה
זֶה בָּא מְדַלֵּג עַל הֶהָרִים מְקַפֵּץ עַל
הַגְּבָעוֹת וְקוֹל הַתּוֹר נִשְׁמַע בְּאַרְצֵנוּ

The sound of my beloved comes, leaping over the mountains, skipping over the hills,
and the sound of the dove is heard in our land.

77. S'U SH'ORIM roshaychem us'u
pis-chay ōlom v'yovō melech hakovōd, mi
hu zeh melech hakovōd, Hashem Tzevakōs
hu melech hakovōd, Seloh.

שְׂאוּ שְׁעָרִים
רָאשֵׁיכֶם וּשְׂאוּ פִּתְחֵי עוֹלָם וְיָבוֹא מֶלֶךְ
הַכָּבוֹד: מִי הוּא זֶה מֶלֶךְ הַכָּבוֹד ה'
צְבָקוֹת הוּא מֶלֶךְ הַכָּבוֹד סֶלָה:

Lift up your heads, O gates, and raise yourselves, everlasting doors, and let the King of Glory enter. Who is
this King of Glory, the God of hosts, He is the King of Glory, Selah.

78. T'HAY hasho-oh hazōs
sh'as rachamim v'ays rotzōn milfonecho.

תְּהֵא הַשָּׁעָה
הַזֹּאת שְׁעַת רַחֲמִים וְעֵת רָצוֹן מִלְּפָנֶיךָ

May this time be a time of mercy and acceptance before You.

79. TŌRAS HASHEM t'mimoh,
m'shivas nofesh. Aydus Hashem
ne-emonoh, machkimas pesi.

תּוֹרַת ה'
תְּמִימָה מְשִׁיבַת נָפֶשׁ עֵדוּת ה' נֶאֱמָנָה
מַחְכִּימַת פֶּתִי

The Torah of God is perfect, restoring the soul; the testimony of God is trustworthy,
making the simple man wise.

Glossary

Aishes Chayil — A woman of Valor. A song of praise to the Jewish woman of the home, authored by King Solomon in Proverbs 31. It is sung on Friday night.

Amidah — The *shemoneh esrei* prayer, consisting of nineteen blessings, said three times daily. *Amidah* literally means standing, a reference to the reverent posture one assumes during the prayer.

Arvus — The principle that each Jew is responsible for his fellow man.

Bais Hamikdash — The Holy Temple. This is a reference for the two earthly repositories of God's Divine Presence. The first was built by King Solomon and the second by King Herod. The Babylonians destroyed the first Temple, and the Romans destroyed the second, both on Tisha b'Av.

Bentching — To bless, a reference to Grace after Meals. *Bentching* is the actual text, *bentcher* is the book which contains the zemiros or songs.

Bereishis, Shemos, Vayikra, Bamidbar, Devarim — The Hebrew names of the Five Books of Moses; Genesis, Exodus, Leviticus, Numbers, Deuteronomy.

Birkas Hamazon — Grace after Meals. The three Torah ordained and the one Rabbinically instituted blessings said after eating a meal in which bread is eaten. Also called bentching.

Birshus — With your permission. The leader of Grace after Meals calls participants to attention before leading the bentching.

Borei pri hagefen ... ha'eitz ... ha'adamah — The blessing recited before drinking wine or grape juice, eating fruits and vegetables, respectively.

Challah — The bread loaves eaten on Shabbos and Festivals. The word challah also refers to an olive-sized piece that is separated from the dough. In the time of the Holy Temple, it was given to the priest, the kohein; today, it is burned.

Cholent — A stew-like dish which cooks overnight. Recipes vary, though it usually consists of meat, potatoes, beans, barley and various spices.

Choson, Kallah — Groom and bride.

Dvar Torah — A Torah thought or discourse, usually related to the portion of the week or relevant topics.

Gematria — Numerical equivalents for Hebrew letters. Each letter represents a number. א = 1, ב = 2. From כ through צ, each letter represents a number from 20-90; From ק through ת, each letter represents 100-400.

Hachnosas Orchim — Bringing guests into the home. The Torah describes the Patriarch Abraham when he greeted the three angels dressed as wayfarers, as one who excelled in this trait.

Glossary

Halachah — Jewish Law. The immutable principles of Torah are the basis for Jewish laws as rendered by *halachic* decisors, or *poskim*. Recognized *halachic* authorities rule on every aspect of Jewish life.

Hamotzi — The blessing recited before eating challah, bread or matzah. *Hamotzi lechem min ha'aretz* — Who brings forth bread from the ground.

Havdalah — The prayer which marks the conclusion of Shabbos. After *havdalah*, work is permitted.

Kiddush — The prayer which ushers in the sanctity of the day after the candles have been lit. Kiddush is recited on Friday night and Shabbos day.

Kiddush Levana — The blessing recited to sanctify the moon. It is recited before the fifteenth of the month.

Lechem Hapanim — Show Bread. These were twelve loaves which miraculously stayed fresh until the following week. They were eaten by the kohanim on Shabbos.

Lechem Mishnah — Two whole loaves of challah or matzah over which the hamotzi blessing is recited.

Leket, shikchah, peah — Gleanings left for the poor and the corner of the field left during harvesting.

Mayim Achronim — Ritual washing at the end of a meal before Grace after Meals is recited.

Megillah — A scroll, usually related to a text, as in Megillas Esther.

Melave Malka — A meal after the conclusion of Shabbos held to respectfully escort the Shabbos Queen.

Midrash — The elucidation of the parts of the Torah, Prophets and Writings by the Rabbis of the Mishnah. It includes allegorical interpretations and statements which take the reader "between the lines" of the text.

Minhag (pl. minhagim) — Custom. These are enactments by the Rabbis of a community to complement Jewish law.

Mishnah — The Oral Tradition handed down from Moses at Mount Sinai, and redacted by Rabbi Yehudah the Prince in approximately 200 C.E. The Rabbis of the Mishanh were called Tannaim, The period of the Mishnah spanned approximately four hundred years.

Mispar Koton — Reduced value *gematria* formula. The ten's and one hundred's value is dropped. $10 = 1$, $200 = 2$, etc.

Netilas Yodayim — The act of ritually washing the hands before eating bread.

Neshama Yesairah — Additional soul. On Shabbos, the Jews are granted an expansive heart to enable them to enjoy the physical richness of Shabbos to complement the spiritual character of the day.

Glossary

Oneg Shabbos — Delighting in the Shabbos. Our Rabbis suggest that physical enjoyment on Shabbos enhances the spiritual dimension.

Revi'is — Approximately 3.3 fluid ounces, the minimum amount to be used for ritual washing before eating a bread meal.

R'tzay, ya'aleh v'yavo — The additions to Grace after Meals, recited on Shabbos and the Festivals respectively. Ya'aleh v'yavo is also said on Rosh Chodesh.

Seudas Mitzvah — The meal tendered at a Jewish celebration, such as a Bar Mitzvah or wedding.

Shacharis, Mincha, Ma'ariv — The morning, afternoon and evening prayers, whose origin is attributed to Abraham, Isaac and Jacob.

Shalosh Seudos — The third Shabbos meal, usually eaten after the afternoon minchah service, as the day begins to wane. Also called seudah shlishis.

Sheva Brochos — Seven wedding blessings recited at each wedding in honor of the bride and groom. Alternately, it is the seven-day period of celebration after the wedding.

Sholom Zochor — A celebration rendered on the first Friday night after the birth of a male child. It is an informal gathering of family and friends held after the Friday night meal.

Simcha — A festive Jewish celebration, as is a bris, circumcision, Bar or Bat Mitzvah or wedding.

Talmud — Tractates of the Oral Law which expound upon the statements of the Mishnah. The sixty volumes of the Talmud, also called *gemara*, contain the wisdom and teachings of our Sages, transmitted by God to Moses at Sinai.

Tefillin — Phylacteries. Black leather boxes worn by males over thirteen years old which contain specific scriptural passages. One is worn on the arm and the other on the head.

Terumah — A portion of the produce given to the kohanim, priests, in the time of the Holy Temple. There were various *terumos* given in different years.

Tzedukim — Saducees. A heretical cult of Jews in the early years of the common era that denied the teachings of the Oral Law.

Zemer (pl. zemiros) — Traditional song sung at the Shabbos table. Most zemiros deal with a Shabbos theme, and many were authored by medieval composers.

Zimun — Three males over 13 years of age are invited to join in Grace after Meals. The group of three is called a *mezuman*.

List of Plates

List of Plates

List of Plates

The Artist

RABBI YONAH WEINRIB SPECIALIZES IN ELABORATE MANUSCRIPT ILLUMINATION, COMBINING RESEARCH FROM TRADITIONAL TEXTS WITH EXACTING CALLIGRAPHY AND ARTWORK. HE HAS LECTURED AND EXHIBITED INTERNATIONALLY, AND HIS WORKS ARE FOUND IN MUSEUMS, PRESTIGIOUS GALLERIES AND PRIVATE COLLECTIONS AROUND THE WORLD.

Rabbi Weinrib has illuminated and authored
numerous volumes of Judaica including:

- Pirkei Avos — Collector's Edition,
  Deluxe leather and standard editions

- The Manuscript Shiron Series (Grace After Meals and Songs)
  Bar Mitzvah Shiron • Bat Mitzvah Shiron • Wedding Shiron

- Bar Mitzvah: Its Observance and Significance,

- Transitions: The Bat Mitzvah Treasury

- Hallel — Deluxe leather and standard editions

- The Haggadah in Memory of the Holocaust

- The Megillah of Redemption — Megillat Esther

- כנפי תפלה / Wings of Prayer

- Shiron Am Echad — Ashkenaz / Sepharadi Bentcher

Additionally, he has been commissioned by major Jewish organizations to create numerous presentation awards, including those for heads of state.

For more information on exhibitions,
art publications or a complete catalogue
of his works including framed wall hangings, contact
JUDAICA ILLUMINATIONS • WWW.JUDAICAILLUMINATIONS.COM
or your local Judaica bookseller.